I enjoy sharing my books as I do my friends, asking only that you treat them well and see them safely home

Peter Stephen

Fly Fishing
for
Salmon and Sea Trout

Fly Fishing
for
Salmon and Sea Trout

ARTHUR OGLESBY

The Crowood Press

First published in 1986 by
THE CROWOOD PRESS
Ramsbury, Marlborough
Wiltshire SN8 2HE

Reprinted 1987

British Library Cataloguing in Publication Data

Oglesby, Arthur
   Fly fishing for salmon and sea trout.
   1. Salmon fishing   2. Trout fishing
   3. Fly fishing
   I. Title
   799.1′755   SH684
ISBN 0-946284-87-3

Typeset by Alacrity Phototypesetters, Banwell Castle, Weston-super-Mare
Printed in Great Britain

Contents

Arthur Oglesby

Preface

In offering yet another book to the frequently bewildered angling reader, I am conscious that vanity or a host of other frivolous motives may have directed me to my typewriter to set all this down. What, you might ask, have I now got to offer that was not given full ventilation in my earlier book, *Salmon*? Well, I feel that I now have significantly more to relate on the problems of fly fishing for both salmon and sea trout. Although many forms of bait fishing are legally permitted in Britain some are falling from fashion and the present trend, and one which I heartily applaud, is for fly fishing to gradually oust all other methods in popularity. The day will come when most of the classic rivers will demand a fly-only rule at certain times of the season — even if only as an unwritten law. In North America, of course, it is the law of the land to fish for Atlantic salmon with some type of artificial fly. In many instances the angler is also limited to a single and often barbless hook. In Iceland a similar code is adopted by most visiting anglers, and only in Great Britain, Ireland and Norway is bait fishing sometimes pursued in preference to fly fishing.

Many of my formative years as a salmon and sea-trout fisherman were spent bait fishing. It took time for me to realise the many joys and advantages of fly fishing and to virtually put aside my bait tackle and become a fly-only fisherman. I suppose a lot depends on where and when we are going to fish. Many of the countries outside the United Kingdom with runs of salmon and sea trout tend to have shorter seasons. In Norway, Iceland and Canada, for instance, the season is confined to the months of June, July and August. Is it any wonder, when the bulk of the fishing takes place at a warmer time of the year, which is conducive to fly fishing anyway, that many waters are bound by a fly-only rule?

The British trend to fly fishing in all game-fishing activity is also being fostered by that growing army of anglers who lay siege to our reservoirs and stillwaters. Fly fishing is no longer merely a snob sport and it is rapidly becoming not only an acceptable but a highly developed method of catching game fish species such as the Atlantic

salmon, sea trout, brown trout and rainbow trout. Across the Atlantic, American and Canadian anglers have seen particular trends in the development of sport with salmon. Many have thrown our traditions out of the window and are now to be seen using diminutive rods of little more than six feet in length. It is little use telling Canadian and American anglers that they are wrong, that we invented it all and that our way is right. We might suggest that we are veterans at the games of golf or tennis and, therefore, better at them than most. Why is it then that the Americans frequently beat us at these and other games and that their top-class anglers are often more skilful than we are? I suggest that it is simply that the serious American sportsman does not settle for mediocrity but seeks excellence in everything he does.

Much British thinking is clouded by tradition. Change comes only slowly in the sphere of salmon fishing and we are stuck with age-old methods simply because they have been handed down and accepted without question. Many anglers still cling to built-cane and some to greenheart rods in the mystical belief that there is something special about them. Indeed, they did once represent the epitome of the rod maker's craft, but the reality is that a well designed piece of plastic tube, be it of fibreglass or carbon fibre (graphite), is more efficient in the two basic tasks it has to perform – that of casting a line and playing a fish – and it is also much lighter. New trends in the manufacture and development of carbon fibre by Bruce & Walker Ltd, of England, which will have revolutionised the concept of carbon-fibre rods by the time this book is in print, are discussed in Chapter 5.

If the die-hard British salmon angler is chained by tradition to the long double-handed rod, then the North American fisherman seems equally unrealistic in his insistence that the short rod will do all that is required. The facts are that if both parties are prepared to yield to common sense there is a real case for fishing with a wide range of rod lengths and actions to suit circumstances – but more of this later.

One of the prime problems for the salmon and sea-trout angler in the 1980s is that pressure on both salmon and sea trout is higher than at any other time in history. In years gone by it was normal to take a crop of this once bountiful resource at any point on the migration route where the fish could be easily intercepted. This usually meant taking the fish as they entered the estuaries and then again at any

point on their upstream migration where they were forced to tarry awhile at some dam or natural or artificial obstruction. The fish were not then intercepted on the high seas for the simple reason that no one knew where they went or on what closely defined routes they made their way back to the river of their birth.

Before the Industrial Revolution in Britain most of our rivers, with easy access from the sea, were reputed to hold so many fish that salmon and sea trout were held in lower esteem as food than many species of coarse fish. Most of us know the fable of the apprentices who, as part of their terms of service, were not supposed to be fed on salmon for more than a specific number of days per week. I have little doubt that such a contract existed, though documentary evidence is as elusive as the Holy Grail. Anyway, it is sufficient to assume that our rivers could stand the levels of predation they were being called upon to endure at that time. Most were virtually unpolluted, while nature always provided bountifully for all the commercial requirements and the new sport of angling which was then just catching on.

One can imagine our rivers in those ancient days! A sight of the salmon resource in Alaska today, for instance, will give some clue to what they might have looked like. Britain has a human population density of about 1,350:1 when compared with Alaska. Imagine a country that is a fifth the size of the continental United States but with a smaller population than a town like Leeds or Liverpool or Fort Worth, Texas. Is there any wonder that in the Bristol Bay area of Alaska alone they can net and trap 20 million salmon for the canneries and still leave another 20 million to run the rivers and ensure superb sport for the anglers as well as a generous surplus for the regeneration of the species.

With the full onset of the Industrial Revolution the salmon's environment was the first to suffer. Many rivers were treated as open sewers. Once-great salmon rivers such as the Thames, Mersey, Humber and Trent were suddenly unable to sustain stocks. Yet the sport of angling was becoming more popular and by the middle of the nineteenth century the dawn of rail travel opened up hitherto inaccessible sporting places to a wider travelling public. The railways also brought the means of transporting large quantities of commercially caught fish to the markets of the highly populated areas. The salmon's fight for survival had already begun.

Throughout the twentieth century the onslaught on our migratory

fish has continued. Monofilament nets, electronic fish-finding equipment, speedboats and other rapid forms of transportation, freezer ships and motorways all assist in delivering fish quickly and in numbers to the marketplace. The salmon is a popular food fish and with increased knowledge of migrations and feeding areas we have been able to harass it at all points of the compass – both legally and illegally. Many observers, like myself, have been protesting for many years, but the establishment does not seem to want to know and the apathy and impotence continues.

If the commercial effort against salmon and sea trout has been magnified tenfold in the last hundred and fifty years then the angling interest has seen similar growth. When I first started serious salmon fishing back in the mid-1950s, it was possible to rent a beat which would only accommodate three rods. That same beat today has been split into three separate beats and each is being asked to carry as many as six rods at a time – a sixfold increase in effort. Is there any wonder that rod catch figures do not yet reflect the fearful decline that has taken place in stocks re-entering our rivers to spawn. Of course, the rod catch on our rivers is still seen to be a tolerable percentage of the total, but the catch per person seems to have dwindled alarmingly.

To compound the problem, we now have a situation where an angler will frequently share his rod with a friend. This usually means that they fish in shifts, as it were, and that maximum effort is maintained throughout a fishing day or night. Also, some estates and owners are joining the bandwagon of time-sharing, by which a week or weeks of sporting rights on a specific river may be bought in perpetuity. The best periods obviously go quickly and make the highest prices, and the owners are then faced with the problem of selling off the poor or useless periods. So, while such schemes appear to offer a get-rich-quick formula for the original owners, the question of how these pieces of water are going to be administered in the future makes the mind boggle. My own long-term view is that time-sharing has to be just about the worst thing that can happen to a salmon river, but time will have to be the judge of that.

The real decline has been witnessed since the end of the Second World War. During this period the sea feeding grounds of salmon have been discovered. At about the same time – incidentally, a time of plenty in our rivers – we in Britain had many of our rivers smitten by the dreaded disease of ulcerative dermal necrosis (UDN). Those

who recall the sight of the many dead and dying salmon will marvel
that the resource could ever recover and be the same again. The
decline in the all-methods catch of spring salmon has continued at a
steady rate since the early 1950s. Figures collated by Mr Gordon
Barr of Bridge of Weir in his submission to the Secretary of State
for Scotland demonstrate this fearful trend. Bear in mind that these
are the recorded figures for the *all-methods* catch on only four of our
classic rivers over the last three decades and that they refer entirely
to spring fish – those which are of the greatest benefit to the
fisheries and the visitors who come to Scotland to spend their
money.

	Dee	Spey	Tay	Tweed
1952–61	196,109	55,873	55,997	223,610
1962–71	107,784	34,119	59,683	111,623
1972–81	82,964	27,197	47,434	41,623

Other than an upward hiccup in the Tay for 1962–71, the figures all
demonstrate a remorseless trend downwards. When might it ever be
halted and reversed?

To add to our problems yet again we slowly became aware of the
horrors associated with acid rain and its devastating effect on the
young ova and alevins which use the headwaters of many of our
rivers as nurseries. Then our attention was focused upon the damage
done to salmon stocks by the increased number of seals we have
marauding off our coasts. Further damage to our rivers is caused by
the outflow of effluent from farms, particularly from dairy farms,
where milking parlours are sterilised with chlorine compounds.
Total available residual chlorine (TARC) levels have been found to
be in excess of those compatible with salmonid life. Now there is
talk of compulsory fluoridation of domestic water supplies in order
to protect our teeth from decay. Has anyone considered the effect
this might have on the fish in our rivers?

Fortunately, as mankind has been slowly ruining the natural
salmon resource there have been groups of enterprising companies
and individuals who have seen and demonstrated that salmon,
particularly, respond almost as well as trout to artificial propagation. This has meant that salmon farming and ranching have taken
off and it suggests that pressures on our wildbred stocks will now
ease. This all remains to be seen. There is no evidence of it yet and

Artificial propagation is doing much to stem the tide of over-exploitation of fish stocks by commercial interests.

the mayhem and general skulduggery continues at sea, in the estuaries and in the rivers. The ne'er-do-wells, eager for quick pickings, are still posing their threat – as evidenced by the increased poaching. Nowhere where salmon swim are they now immune from the greed of mankind. They are totally vulnerable and it might be argued that mankind does not deserve to have this once-bountiful resource anyway. Be that as it may, it is up to the angler, as the last predator in the chain who claims to have any feelings of responsibility for the quarry he hunts, to show a disciplined attitude and maintain the best traditions of good sportsmanship. This may mean greater self-control on the methods adopted to take salmon and sea trout. No longer can we tolerate the so-called angler who is content to get his salmon and sea trout by any means. There must be a greater deterrent for those who 'sniggle' or foul-hook fish, together with the bombers and cyanide merchants.

It will not do either to assume that it will all come right in the end. The heavy rainfall of 1985, for instance, has deluded some anglers into thinking that all is now right again. Indeed, there were

some good runs of fish following the rain, fish which could escape some of the nets in high water. But the cancer is still there. One year's medicine has not effected a cure; it has merely reduced some of the pain.

However, it has to be recognised that fair angling is about the most inefficient method of catching salmon and sea trout. In times of plenty we could well afford to net and trap a few fish. Indeed, it made commercial sense to crop a percentage so that a highly valuable resource was not wasted. Today the matter is much different. Many Scottish glens and straths rely heavily on the visiting angler and it is the sporting resource that is now of the greatest value to the economy of the areas in which salmon and sea trout are generated and nurtured.

Throughout this book, therefore, my reader will be aware of my plea that he should adopt a highly responsible attitude in the capture of salmon and sea trout by rod and line. In the last thirty years I have noticed an alarming decline of stock in many rivers which were previously full of fish. We need to develop a more conservationist attitude and think in terms of fish being a bonus rather than an entitlement. I have caught a lot of fish on spinners and natural baits in the years gone by and it may seem easy for me to pontificate and advocate a fly-only philosophy. Sadly, times are vastly changed since I first fished for salmon and sea trout. Fish were there for the taking without the slightest worry that by fair angling even a big catch would jeopardise wild stocks. Today, however, the wild fish may well be an endangered species and we owe it to future generations of sportsmen as well as to the salmon to demonstrate some semblance of responsibility in our management of this wonderful resource.

No sporting life as successful as the one I have enjoyed could have been possible without the assistance of many friends. My early thoughts and skills in angling were honed and polished by one of the greatest friends I had. I refer to the late Eric Horsfall Turner, for he was the one man to take me on, after the fashion of master and apprentice, and steer me through to some form of maturity. The next great influence came when I met the late Captain T.L. (Tommy) Edwards in the mid-1950s. Tommy did not suffer fools very gladly and had I been of faint heart I might have let him reduce me near to tears shortly after our first encounter. To my good fortune he warmed to me slightly and in later years not only did he

improve my casting abilities but he gave me an insight on how to pass on some of those skills to others. Upon his death in 1968 I was honoured to be asked to take his place as chief instructor on the angling courses held annually in Grantown-on-Spey.

With a firmer base I was then most fortunate to get access to superb fishing on the Spey at Castle Grant. Thanks are due to the factor of this estate, Mr Hugh Blakeney, for all his kind help. Thanks are also due to Lady Pauline Ogilvie-Grant, daughter of the late Countess of Seafield, for all her kind hospitality, and to the Strathspey Angling Association, on whose waters I now do most of my instruction.

Thanks are also due to the editors of *Shooting Times and Country Magazine* and *Trout and Salmon* for permission to reproduce, if only in part, some of my articles which have appeared in these journals; to R. V. Righyni for all his wise counsel on how best to fish the Newton water of the Lune; to Odd Haraldsen for his annual invitations to fish some of Norway's famous rivers, opportunities which have enabled me to catch some huge salmon; to Gerald Panchaud, who also gives generous hospitality to my wife and me with annual invitations to the Outer Hebrides to fish the renowned lochs of the North Harris Estate at Amhuinnsuidhe Castle; to Andrew Mackintosh for patient assistance with the diagrams; and to that talented sea fisherman and photographer, John Holden, for helping me with some of the photography.

It would not do to close this introduction without some mention of other anglers and writers who have influenced my philosophy. Formative years were spent reading the works of G. P. R. Balfour-Kinnear and Richard Waddington, but it was a little known writer, J. Hughes Parry, whose book *Fishing Fantasy* first prompted my real hunting instincts and who caused me to start much of my salmon fishing with baits and spinners. Much practical help in this activity was also obtained from David Cook, a one-time river keeper on the little Esk near my home in North Yorkshire. But fly fishing brought few mentors other than Tommy Edwards and I have been most fortunate in that I learned to cast to a reasonable level of competence, for this is the prime requirement in all fly fishing.

Of course, there have been many friends to whom I am eternally grateful for their professional advice or their kindly criticism and encouragement. I am thinking initially of those great American sportsmen such as Clare Conley (who engaged me as European

editor of *Field & Stream* magazine), Al McClane, Lee Wulff, Ed
Zern, Gene Hill and Jack Samson, who have all influenced me in
modifying my rather conservative British angling philosophy. I am
also particularly indebted to Tony Chattaway for his advice on
salmon management and fish farming and to Jim Bruce and Ken
Walker of Bruce & Walker Ltd, who have been so helpful in
permitting me to play about with prototype rods and tackle until we
got the desired performance and for commissioning me to make a
series of angling films and videos for them. My thanks are also due to
my friend and family doctor, David Goldsborough, to my patient
publisher, John Dennis of the Crowood Press, and to all his staff,
who took my manuscript from the rough into final publication
form.

Other anglers and writers I have noted with more than passing
interest include Charles McLaren, Neil Graesser, Bill Currie, Philip
Green, R. V. Righyni, John Ashley-Cooper, Jack Chance and Hugh
Falkus. Falkus in particular has given us some classic writing on
salmon and sea trout and it was a great pleasure for me to be
involved in doing much of the photography for his most recent
book, *Salmon Fishing*.

Perhaps the finest practical fly fisherman I ever met is that great
American veteran, Lee Wulff. Wulff combines the three talents of
writer, angler and photographer, not necessarily in that order, and I
regard his book *The Atlantic Salmon* as essential reading for anyone
who has a specific leaning to seeking salmon only on the artificial
fly. The fact that Wulff is an American and his book is largely about
North American waters, where he has caught over 5,000 Atlantic
salmon on fly, does not detract from the value of his thinking and
experience. In the short times he has spent in Britain he has amply
demonstrated to me and others that his technique works when
others falter or fail. He is an advocate of the ultra-short rod, but is
the first to admit that he only fishes with such a rod because he
prefers it that way. Nowhere is there any instruction that it is
necessarily the best way. In recent correspondence he admits to
recognising the great advantage of the long rod and the Spey cast for
the big rivers of early spring and late autumn.

Al McClane is yet another American who, in his own country and
like Lee Wulff, enjoys some of the reverence we might bestow on the
Almighty. McClane is also a great devotee of the single-handed fly
rod. I am reliably informed that he has fished in 140 countries (I did

not know that there were so many) but then as a man who, since the
end of the Second World War, has devoted his entire life to angling,
I would expect him to know a little bit about it all. On one occasion,
when he fished the Spey with me on one cold spring day many years
ago, I timidly suggested to him that he would do better with my
spinning rod than with his fly rod. The spinning rod was refused
with quiet scorn and I was thereupon politely informed that anyone
who would spin would also steal!

Although I do not now fish with quite the great fervour I had
when I was a novice, I do spend the best part of two months on the
Spey, which is then augmented by sundry other periods on a wide
variety of salmon and sea-trout waters in this country and abroad.
My total fishing time must run into more than five months in a year,
but I am still learning and ever-grateful to those whose paths I
crossed all those years ago who steered me onto a different course.

At this stage it might be appropriate to mention the several
organisations which support the cause of salmon conservation. The
prime movers in this cause are the Salmon and Trout Association,
the Atlantic Salmon Trust, the Salmon Conservancy and the
Scottish Salmon Anglers' Federation. I am a member of all these
organisations and on the committees of two of them. In many
respects, however, I am one of their greatest critics. It is only in very
recent times that the S&TA has emerged with a strong mandate from
its membership to represent only the angling interest. The AST, on
the other hand, tries to sit on the political fence and remain
unpartisan, while the Salmon Conservancy is entirely new in the
arena of salmon skulduggery. The SSAF, while having some influen-
tial names among its membership, has always seemed to lack the
teeth to bite effectively, and the latest news is that it is going to
amalgamate with the S&TA anyway.

The Salmon and Trout Association, therefore, seems to emerge
as the organisation that best upholds the interests of the angler, and
it is a great pity that it seems unable to raise its membership any
higher than 10,000. This demonstrates the almost total impotence
of anglers to defend their sport. It would be much better if there
were only one such organisation, with at least 100,000 members.
Surely, with an estimated three million anglers in this country, that
is not asking too much?

However, there are many individuals within these organisations

who are working hard to defend and champion the angler's cause. Those firmly on the side of the angler include such resourceful people as Gordon Barr, David Swatland, David Shaw and James Ferguson, along with a few MPs who are also keen salmon anglers and conservationists. Meanwhile, it will take a long battle to defeat the commercial fishing interests.

On the techniques of angling, however, I can do little better than paraphrase the closing lines of Richard Waddington's book *Salmon Fishing*, where he pays a back-handed tribute to the gaffers, rod wagglers, and others: I now go salmon and sea trout fishing not so much for the pot as to enjoy the exercise with the minimum of encumbrance and clutter. My bare hands have usually proved sufficient in extracting my fish and I wade the rivers and streams with no more encumbrance than my breast waders, a box of flies and a spare spool of nylon leader in my pocket.

In this book I shall examine the few facts that are known and speculate on the many fancies and theories that have been put forward from time to time. Although I am now on the wrong side of sixty I hope that I shall have the wisdom to continue to learn and that never will I convey to my reader that my thinking is omnipotent or that there is no other point of view worth noting. I have now fished for over fifty years and I have learned what sometimes seems profitable to do and what sometimes appears to be a total waste of time. But I love being beside the river – sharing it with my rod, cameras and friends, and the serenity it all brings. That is the true joy. A fish now is a great bonus, and that is the way I suspect more of us are going to have to think if this wonderful resource of migratory salmon and sea trout is to be spared for another generation.

1

The Fish

The salmon is accounted the king of fresh-water fish: and is ever bred in rivers relating to the sea, yet so high or far from it as admits of no tincture of salt or brackishness.

Izaak Walton, The Compleat Angler

Much more is known today about most of our salmonid species than was known even ten years ago. The Atlantic salmon, *Salmo salar,* the wanderer of the vast oceans and the source of leaping legends, has particularly had its lifestyle carefully and accurately documented. In the past ten years we have learned more about *salar* than we ever knew before. This is due entirely to the commercial fish farmers, who were quick to see an opportunity of rearing salmon in an artificial environment and who, equally resourcefully, saw the vast commercial potential.

THE LIFE-CYCLE OF
SALMON AND SEA TROUT

Although I am not a scientist and can only express a layman's opinion it seems reasonable to suppose that all the salmonid species had a similar origin; that environmental changes brought slight behavioural and physical modifications and that the salmon, sea trout and brown trout we have today share a common denominator. Indeed, one does not need to be too perceptive to note the hallmarks of the species of *Salmo* – similarly shaped bodies, the adipose fin and the ability to develop spotted flanks as nature or the time of season dictates. All require a similar degree of water purity and all seek the faster-flowing rivers of our uplands for their spawning ritual. All, without exception, rely on a rich protein diet, which they get by preying on smaller fish or on the abundance of aquatic insect life which is still to be found in many of our rain-fed and spring-fed rivers. All survive and thrive best within the narrow

confines of a water temperature between 5° and 20°C. Of course, they can exist in temperatures just outside these limits, but their rate of food digestion and metabolism seems to be at its best between 10° and 15° and many of the species start to show distress at prolonged temperatures much in excess of 20°C.

Salmon and sea trout, the principal anadromous species, also start their life-cycle in a similarly highly oxygenated stream to that sought by trout, approximately six weeks after the laying and fertilisation of eggs or ova in the nest or redd. This is usually a trough scooped out of the gravel by the female. As she lays her eggs in it, the male comes within close body contact and sheds his milt over them. On completion of the orgasm the hen re-covers the redd with fist-sized stones and it is then left to the vagaries of nature to dictate when the ova or eggs will fracture to permit the young embryo to emerge. Water temperatures have a direct bearing on this, but six weeks seems to be about normal.

Following this the young fish live on a built-in food supply in the form of a yolk-sac. This will sustain them for a few more weeks, but the time will quickly come when they must force their way out between the stones and face the full fury of their new and hostile environment. At this stage they will offer easy pickings for the many predators which abound. They will be expected to face the full onslaught of a flood or whatever else nature has in store for them. Many will not even survive to acquire their first natural meal. Nature is ruthless, only demanding that one spawning pair produce another spawning pair in a few year's time.

For those which are to survive for a while longer there will now be the best part of two years to be spent hiding and escaping from predators in the river while grabbing every morsel of food to come their way. In the wild state, only slowly will they develop their parr markings (faint black bars down their sides) and even more slowly (two years approximately) will they come to that moment when they don a silvery coat and nature will tell them to drop downstream towards the sea. Now known as smolts, the young salmon and sea trout have at last acquired the migratory instinct and nature ordains that they must proceed to sea to meet whatever fate has in store. During the downstream migration they may suffer untold hardship and exploitation. Waterfalls and dams must be passed; the turbines of hydroelectric schemes and the ever-increasing filth of the effluent dumped into the river from housing and industrial areas

must be negotiated. Indeed, it is possible for the migrating fish to find a downstream environment so hostile that they will not survive the filth and effluent when they reach it. In such a situation you may well wonder how the adult fish make it upstream in the first place. Usually, of course, the adults returning from the sea test the quality of the fresh water they intend to enter. At times of a big flood, for instance, the pollution levels may be sufficiently diluted for the fish to pass with comfort. Then, within hours rather than days, they can press on upstream into the higher reaches of the river where the water quality is generally of a high order. The migrating smolt, on the other hand, has no prior information on the effluent levels awaiting it in the lower reaches (usually around the month of May). It can only drop downstream as nature demands and if it drops into water with a high biochemical oxygen demand (BOD) it may well succumb and die.

Once salmon and sea trout have obtained the migratory instinct, they must proceed to sea to meet whatever fate nature has in store ... These seals were spotted just off the Isle of Harris, Hebrides.

Only during periods of a big flood, when pollution levels are
diluted, will migratory fish face the filth and effluent
disgorged in housing and industrial areas. Few of their
progeny ever make it back to the sea.

Those mature salmon which survive the spawning act are known
as kelts. Frequently they may be readily recognised by a lean and
hungry look, ragged and torn fins, a distended vent and an abundance of maggots under the gill covers and in the membranes. Some
fish may have patches of white fungus on their bodies and all tend to
look slightly 'tinny', as if the silvery coat which they were slowly
forced to abandon, prior to spawning, is trying to come back. It may
be very much a metallic appearance as opposed to the silver
freshness of a recently run salmon. Many of the males will stay on
the redds, either fighting off other spawning pairs or merely seeking
another mate. Most males eventually succumb and die, but a good
percentage of the females – those which are soon fully spent
but which have the sense to seek rest in quiet water – will survive

Note the marked difference between a fresh-run salmon and
a kelt. Fish will not always be so easy to identify.

Sea lice on a salmon, the hallmark of a fresh-run fish. Sea
lice are said to lose their tails within 24 hours of entering
fresh water, and to die and fall off within 48 hours.
However, sea lice have been known to stay alive for up to
seven days in fresh water.

to make it back to the estuary and resume their sea feeding.

Many of these kelts are caught by anglers fishing for spring fish during the early months of the season. It is also possible to encounter other fish whose real status gives rise to some perplexity. For instance, it is possible to hook a baggot or a rawner – a female that has apparently not yet found a mate and still has all its ova intact. Many of these females may have the appearance of being fresh-run; indeed, some may have sea lice on them. There are many occasions when they look so fresh that it seems the only way they can be identified with certainty is after they have been knocked on the head and left around for a while. Then their colour will darken and, when they are picked up by the head, they will shed their spawn without any other influence. Partially spawned male fish, known on the Tweed as kippers, may also be caught. These were once regarded as the boatman's perks but, like the kelt, all are regarded as unclean fish and the law states that they should be returned to the water with as little damage as possible.

For those salmon smolts of the new generation which survive the trauma of the transfer from fresh to salt water some form of shoaling must take place. Large shoals of smolts then proceed to sea and start a vast feeding spree which will take them from mere fingerlings in one year to fish of about 5lb or over in the first sea feeding year. No one knows just what influences are brought to bear, but the fish may then return to fresh water after only one year at sea. These fish, known as grilse, come back as mature spawning fish. Most do not appear until the first floods of summer and then tend to run the rivers rather quickly and be of little overall value to the angler. Many are caught by the inshore coastal and estuary netsmen, but those which escape this mayhem are regarded by some as the pimpernels of the river – here today and gone tomorrow.

To those fish which prolong their sea feasting beyond a year we can now award the title 'salmon'. These fish may spend up to three or even four years at sea before the urge to spawn comes upon them and they start their wearisome journey back to the rivers of their birth. Just what triggers off this homing instinct and gives them the ability to find the river of their birth is one of nature's mysteries. As they start the return migration they stop feeding and their stomachs begin to occlude or atrophy. Much speculation has been generated on the question of which comes first. Does the stomach occlude and cause the fish to fast? Or is it the voluntary fasting

which causes the stomach to occlude and become inoperative? Many believe that it is the mounting sexual urge which causes the fish to fast and that the occlusion of the stomach is a secondary manifestation.

Hugh Falkus in his excellent book, *Salmon Fishing*, and in consultation with my friend and family doctor, David Goldsborough, proposes the theory that salmon develop appetite suppression with sexual maturity which may be likened to anorexia nervosa (the slimmer's disease) in humans. The inferences are quite fascinating and the mind boggles at the possibility, however remote, that those humans who have developed appetite suppression may, in reality, be over-sexed. Does this imply that a cure for anorexia nervosa might be found in a bromide? Or that the day might dawn when anglers seeking to catch a lot of fish will be able to release a chemical into the water to subdue the sexual urge in salmon and thus cause them to start a feeding spree?

There are several examples in hatcheries where salmon have been neutered. In some instances these fish respond like other animals, such as cats and dogs, which have been similarly treated – they feed voraciously and grow to be larger than average. Indeed, I am reliably informed that Atlantic salmon weighing over 100lb have been produced in totally artificial conditions. On the other hand, there are many recorded instances where male salmon parr, feeding as voraciously as they do in fresh water, can and do fertilise the eggs from adult females quite effectively.

The basis of the Goldsborough hypothesis is that appetite suppression of salmon is caused by changes in a portion of its brain – the hypothalmic/pituitary axis – and that in some fish the suppression is only partial. Thus, it is postulated, some salmon not only respond to an angler's lure, but they do so in a number of widely differing ways. Additional inferences would indicate that if there are some salmon which are more prone to take an angler's lure than others, these same fish might also be induced to take food while in fresh water. Alas, there is still no evidence that wild salmon ever take food for nourishment on their spawning run. Even so it is an interesting speculation and it may just account for the fact that some salmon seem to take our lures more readily than others. Sadly, however, this information may be of much more interest to the medical profession than it is to anglers. Even full knowledge is unlikely to help us to catch more fish.

Hugh Falkus fly fishing for sea trout on the Cumbrian Esk.

Those fish which remain at sea maintain a steady growth rate. A lot depends on water temperatures and the availability of food. Many of our salmon are known to migrate into northern Arctic waters, where they may go under the ice. Some go to Greenland, the Faeroe Islands and north Norway. Some may well attain weights in excess of 30 or 40lb, but the big British salmon of bygone days are now more rare while fish in the 10 to 15lb bracket are more frequently encountered. Much is still unknown of the minutiae of the salmon's life-cycle, but in all instances the return to fresh water is prefaced by a loss of appetite and a firm preoccupation with the business of survival of the species and ultimate mating.

There is much speculation on why mature salmon re-enter the rivers of their birth at different times of the year. From our point of view those fish which return and enter the rivers during the spring are among the most desirable. Known as springers, they may well come back at any time between February and May. Indeed, it is well known that some spring fish will enter fresh water as early as November. What induces them to do this when they do not intend spawning until the following November and when they must sustain themselves on nothing more than built-up food reserves in the body

A back-end cock fish with well-developed kype. A fish which is past its prime and is possibly better spared.

tissue? Why do other salmon wait at sea until autumn, when they are on the threshold of spawning, then run the rivers and complete their spawning act within a few weeks rather than months?

If we lean to the view that like breeds like, it would seem reasonable to suppose that fish with spring-running tendencies will beget fish with a similar habit. Fish which come in during the late autumn, on the other hand, may well bequeath to their offspring the instinct to come back at that time. Of course, it is the spring fish which is the most desirable for the fishery and it is also this same fish which comes under most attack from the commercial fisheries. Does this not adequately explain why our spring fish are disappearing and why the autumn runs are being sustained and augmented?

In many instances the running habits of fish may be linked with the length of the river system. Most of our classic and longer rivers get runs of early springers. The Tweed, Tay, Dee, Spey and Wye are good examples. Other, shorter, rivers – such as the spate rivers of the west coast of Scotland – may not see the first fish until the floods of early summer. My earlier book, *Salmon*, contained much speculation on this subject and it is not my intention to repeat too much of what I have already written. Most authors on salmon and sea trout devote at least one lengthy chapter to the known facts and to their speculations on the life-cycle of the fish. I was never much of a man for theories. The best theory ever propounded on any subject usually only has to wait around awhile for destruction or demise.

With its return to fresh water, we know that the salmon's appetite continues to be suppressed. It is perhaps a little ironic that the longer the fish resides in fresh water the less it is inclined to take our lures or any item of food. Of course, other influences might induce a fish to take our lures and we will examine these in a later chapter, but the actual consumption of food for nourishment is virtually unknown.

How long it takes a salmon or sea trout to proceed upstream is a source of further speculation. Evidence is strong for the assumption that the early spring and late autumn salmon move only slowly through the lower beats of a river when the water is exceptionally cold. There is equally convincing evidence that later spring and summer fish, in warmer water, may run fast and far. During their sea lives most salmon attract parasites known as sea lice. These can survive for only a short period in fresh water. The actual period varies considerably and in laboratory conditions these parasites have

A diseased spring salmon from the River Tweed.

been known to remain clinging to the host for up to seven days. In the hurly-burly of a turbulent river, however, it is assumed that they only survive for up to forty-eight hours. But this is only a supposition and there may be no real way of establishing the truth. On the assumption that sea lice may exist on salmon or sea trout for up to forty-eight hours, however, we may draw some interesting if tentative conclusions. A week before writing this chapter I caught a 7½lb Spey salmon with sea lice on it at least forty-five miles upstream from the estuary. This suggests that my fish had run upstream at a speed of nigh on one mile an hour or twenty-four miles in a day. It also evokes questions such as what might induce it to stop for anything other than a short rest, and when it might regard its upstream migration as at an end until spawning time. Do rivers fill from the top, as some authorities suggest?

Along with all the other pestilences and trials which salmon and sea trout have to endure, there has been an occasional and deadly plague which strikes them down from time to time. Originally named *Bacillus salmonis pestis* in the late nineteenth century, it now enjoys the more exotic title of ulcerative dermal necrosis, or UDN. No one yet seems any wiser on the origins of the disease, but it broke out with dire effect in the 1880s and again in 1966. In both instances it took nearly twenty years to abate, but it was back again with a very bad outbreak on the Tweed in November 1985 and who

might say with any conviction that it will not come back in plague proportions at any time in the future? It is assumed that UDN occurs with more deadly effect in cold water conditions and that it is of viral origin rather than bacterial or fungal. Whatever else it might involve, it seems that the final fungal growth is the last and most deadly symptom in the chain. While it might be only coincidental, the 1966 outbreak came to many rivers at a time when they seemed to have highly abundant stocks. We still had to wait for the main onslaught of the Danish high-seas netting to further deplete our stocks and it may be that the disease was merely nature's way of eliminating an excess. When it hit the Lune in October 1966 I was one of the first anglers to catch a fish with a small patch of fungus on it, about the size of a penny piece. Within days there were fish dying **in their thousands. It was a sickening sight.**

No one yet seems any wiser on the disease UDN, but it broke out with dire effect in the 1880s and again in 1966. In both instances it took nearly twenty years to abate.

THE EXPERIENCE OF FISH FARMERS

Sadly there are altogether too many questions about our migratory fish species to which we do not yet know the answers. Most are only of academic interest, but we may learn a lot more in the near future from those who exploit the salmon as a farmed species. For instance, it is known that wild salmon do vastly different things in differing environmental situations. Just a few rivers may be able to produce smolts which will migrate seawards after only one year in

fresh water. Many more rivers produce smolts that are at least two years of age and there are a sprinkling of other rivers – notably those of northern Norway – which may take up to four years to produce a sea-going smolt. Doubtless a lot has to do with the temperature of the water and the consequent availability of food. The period of a winter freeze-up must be considered, but a four-year smolting pattern would be of little interest to the hatchery manager whose prime task is to create a fish of saleable size in the shortest possible time and with the minimum production cost. With selective breeding most hatcheries are now producing salmon fry and parr which become smolts at one year. These are quickly transferred to the sea feeding cages where – depending on water temperatures – a rapid growth can result from artificial feeding. Fish may be graded throughout the growing process and it is then a simple matter for the hatchery manager to produce fish of the most acceptable size for the market. Unlike a commercial netting station for wild salmon, where the quantity of fish seems more important than their size, the hatchery will be able to supply large quantities of fish of identical size for easier packing, marketing and transportation.

Fish which go off their food as the spawning instinct develops are clearly undesirable in commercial farming. Hatchery operators try to breed this characteristic out of their salmon, and they are now producing smolts at one year of age and fish which grow to marketable size long before any sexual development slows down their growth. Of course, these fish never have to face the hardships endured by wild salmon. They are cosseted from the womb to the tomb, as it were. Not for them the rigours of natural spawning and the distinct possibility of an untimely death at the end of it all. In the wild state a lot of the females and most males die from exhaustion after spawning. Those which survive – kelts – may just make it down to the estuary and back to the sea feeding grounds, but most will succumb at some point on their return migration, and the depredations of the ever-increasing packs of seals are increasing this toll. Fish born in a hatchery, on the other hand, are protected from all known predators. Water temperatures can be adjusted to give the best rate of growth and, when the smolts are transferred to the sea feeding cages, growth rate may be little short of phenomenal. Thereafter, only those fish with the fastest growth rate are kept for brood stock. They will not have to run the gauntlet of predators or the myriad of netting and trapping devices that man has established

up and down our coasts, in the narrowly defined sea lanes and estuaries, nor will they have to negotiate the natural and man-made obstacles in our rivers.

However, it is questionable whether any amount of salmon farming will ever eliminate the market for wild-bred fish. This is sad for those of us who looked to salmon farming to reduce pressures on the wild-bred stocks. These pressures are now higher than at any time in history. Amazingly, there are still people who believe that this manna will continue to pour down as if from heaven and that mankind can go on cropping the resource without a thought for good husbandry or the future well-being of the species. It is argued that nature always provides; that there are always enough salmon for the netsmen to catch all they can within the permitted hours and seasons; that the chain of predators can continue to take its quota and after the angler has taken his lucky dip there will still be sufficient fish left in the rivers for adequate survival of the species. I wish that this were so, but the wild salmon is under severe threat of overcropping and few people, if any, are prepared to acknowledge that there is a problem or, if they do, attempt to do anything about it.

It is now impossible for us to enlist public sympathy with the claim that the salmon is a threatened species. So long as the hatcheries operate, the salmon will be less of a threatened species than it has ever been. Salmon will be as plentiful as broiler chickens, chipped potatoes or baked beans. We do not need to have a single mature salmon in our rivers to achieve this, but it will be a sad day for the sporting angler and those of us who thrill at the sight of the wild salmon's leap and the sheer magic of its natural life saga.

The future may see an even greater quantity of wild salmon being netted on the high seas and round our coasts and estuaries. A few fish may be retained alive in pens as brood stock for future generations and stripped at spawning time of their ova and milt. The next generation would be reared to the smolt stage in hatcheries. The one-year smolts would go to the sea feeding cages, while fish which take two years to reach smolting stage may be dumped in the upper reaches of the rivers to take their chance with nature and provide the commercial fishermen with their share of the catch. Any survivors to come back to the river of their apparent birth could easily be scooped up, a further brood stock retained, and the whole process repeated. This, in my view, is not a nightmarish dream. It

could happen. But, if and when it does, I hope that I shall have passed on, for the sport of angling as I have known it will be a thing of the past.

It is my view that it will be impossible to maintain the sport of angling as it has been for wild fish, and at its present level, unless and until there is full awareness of the necessity to indulge in good husbandry. The owners of most sporting estates know full well that if their land is to produce big bags of pheasants for the shooting fraternity then it is wellnigh impossible to rely on a wild-bred stock. On those rough shoots where more modest bags of game are sought or expected it is frequently possible to rely entirely on natural production, provided there is help in the elimination of predators and that the balance of nature is maintained. The snag is that with migratory fish we have no idea how to maintain this balance. We do not have a clue what production we get on our spawning beds, what happens to the survivors or the product of a particular year, how many get preyed upon in the dark vastnesses of the oceans, and just how many get mopped up by the antics of mankind as he nets and traps them at any point where they may be located.

Even when the survivors make it back to the river we have no notion of the numbers, or what might be a sensible percentage to net as a commercial crop at the mouths of our rivers. How dare anyone claim, in the most remote sense, that the resource is *managed*? It is totally mismanaged, and I would be ashamed if I were one of those people who stood before the public at large and proclaimed that I was actively engaged in salmon management, that everything was all right and that I was really doing a good job. Most of those involved merely speculate on matters which they do not fully comprehend.

One way of increasing the stock of near-wild-bred fish is to take the excess of parr from the hatcheries (those which are to take two years to become smolts) and release them into the headwaters and feeder streams of our migratory fish rivers. Food might be at a premium and there would be all the other hazards of the wild to endure, but there would be a reasonable chance of those fish becoming imprinted with those waters and, after their sea-going migration, seeking the same river system in much the same manner as any wild-bred fish born there. Some scientists suggest that we should not meddle. In a short article in the *Daily Telegraph* of 18 November 1985, titled 'Fear over Salmon Stocking', we read:

Indiscriminate stocking of salmon rivers with hatchery fish might destroy the salmon's homing instinct . . . Prof. Noel Wilkins, dean of the science faculty at University College, Galway, explains in a booklet published by the Atlantic Salmon Trust that the hatchery fish may be genetically different. He writes in 'Salmon Stocks – A genetic perspective' that there are two distinct races of Atlantic salmon in the British Isles, and important genetic differences between salmon in separate rivers. 'The Atlantic salmon is far from a single interbreeding and remarkably homogenous species as was once thought. On the contrary, it can be divided into a large number of local spawning populations which differ genetically from one another,' said Prof. Wilkins. The homing instinct of salmon to return from feeding grounds to spawn in their native rivers is particularly well developed in Atlantic salmon, he explained. This maintains the gene pools of separate stocks, so that they can evolve differently. An early effect of indiscriminate transplantation of non-native fish or hatchery-reared fish to such rivers is interbreeding, 'with consequent alterations in genetic composition and reducing homing precision of the offspring'.

All this, of course, is possible, but the first day man stripped a hen fish of its ova and added the milt of a male to fertilise the eggs was the very moment when we meddled and produced offspring which had been created by our selection and not that of the fish.

In view of the history of artificial replenishment of our salmon rivers so far, therefore, I suspect that the scientists are being unduly cautious and that some continued experimentation would not do any more harm than we have already done. In this context, an interesting incident was related to me by Tony Chattaway about some parr dumped by a west coast Scottish fish farm to fend for themselves because they were not due to become smolts until they were two years old. The only outflow of fresh water from the farm to the sea – and therefore the only access to the sea the parr had when they became smolts – was a culvert of little more than normal size. Imagine the surprise and delight of the fishery manager three years later, therefore, when a shoal of fresh-run salmon, including a fish estimated to weigh 50lb, tried to run back up the culvert. Of course, brood fish in excess of 50lb are not uncommon in the feeding cages of these hatcheries. Constant feeding in controlled hatchery conditions will soon give us larger than normal

fish. But the rub came when it was realised that the original stock of ova of that run had been taken from a Norwegian river where fifty pounders are not uncommon.

Much the same happens with red deer brought off the hill and kept in cosseted surroundings. They not only grow to weigh more than their wild brethren, but they also develop some of the finest antlers it is possible for red deer to have. Anyway, the incident of salmon returning to a drainpipe is sufficient to convince me that we would not be taking any grave risks by the release of surplus parr into the headwaters of some of our migratory fish rivers, merely for experiment.

Of course, until something is done about the indiscriminate netting and poaching it might need a group of philanthropists to finance such an operation. As an exercise in business prudence it does not yet make much sense. But water authorities or district fishery boards might usefully undertake some modest expenditure and at the same time give a good and useful home to a type of fish unwanted by the hatchery. Of course, the scientists will continue to tell us that it is all highly dangerous, that we are messing about with genetic engineering and upsetting natural patterns. Well, we have already done that and no one is doing it more than the commercial fishermen and the poachers on the high seas and elsewhere. Even the legitimate netsmen don't seem to care if they take the entire stock returning to one specific river system. They are interested only in taking all they can find within the permitted times and seasons. As for the poacher, he has no such scruples and regards all as fair game at any time or place.

If any group of people are prepared to make some attempt to do something positive about safeguarding the salmon and sea trout resource, there is still time to get on with it. But at the moment, except during those years of heavy rainfall such as we had in 1985, when a lot of fish were able to escape the ravages of the netsmen, the efficiency of those who take the crop of migratory fish exceeds that of those charged with the management of the resource. And what of those who should be protecting this resource for the future? How do we get them away from their desks and their committees and their conferences? It all reminds me of my father's definition of a committee as a group of people who, as individuals, could do nothing, but who formed themselves into a committee to decide that nothing could be done!

2
Catching Methods

Every child is born with inclinations of some sort. But the field must be open for their recognition and development. A deaf child cannot become a musician, nor a blind one a landscape artist. So it is with angling. If it is in the blood, the fish must still be there to be caught.

Eric Horsfall Turner, Angler's Cavalcade

From Roman times and beyond mankind has regarded salmon and sea trout as a resource he could crop without a thought for the future. The fish would come in on the restless tides and, at all points on their upstream migration, nets and traps would ensnare the unlucky and the unwary. Indeed, salmon and sea trout were so plentiful that in earlier times they sometimes made less of a market price than some coarse fish. Even the returning kelts which survived the rigours of spawning were netted and trapped. Perhaps there is little wonder that those apprentices grew weary of salted kelt.

Imagine the size of the resource in those far-off days – days before the dawn of rail travel when an angler like myself living in northern England might have taken the best part of a week by stage-coach to get to somewhere like Grantown-on-Spey. The Highlands represented a hostile environment in those days, and few would venture even beyond their clan borders without a veritable army to accompany them. The fish in our rivers were so plentiful that it seemed impossible to overexploit the resource and no amount of netting, trapping, spearing or leistering could possibly reduce it to endangered proportions.

Although it is difficult to determine just when the sport of angling for migratory fish really got into top gear, it must be assumed that it coincided pretty closely with the advent of rail travel. Before that the bulk of all migratory fish caught were taken by nets. In the 1921 edition of Scrope's *Days and Nights of Salmon Fishing in the Tweed*, edited by H. T. Sheringham, we read that in 1816, one of the years of record catches by the nets on the Tweed, the figures were: 54,041 salmon, 120,596 grilse and 62,074 sea

trout. Thereafter the catches tended to decrease and from 1845 to
1849 the average return was 8,909 salmon, 39,409 grilse and 35,641
sea trout. From 1895 to 1899 the average return had gone down to
7,366 salmon, 8,458 grilse and 23,746 sea trout. Sheringham goes on
to comment:

This indicates a serious decrease in the total, though the salmon
have not fallen off so much as the others. Pollution, the increased
land-drainage [of which Scrope complained even in 1842] and the
operation of the nets – all, no doubt, have played a part in the
decline.

There is also no doubt that the nets were comparatively inefficient
in those days. Methods today are much more sophisticated and
consequently the catches are now much higher.
    Earlier in his introduction to this classic book, while commenting
on the increasing shortage of salmon which was then (1921) quite
apparent, Sheringham wrote:

The next evil – and it is hardly less serious – is the fact that in the
estuaries or lower reaches of many rivers which still hold salmon
there is so much netting that an undue proportion of the stock is
killed off year by year, leaving too few for the reproduction of the
species to the extent designed by nature. This netting takes special
toll of the most valuable classes of salmon, those which run into
fresh-water in the early months of the year, and in too many cases
leaves no chance to any except the late autumn class which runs
after the netting season is over. Some rivers are said to be getting
'later and later', which is merely a euphemism for 'over-fished'.

My view is that until the end of the Second World War netting
and angling interests made reasonably comfortable bedfellows.
Most angling was confined to that done by the riparian owners and
their guests and pressure was never very high. Commercial fishing,
on the other hand, had been severely curtailed by the Act of 1861
and was now confined to the operation of estuarial and coastal nets
at specified times and seasons. Of course, the netsmen could still
kill all they could catch, but the nets were made of hemp and not so
easy or so effective in operation as are the monofilament nets we
have today.

Since the war there have been dramatic changes in the pursuit of salmon and sea trout and in the methods by which we catch them. Angling is one of the most inefficient methods there is of taking these fish. Fish which do not feed in fresh water on their return from the sea are highly unpredictable in their response to our lures. Given an opportunity of fishing for a particular species of fish, one of the first questions we would ask is 'What does it feed on?' Armed with the right answers we can then go forth hopefully in the knowledge that our chosen baits or lures might hold some interest for the fish. To be told that the fish does not feed on anything does not give much assistance in the choice of baits or lures. We might glean some information on a choice of lure by a study of the type of prey the fish sought during its feeding period and there can be little doubt that the lures and flies we offer to salmon and sea trout today are designed to arouse the predatory instinct rather than the appetite.

My practical knowledge of salmon and sea-trout angling is confined to the period since release from military duty at the end of the war. In the early years it was possible to go fishing in much more certain knowledge of a catch than it is today – although my first salmon was caught entirely by accident when worm fishing for trout. Slowly I acquired the necessary skills to catch salmon and sea trout more predictably, but it was not until the advent of the salmon disease in the autumn of 1966 that many of us became aware of the mounting pressure on the salmon resource from many quarters. About the same time there came news of the discovery by the Danes of some of the sea feeding areas of salmon in the vicinity of Greenland. Until then it was virtually unknown exactly where salmon migrated for the bulk of their sea feeding activity. Nuclear submarines gave us the next clue when they reported packs of salmon feeding under the Arctic ice shelf. Indeed, if this is where the bulk of the fish go it is a merciful blessing that the thick ice protects them from the destructive tactics of the commercial fishing world.

Be that as it may, nowadays a plethora of electronic fish-finding equipment and sophisticated netting systems is operated on the high seas to intercept large stocks of salmon. Many of the routes used by the fish to reach the sea-feeding grounds are now known and their co-ordinates recorded. Most of these are comparatively narrow channels which may be easily obstructed by long monofilament drift

nets. Some of these nets are reported to be vast. One corres-
pondent, a serving officer in the Royal Air Force, wrote recently to
say that the high-definition radar apparatus of Coastal Command
surveillance aircraft has detected marker buoys of nets extending up
to fifteen miles. An entire run of fish could be intercepted and
annihilated. Worse still is the fact that in a period of stormy weather
the net may break loose and be lost to those who service it. Being of
rotproof monofilament, it will continue as a fishing instrument,
roaming the seas like some legendary Flying Dutchman and ensnaring
all the fish to come within its orbit. The caught fish would doubtless
die and rot, leaving space for the mesh to ensnare again.

Salmon are now being intercepted at all points of their migration
out to and back from the sea feeding areas. Rumour has it that
Russian factory ships can 'hoover' up vast shoals of migrating
smolts, but there is enough real evidence of general mayhem and
skulduggery without listening to rumour. Much concern is ex-
pressed by the Scots at the large drift-net fishery which is still
permitted to operate legally off the Northumberland and Yorkshire
coast. The Scots claim that the bulk of these fish are destined for
Scottish rivers and they are highly indignant about it all when drift-
netting for salmon is now banned by law in Scottish coastal waters.
The Northumbrian netsmen claim that theirs is an age-old entitlement; that with a six-mile limit from the shore and a net length of
600 feet they are not doing a great deal of damage. They also point
out that a cowboy element of commercial fishermen is ready and
waiting for the laws to be altered so that they can move in and fish
illegally. Meanwhile, they claim that so long as it is legal to net the
North Sea off Northumbria they, the present netsmen, keep the area
well policed. It's a bit like them saying that so long as you let us
continue we will only burgle your house and thus prevent the
cowboys coming in to murder you.

I don't know the full saga of the Northumbrian drift-net fishery,
its effect on Scottish salmon migrations, or the effect of illegal drift-
netting in the Moray Firth and all around the west coast, but I do
know that it is yet another link in the ever-growing chain which is
used to take more salmon for the market. In addition to the crop
now taken by the Danes off Greenland, there is a growing fishery
operated by the Faeroese and more long-line fishing by the Nor-
wegians off the Lofoten Islands. Their argument is that if fish bred
in British or other European waters then come into other territorial

waters to feed, those with fishing rights in the non-producing countries should at least be entitled to a 'grazing fee' in lieu of payment for the fish which the salmon take as food. This is all understandable but it does not help, in any way, to reduce the continued pressure on the salmon resource at all points where they are found.

On their return to the rivers of their birth salmon and sea trout are again harassed by both legal and illegal netting systems. While much illegal fishing still goes undetected, it is an age-old right of many estuarial proprietors to net their rivers at set times and seasons. Some of these riparian owners literally rely on the income generated from the salmon and sea trout that are netted and sent to market. All salmon and sea-trout fishing in Scotland is a heritable right and there is no public right of fishing anywhere. The riparian owners may, if they wish, retain these rights for themselves and not allow a single angler to trespass on their territory. That many of the owners now choose to let their fishing rights to tenants, syndicates, clubs and hotels does not alter their private right to keep them to themselves. Similarly, the right to net and trap goes back into ancient history. It would need drastic changes in the law and the ability to enforce them before any alteration in the status quo could be achieved.

Much the same situation applies to Scandinavia and Iceland, but at least the socialist government of Iceland, recognising that the angling resource brings the greatest benefit to the economy of the country, imposes a ban on most commercial fishing. On the eastern shores of North America the situation is vastly different. Here the riparian rights are all held by the Canadian and US governments and both netting and angling are subject to careful management. In recent years there has been great concern that the commercial effort has been taking too big a crop. Much commercial fishing has now been curtailed and there are strict limits on the numbers of fish which may be killed by anglers. There are trends which indicate that catch-and-release policies will soon become normal rather than exceptional. There may be an insistence on barbless hooks. This may prompt some of us to analyse exactly why we go fishing, and raises other – ethical – questions about the morality of playing fish merely for fun and abandoning the choice that any hunter likes to exercise – that of tackling our quarry in a sporting manner, but with the right to kill occasionally for the pot.

I lean to the view that unless we maintain our right to kill a few fish we are on very dangerous ground with the ever-growing fraternity of those who see angling merely as another form of animal cruelty. There can be nothing unethical or immoral about wishing to exercise our age-old instinct in the catching and killing of our own food. Being one of those rare people who retain a belief in God, I am reminded of the permission which God gave to Noah:

And God blessed Noah and his sons, and said unto them, be fruitful, and multiply, and replenish the earth. And the fear of you and the dread of you shall be upon every beast of the earth, and upon every fowl of the air, upon all that moveth upon the earth, and upon all the fishes of the sea; into your hand they are delivered. Every moving thing that liveth shall be meat for you; even as the green herb I have given you all things. (Gen. 9:1–3)

Whatever is to happen to the sport of angling, there can be little doubt which of the methods of exploiting or enjoying the salmon resource is the most profitable to the general economy. Socialist Iceland soon recognised the priority and it is clear that the visiting angler to a Scottish river (or any other river for that matter) is going to pump a great deal more money into the local economy than is gained by the sale of commercially caught fish sent to the market-place. At best, the commercially caught fish will provide only a living wage for the small number who operate the nets. The larger profits will go to the owners or the tenants of the netting rights and those faceless ones in faraway places who market the fish in our large cities and towns. Very little benefit will accrue to people living in the areas where the salmon and sea trout are generated and nurtured.

A rod-caught fish, on the other hand, has to be worth many times the value of a commercially caught fish. There is the initial benefit paid in river rental to the owner or his agent. This is followed by the sums handed over to the local hotel, garage and tackle shop and salaries and gratuities to the many gillies – not to mention all the other ancillary connections these and other trades have with each other. It was recently said that a rod-caught salmon might be worth as much as £2,000 to the local economy, but I suggest that the real figure might be higher – particularly in times of a shortage of salmon in our rivers. One angler of my acquaintance claims that it cost him

nearly £3,000 in salmon fishing expeditions before he caught his first fish.

Most salmon anglers, even those with a modest income, do not count the cost when they come away on a holiday. They are the big spenders in every sense and ask little more than the opportunity of fishing in scenic places with a bonus chance of taking a salmon home with them. Deny them that opportunity or render the fishing so poor that even the sight of a salmon is a rare event, and you may well deprive the Highlands of a useful and highly welcome visitor. At a time when the Government is under great pressure to maintain maximum employment, it must see that the employment of a few netsmen – and the lining of the pockets of those who have inherited the netting rights – is as nothing compared with the employment and income generated from the visiting sportsman.

If some of the age-old methods of fishing for salmon and sea trout are now too effective, what should the angler do to avoid coming under the suspicion of over-exploitation? First, I think that we must accept that there are many so-called anglers who are not content merely with the odd fish to take home. Some have developed a fishmonger mentality. There is little place for this type of angler in the sport as I see it in the future and it may be that the imposition of strict limit bags – which apply with practically every other species of fish – will eventually get the support it needs from salmon and sea-trout anglers. Traditionally, both the netsmen and the angler have killed every fish they could catch. Those surplus to requirements are sold in the marketplace. Those caught by estate guests are handed in for similar sale and it was always assumed that the resource could take all, and more, of the demands we made of it.

I suspect that the time is not too distant when we shall be encouraged or even compelled to put our own house in order. This may mean adopting a fly-only rule on some rivers. It may also mean a limit on the numbers caught and the quality of the fish killed, together with further restrictions on the duration of the season. Many of us feel that we must start imposing some form of self-discipline and I have been happy to abandon all forms of bait fishing in favour of the fly and to return all those fish – particularly the gravid females – which tend to be past their best at the end of the season. We may even think of altering some of the closing dates, but this will require firm and enforceable changes in the law or more self-discipline than can apparently be found at present. Few riparian

owners will be willing to restrict their income by a voluntary shortening of the season, but there are precedents in the curtailment of sport in the shooting world. Grouse shooting is frequently curtailed or abandoned and wildfowling is frequently banned in times of hard weather or when there is a threat to the species. Why is it that no one has ever come up with a ban on salmon fishing at times of great threat to the fish? The answer is simple. There are few if any vested interests in wildfowling and grouse shooting other than for sport, there is an immensely powerful lobby for the commercial salmon fisherman.

At the present moment, therefore, there are just too many legitimate methods of catching salmon and sea trout for the future well-being of the species. Add to this all the illegal skulduggery and we have a totally intolerable situation. History suggests that things get worse rather than better, and I suspect that I might be living in the autumn of the wild salmon resource. Fifty years ago, when I first started fishing for trout, it was a rare event to encounter a trout that had been reared in a hatchery. Today the hatchery-reared trout is relied upon almost totally to provide sport for the masses. The wild fish can occasionally be encountered in remote and inaccessible places, but it is the hatchery fish which dominates on most of our rivers and streams and certainly on all the man-made stillwaters. Might the next fifty years see the same trend with salmon and sea trout?

We have already seen the development of stillwater impoundments and artificial rivers stocked with hatchery-reared salmon. There will not be many of my generation who will seek to fish them, but they might well provide a coming generation with the only type of salmon fishing which will be readily available and at modest cost. We have seen it happen with our stocks of wild trout. What is there to stop it happening with salmon?

So far I have given little attention to sea trout. These have escaped some of the ravages wrought on the salmon, but salmon and sea trout frequently assemble together in our estuaries before running the rivers and in the years ahead sea trout may well come in for much the same exploitation as the salmon. In the Hebrides I have frequently watched vast shoals of salmon and sea trout intermingle as they move in and out with the tides waiting for a rise in the small rivers entering the sea. Both have a similar behavioural pattern, but there are sometimes subtle differences in the way they take lures.

Many methods, both commercial and sporting, apply equally for salmon and sea trout. But the fish do not seem to take the same migration routes in the sea and sea trout are known to run the rivers on more frequent occasions than salmon seem to – and to survive these spawning runs. For much of their lives, however, sea trout come under the same pressures as salmon. Both may be legally angled for with a wide variety of baits and lures and I suspect that the time is overdue when we must think of sterner measures of conservation than we have at the moment.

Legal methods of angling for salmon and sea trout presently include the use of many forms of natural bait, any type of spinning bait and any type of fly. The use of ova as bait is banned and other restrictions may be imposed at certain times to conform with an owner's policy or that laid down by the ruling river authority or district fishery board. Multi-hook lures are still permitted in Britain and it has to be admitted that the treble hook is a most efficient instrument. Sadly, there are also too many unscrupulous anglers who use these in conjunction with lead weights merely to rake the bed of a river and foul-hook any fish which may be lurking there. Foul-hooking, or sniggling, seems to be accepted practice on too many rivers and particularly in such locations as the upper Tweed. Just why those in authority do nothing about it remains a mystery. Is it that they are intimidated by gangs of hooligans who might threaten, or do they just turn a blind eye?

If there is to be a miracle, and our wild salmon and sea trout are to survive for future generations of sportsmen, then I suspect that on many rivers a fly-only rule will gradually take over. It is the law in North America and it would seem to be a natural consequence here if the fish are not to be fished out before this century is over. With that firmly in our minds, therefore, I shall examine only those fishing methods which are in the best sporting traditions – fishing for salmon and sea trout with an artificial fly or lure.

3
Facts and Fancies

I don't mind middle-aged fishermen airing their pet theories, which doesn't do any harm, and one needn't pay attention, but I do object to their telling downright lies!
John Ashley-Cooper, The Great Salmon Rivers of Scotland

Most of us who claim to know a little about salmon and sea trout are all too aware of the limited knowledge we really have. Much has been added in the past ten years by those entrepreneurs who have taken up salmon farming and ranching. Most have come to accept the harsh realities of the commercial world where success brings reward and applause while failure brings bankruptcy and obscurity. In their wild state, however, we know that, at times of their own choosing, the fish move in from the sea and are only then able to negotiate those rivers whose lower reaches have the requisite water chemistry, dissolved oxygen content and freedom from pollution. We know that for reasons best known to themselves they make erratic progress up to the spawning redds and that, in the autumn of the year, the hens eventually shed their ova to be fertilised by the males on the redd, and thus the new life begins.

These are the basic facts of the upstream movement of salmon and sea trout. But we have had to suffer untold and often idle speculations about how many salmon and sea trout are needed to replenish the stock sufficiently well to enable it to withstand all the ravages made upon it. My contention is that it is virtually impossible to have too many fish running a river. Of course, there might be overcrowding, disease, over-cutting of the redds at spawning time and an apparent loss of the crop which mankind might have taken elsewhere. Our fishery specialists (perhaps those with their eye on the commercial fishery) will tell us that over-cutting of the redds is undesirable in that it merely represents waste. They do not tell us that shortly following fertilisation a salmon egg is one of the toughest objects in nature; that if dislodged from the redd by another spawning pair it has as good a chance of lodging elsewhere

and hatching out as of being eaten by a predator. Many trout hatcheries bombard their newly fertilised ova in a tumble-mill merely to kill off the weaklings. Why should nature be less demanding? No, the over-cutting jibe is merely a hoary old chestnut which comes from those who would like to find excuses to take an even higher commercial crop.

It is said by some that many salmon rivers are stocked from the higher reaches downwards. This implies that all the early-run fish make for the headwaters and the tributaries and that the late-running fish merely fill the lower beats so that all of the available space in a river system is used for spawning. If I were to lean to any theories on fish and fishing, this one would appeal to me. It fits in with my thoughts and idle speculations, but I am not convinced that it even remotely approaches the truth. I just do not know if a river fills from the top. I do know that some very late-running autumn fish on the Tweed can travel a long way in a very short time. Whether nature demands that they are merely a back-up stock for the depletions which have occurred upstream to the early-running stock is yet another idle speculation. Sea trout particularly will run fast and far late on in the season, even if there is barely sufficient water to cover their backs. But just where and why they choose their spawning rendezvous is yet another of nature's mysteries.

For instance, why is there a vast run of immature sea trout into such rivers as the Spey in the autumn? These fish, known as finnock, do not seem to spawn but merely overwinter on a starvation diet and then migrate back to the sea about the same time as the surviving kelts are trying to get back. These finnock may be easily caught in vast numbers by early anglers on the Spey, but who is to say that they would not be better spared to become mature sea trout? What purpose is served by their being in the river?

It is perhaps a fair assumption that both salmon and sea trout were once entirely resident in fresh water. The fact that the salinity and the specific gravity of sea water would cause their hatched eggs to float must imply that fresh water is essential for reproduction. Their initial sea-going migration may have been the result of a tremendous shortage of food in our rivers at some time in history and it must be for the same reason that salmon and sea trout do not need to feed upon their return to fresh water. If they did need to feed, the average salmon river would simply lack the resources to support the stock. It is also reasonable to suppose that somewhere there is a

link between sexual maturity and appetite, but I am not sufficiently well informed to comment. There is also evidence to suggest that a return to fresh water, even in the absence of any sexual development, may trigger off some appetite suppression. For instance, let us examine the pattern of behaviour of those salmon which are taken from a sea hatchery and released into one of the new artificial salmon fisheries in the Midlands and elsewhere.

The hatchery fish are required to become smolts as quickly as possible. These smolts are then transferred to cages or fenced lochs in the sea where they are fed a diet similar to that sought by sea-going salmon in the wild state. Experienced hatchery operatives can vary the diet to create the type of fish desired in the marketplace. Some may make superb smoked salmon while other fish may be more suited to the fish-kettle. I do not pretend to know the intricacies of salmon farming, but I am most interested in learning all that I can about behavioural patterns of the fish.

Most of the fish which feed in the sea lochs and cages will be grown to a specific weight or dimension, starved for a few days to enable the gut and bowel to get rid of the residual faecal matter and then knocked on the head and dispatched to the marketplace. Fish which are required for restocking, however, may again be fed until they have attained the required size and then starved for a few days before transfer to their new home. Starvation is necessary if only to eliminate fouling of the water in the transportation tanker. But, curiously upon their release into fresh water the fish may show little sign of wishing to renew the hectic feeding they had indulged in a few days earlier. It seems that the very act of transporting them from sea water to fresh triggers off the same appetite suppression as occurs in wild fish. (This behaviour is not typical of all salmon. For example, in some states of the north-eastern USA many waters contain stocks of land-locked Atlantic salmon, which use large freshwater lakes as a sea and run into the smaller feeder streams to spawn. These fish do not attain the weight of sea run fish, but they are a highly valued sporting species in such states as Maine and New York.)

One man who has done much in the development of artificial salmon fisheries and fish culture generally is Mr Tony Chattaway. In many conversations with him I have tried to establish a link between the behaviour of hatchery fish and wild fish – but it has not been easy. Contrary to the school of thought which holds that salmon

cannot feed in fresh water, there is ample evidence that hatchery-reared salmon can and occasionally do. Decaying food is sometimes found in the stomach as well as the gut of fish caught by anglers in these artificial impoundments. The same fish also retain their vomerine teeth for as long as they might continue to feed. Thus it might well be that it is the advent of sexual maturity that is the prime cause of loss of appetite. There is no evidence to suggest that salmon in an artificial freshwater environment continue feeding to grow, but there are hints that they do occasionally take the small amounts of natural food available.

Of course there is no sexual development in these fish taken from the sea cages. They have merely been compelled to stop feeding for a few days and then subjected to the trauma of transportation down the highway to their new freshwater home. It may be that the stress created by the overland journey is sufficient to cause the immediate appetite suppression, but if we believe that it is really sexual development that inhibits wild fish from feeding on their return to fresh water it is difficult to accept that there can be many other reasons for total appetite suppression.

As an aside – one which I offer merely to add to the confusion – I was once fishing a broad estuary of the Branch river in south-west Alaska. Pink salmon (one of the five Pacific species) were pouring upstream on the flood tide. I was with a party of Texans who wanted to catch their limit bags of five fish each. All of us caught our limits in less than an hour and it was then that our guide began his task of cleaning and gutting the fish for deep-freezing. The offal and guts were thrown into a small backwater adjacent to the river and could be clearly seen lying on the bottom in the shallow water. Within minutes a vast shoal of salmon moved into the backwater and proceeded to gobble up all the discarded guts and offal. It was an amazing sight and may well add some power to the elbows of those who claim that salmon can and do feed in fresh water. At that state of the tide the water was still brackish or semi-saline, and of course the fish were Pacific salmon and not Atlantic salmon.

Most of us who go fishing for salmon and sea trout soon become aware of the sharpness or otherwise of salmon teeth. I have caught very fresh-run Norwegian salmon, covered in sea lice, with very sharp vomerine teeth; but I have also caught fairly fresh-run fish in Britain where the teeth are almost totally absent. As far back as 1888, in a letter to a London journal, one Colonel C. G. Colling-

wood of Alnwick, Northumberland, writing of his visit to fish the
River Moisie in Canada, wrote:

We were all standing together on deck talking when someone asked
the best way of telling how long a salmon had been in the river. After
the discussion had gone on for a few minutes, Halliday, who was
standing a few paces apart, said, 'Don't you know the way to tell
how long a salmon has been in the river? Why, I could tell in the
dark with my eyes shut .... I should put my finger in the fish's
mouth and feel round his teeth ... when a salmon comes into
freshwater it sheds its teeth. After three or four days it will have lost
one or perhaps two teeth, at the end of sixteen or seventeen days it
will be entirely toothless.

So much for Collingwood's contribution. I offer it as another bit of
folklore which may or may not be based on truth.

  Wherever the truth really lies, and there may be large patches of
grey within the more sharply defined areas of black and white, there
is a lot of evidence to suggest that the behaviour of fish resident in
fresh water is vastly different from those resident in salt water. On
many visits to Norway I have frequently stopped off at the fine
aquarium they have in Bergen. Here there are many species of fish
from both salt- and freshwater environments and I was fortunate to
be able to see large, fresh salmon feeding in saltwater tanks and also
watch slightly leaner-looking fish resting in a tank of fresh water
where a current had been induced. The most remarkable feature is
that the fish in salt water were continually roving round the tank in a
very alert manner. When I photographed them with a flashgun on
my camera, the flashlight triggered off an immediate show of fright
in that the fish instantly charged all over the tank for a few seconds.
Flash photography of the fish resident in fresh water, however, did
not bring so much as a blink. They continued to lie there as if
nothing had happened. This leads me to the belief that there may be
some measure of reduced mental alertness in the freshwater
residents which may account for the fact that, quite apart from
appetite suppression, these fish can and often do totally ignore the
lures we present to them simply because they are in a state of semi-
hibernation.

  If we accept that salmon and sea trout do not in the full sense feed
in fresh water, the question of why and when they might take lures

or flies immediately arises. That salmon and sea trout will readily grab lures when feeding in salt water is evidenced by the few people who have had an opportunity of longline fishing for salmon at sea or of casting a lure or fly into the sea lochs where hatchery-reared salmon are being fed. Although I have not done it, I am told by those who have that it is instant sport, that the fish immediately grab any lure or fly that looks like food. And commercial fishermen on the high seas regularly catch their fish with longlines and baited hooks. Can we assume that when the fish are having a feeding spree they will take anything which even vaguely resembles food?

With the knowledge that salmon and sea trout in salt water are highly predatory animals, coupled with the knowledge that their close brethren the trout are equally rapacious, it may be safe to assume that it should not be too difficult to create some lure to which fish might react if we could initiate a feeding or predatory reflex action. Doubtless there is some logic in the fact that a wide variety of flies, lures and baits have proved successful in catching salmon and sea trout. Might it be reasonable to presume that at times they will take anything that even vaguely resembles food? For instance, there is nothing in nature that moves with the rapidity or the motion of a Devon minnow spinning bait. But the Devon has proved itself to be a superb catcher of salmon at certain times and seasons. Who is there who will tell us that, because it does not move like anything else in nature, it is useless? No. I suspect that we merely endow many of the species of fish we catch with more guile than they can possibly possess.

When thinking, therefore, of the impulses which might initiate reaction from a non-feeding migratory salmonid we may rule out the necessity for them to accept our baits, lures or flies as some form of food for sustenance. Salmon and sea trout do not have need of them and we must look elsewhere to try to deduce what might prompt sufficient reaction for a fish to take our lure or fly.

In my earlier book, *Salmon* I frequently likened a salmon in fresh water to a half-sleeping cat or kitten. I still cannot think of a better analogy to explain why a salmon will occasionally take a fly or lure. Imagine a half-sleeping cat outside the house. It has been well fed and needs little more than a bit of exercise and some sleep. It curls up, in the fashion of cats, sheltering from a cool breeze. Bits of dross and fluttering leaves get blown past it. For most of the time they are totally ignored, but there comes the occasional moment when a

fluttering leaf has a tantalising and magnetic effect and then the cat will quickly leap to its feet and chase the leaf as it would a bird or a mouse. Thereafter it will dab the leaf with its paw (its principal means of attack) and take some satisfaction not in eating the leaf but merely in having successfully exercised a predatory instinct.

Imagine, therefore, a lethargic salmon lying in a pool with no thought of food on its mind at all. It detects a tenuous-looking fly dangled from a rod and will frequently ignore it. The fly dances furtively in the current but, as with the cat and leaf the fish is not greatly concerned with the appearance or pattern of the fly – merely that it represents prey and something that might exercise the fish's ability to intercept it and attack it with its mouth (its principal means of attack), and thus gain the satisfaction not of eating or trying to swallow the fly but merely of demonstrating its basic hunting instinct.

That is one of the best theories I have heard of why a salmon or sea trout might take a fly or lure. However, I do not like theories very much and were there some factual information I would prefer to build on that rather than on the basis that the pattern of my fly or lure does not matter so much so long as I can arouse the predatory instinct.

The fact that a cat is never likely to eat a leaf tells us that it is the movement of the leaf that arouses the attack or curiosity reaction. It merely dabs the leaf with its paw. A salmon or sea trout, on the other hand, only has its mouth or its tail to demonstrate aggression or curiosity. So what lure do we devise and how do we manoeuvre it to help stimulate these reactions? A fish needs only to give a lure a firm nip for it to have every chance of being hooked. It does not need to swallow it. It merely has to intercept it with its primary attacking weapon and we may have sport on our hands. This may account for the fact that salmon and sea trout frequently nip a fly or lure without being hooked – they are just not taking it as food.

What then of the behaviour of a salmon with a rolling worm bait? This does indeed confuse the picture. Indeed the fish is occasionally inclined to play about with the bait, to mouth it, chomp on it, blow it out again, and even take it well down into its gut and get itself hooked where, without major surgery, the hook cannot be reclaimed. Some argue that even then the fish only sucks at the bait and that if left long enough it would eventually expel it. I must admit that I don't know, but I don't think that the fish takes the worm as

food in the full sense.

With trout, of course, it is possible to watch fish rising to the surface to feed on the flies that are hatching. By keen observation it is possible to identify the insects hatching and establish the times of day, month and year when such hatches can be expected and when the trout might seek them. With the help of some skill in fly dressing we can then reasonably present to the fish a suitable imitation. If we possess the necessary skills of casting and presentation and can make a reasonable assessment of the pattern of fly required, we have an excellent chance of making a good catch of fish. With salmon and sea trout, on the other hand, there can be no such knowledge. An odd leap or a head-and-tail rise might betray their presence, but we usually have to rely on other information to know if fish are present in any quantity in water we intend to fish. We then need further information on which to base our choice of fly. With no feeding or taking habits to guide us, as with trout, we are left with little more than folklore inherited from books and our forefathers – or some inspired guesses.

Much of our knowledge of what we might offer to salmon and sea trout, and why, has been established on an entirely hit-and-miss basis. It has been established that salmon will sometimes take a variety of baits and lures. In years gone by the mussel was a bait favoured by some fishermen. In olden times it was said that salmon ova were a highly effective bait. The lowly worm has long been an anglers' favourite, as have the natural prawn and shrimp. Preserved natural sprat baits, dyed silver or gold and mounted on a spinning flight, have seen the downfall of many salmon. Sea trout respond well to a worm at times, but they do not take large natural baits very well, preferring smaller lures such as a Mepps spoon. Both salmon and sea trout will occasionally take the so-called 'flies' we offer them and both species seem prepared to accept these flies in a wide variety of sizes. What logical or scientific basis is there to help us with our choice of fly?

Sadly there is none which is apparent and we have to rely on the lore which is handed down or else generate our own. Inevitably, most novices rely heavily on what they read in books and articles, but a would-be tutor in these matters requires no qualifications and it is possible, even in these enlightened days, to read large tomes of theory and dogma which bear little relation to the realities of salmon and sea-trout fishing. Many of these writers are or were more gifted

with the pen than ever they were or are with a fishing rod and I have always argued that an angler should have caught very large quantities of a particular species of fish before he begins to pontificate on how to fish for them. The one-week-a-year angler may have some snippet to contribute, but he must refrain from serious piscatorial philosophy until he gets a lot of experience. People who devote their lives to fish and fishing and who spend at least four or five months of the year on or in the water may be permitted a little more speculation and reflection. It is one thing to propound a theory off the top of one's head or repeat it from a book; it is quite another to base that theory on some proven facet of behaviour.

One writer on salmon not only held that the fish might tell the difference between a fly with a ginger hackle and one with a blue hackle, but that such a difference might be the deciding factor in whether the fish would take. Other writers have been equally adamant on the sizes of fly to use on specific occasions. Had they been able to base any of these theories on known facts I might have given them some hearing. But it is regrettable that angling, and particularly angling for non-feeding salmonids, gets more than its fair share of nonsense talked. Other than the half-sleeping cat analogy, I do not know why a fish might take my flies and lures. Much speculation and many theories have been put forward, but it is not my plan to attempt critical analysis for the simple reason that I would be just as guilty as those whom I accuse of the perpetuation of doctrines which cannot be proved or disproved. All I know is that I have caught a lot of salmon and sea trout over the past thirty years. I have been fishing now for over fifty-five years and have developed some of the skills of the hunter and the ability to handle my tackle in a fairly dextrous manner. I have had the wonderful opportunity of fishing on some of the finest waters in the world – and a few that are of not much account. And I have learned just a little about when it might pay to fish hard and when it seems preferable to sit and watch or go home.

I am left, therefore, with the broad-based lore that has been handed down over the generations. This lore declares that salmon in cold water will only take a big fly on a sinking line and that salmon in water over 50°F need to be offered a small fly on a floating line; that sea trout are shy and can only be caught at night; that they might then take a big tandem lure on a sinking line or a small fly on a floating line. Of course there are many permutations on these

themes, but as a broad-based lore they form the basis of much of our angling philosophy. Indeed, it could be argued that for all our experience of salmon and sea-trout fishing we have found little in the lore that can be refuted. Many anglers of my acquaintance stick to it rigidly and catch their share of fish. Who am I to tell them anything different or to suggest other methods for trial?

The earliest ideas about salmon flies were based on the belief that if trout could be caught on small, imitative flies it seemed logical to expect to catch salmon and sea trout on slightly larger flies. Of course, we all recognise that throughout their infant lives all salmonid species feed avidly on flies and small insects. As they grow larger they may well devour small fry of their own kind, but following the smolt stage and their migration to the sea they will begin a new feeding pattern, one about which, even to this day, we may not be fully informed. It seems, therefore, that in offering large and small flies to the fish we are attempting to do two things. The small fly offering may even represent a natural fly on which the fish once fed – we all know of instances of salmon taking small flies intended for trout. Alternatively, the slightly larger lure or fly may suggest the representation of a minute alevin, minnow or fry of some type, while a larger salmon fly or lure undoubtedly represents a small fish. There can be few known instances of exact imitation such as we employ in trout fly fishing, so we just hope that the various lures we have inherited or devised will arouse a predatory, curious or playful instinct.

To a large extent I have been prepared to accept the flies and lures handed down from our forefathers or recommended by contemporary anglers of experience. I have a preference for hair-winged flies against feathered wings merely because back in 1960, when I made a film sequence of both types of fly in a tank of running water, it was plain that the hair-winged variety had much more animation and lifelike movement than did the feather-winged flies. Some hairs and fibres proved to be more lifelike than others. Goat hair and heron-wing fibres, for instance, gave greater animation than bucktail. But a heron-winged fly does not stand up to the rigours of casting and playing fish for very long, whereas bucktail seems almost indestructible. With smaller flies, squirrel hair produces vivid animation and I have tended to rely more on flies constructed with squirrel and goat hair than those with stiffer, and probably longer-lasting, fibres. Indeed, I have come to think that the degree of animation a fly offers

is of much more importance than the style or colour of the dressing, and that the lore may be right when it suggests that we need big flies for cold water and small flies for warm water, bright flies for cold, bright days and dull flies for warm, dull days.

One of the basic reasons for the wide range of fly sizes is different reactions of salmon and sea trout in water of varying temperatures. In my opinion a lot also depends on the height of the river and whether it is basically a shallow river or one of the deeper, classic spring rivers such as the Tay, Tweed and Wye. The Dee and Spey are comparatively shallow and I do know of anglers who insist that Dee salmon will take a small fly from the opening day of the season on 1 February, no matter how low the water and air temperatures may be. Conversely, I would not dream of using a small fly on the lower reaches of the Tweed in February or November but I might well use one on the Spey in April, when water and air temperatures may be only a little warmer. I have also known occasions in mid-June or July when a sinking line and the same large fly I would use in very cold weather may be the only *apparent* method of taking a fish on the fly. This situation may follow a small rise in the water from summer rainfall, which can raise the level of acidity in the water and make the fish slightly reluctant to take flies near the surface. But there can be no hard-and-fast rule.

This, for me, is the great fascination in fishing for these non-feeding migratory fish. Not only are they highly prized as sporting fish, they are also, when fresh-run, a culinary delight. The challenge of outwitting them often seems greater than with many other species of fish which have known feeding and behaviour patterns. Of course, there is a great deal of the lottery about it all. Just as we may never know the moment when the cat will wake up, yawn lazily and immediately dash off to intercept that blown leaf on the wind, we may never fully understand or predict the influences required to initiate reaction from a salmon or sea trout. The reality is that the most important factor in successful salmon and sea trout fishing is being in the right place at the right time.

4
Where to Fish

At first glance it would not seem to be a difficult matter to decide upon a fair price or a reasonable rent to pay for a salmon fishery. It is, however, not so simple as one may think, because there are so many factors to be considered.

G. P. R. Balfour-Kinnear, Catching Salmon and Sea Trout

As a salmon and sea-trout angler of long experience it might be thought that most of the questions I am asked would concern techniques and tackle. Not a bit of it! The question I am most frequently asked is where to go, and when, to have the best chance of catching fish. This question assumes paramount importance in the minds of many anglers but, sadly, it is not easily answered. Unlike the situation in much of North America, where all the sport and commercial fisheries are controlled by the state and paid for in licence dues, most of the fishing rights in European rivers are held by private individuals. Theoretically, even with a licence – as required in England and Wales, but not Scotland – the sporting angler has no right of access or freedom to fish anywhere without first seeking permission and paying any charge. While other influences may also inhibit access, it is fair to say that an angler with a large bank balance usually has a better chance of gaining access to good water than one of more modest means.

The best and most certain way of guaranteeing rights to salmon and sea-trout fishing is to own a suitable piece of water on a good river and to keep constant access to it throughout the season, either living on it or being able to down tools quickly and go to it when the gillie or keeper says that conditions are just right. If ownership is not possible or convenient, the next choice is to take a long lease on the best that is available, have a house, lodge or hotel within easy reach, and go when conditions are right. Most people, however, settle for renting a beat or section where, in the company of one or two friends, they may stay in the local hotel and fish the water for the week of their choice. Often, of course, the water is unavailable

during the best weeks, being already snapped up by regular tenants. It is an unwritten but closely followed rule that a good tenant will usually be offered the same piece of water for a similar period the following year. The only time that this rule may be altered is when a tenant of long standing drops out and there is a comparative newcomer on the ladder, so to speak, looking and hoping for promotion to a better time of the season. Therefore it will often pay a newcomer to take a piece of water when it becomes available, even at a less favoured time of the season. If he continues as a welcome tenant it should not be too long before he is upgraded and offered first choice of a vacancy in a better week.

In this context it is as well to remember my qualification of *welcome tenant*. Some anglers lack a little guile in this respect and think that they can behave badly and get away with it. Most owners of good water have no problem letting it from year to year and have a long waiting list of potential clients. Imagine their irritation when a particular individual behaves badly or is a known bad sportsman! On at least two occasions I have been able to acquire better weeks as a tenant simply because the gillie or boatman complained to his landlord about the behaviour of another tenant, who was then subsequently not offered the fishing the next year. Whatever else, it is important that you make friends with your gillie or boatman. Fall foul of either of these and you may well find that future access to the water is not easily acquired.

Some of the best salmon and sea-trout anglers I have ever met started life as coarse fishermen. This enabled them to think and react in the third dimension much more readily than some fly-only fishermen who are content merely to cast their flies across and downstream and wait for a pull. I was glad that I served a youthful apprenticeship in coarse fishing, for it gave me a feeling for the strength and depth of water and where fish might choose to lie. The knowledge stood me in good stead when I made a start as a salmon angler, particularly just after the Second World War when I was newly married and finding that the realities of life demanded that I earned more money than I seemed to be spending. My first forays in search of salmon, therefore, tended to take place on those

Right Arthur Oglesby fishing for salmon on the Knockdolian estate water of the River Stinchar, Ayrshire, a superb autumn river.

The Ballynahinch river and castle, Co. Galway, Connemara,
Ireland, excellent for salmon and sea trout.

inexpensive and much-fished association waters which can be found
on some of our early spring rivers. The first to receive some
attention was the Eden in Cumbria, but I was to make many visits
there before it yielded a salmon for me. Indeed, my first (a red-
looking late summer fish) was caught while I was fishing for trout
and it was quite some time before I turned my full attention to the
problems associated with more regular encounters with salmon. My
first sea trout was caught on the little River Liddell, a tributary of
the Border Esk, back in the mid-fifties, but I have never applied
myself quite so diligently to sea trout as I have to salmon. For many
years, incidentally, the epitome of fishing for me came when I was
the secretary of a small club with chalkstream trout fishing near
Driffield in East Yorkshire, where I developed some expertise in
dry-fly and nymph fishing for trout. Now, of course, I have become
type-cast primarily as a salmon fisherman, but this does not fully
reflect the alternating joys I get from all forms of game fishing in
their seasons.

Many of my formative years as a salmon and sea-trout fisherman were spent on modestly priced waters where access was available at short notice and where one fished in competition with many other anglers as well as the elements. In these circumstances it is important to remember the etiquette of salmon fishing and not bulldoze your way in front of another angler and hog the water he would soon be fishing if you had not intruded. Where wading is involved I like to wait until the other angler is far enough downstream of me that my line and fly, when cast to its full extent, will not swing round him and possibly hook him in the waders. Thirty yards is a respectable distance but at times, on hard-fished water, particularly following a flood when the spinning fraternity will be out in force, you might have to settle for less.

It was not until the mid-fifties that I started catching salmon more by design than accident. A few mid-August visits to Argyll's River Awe gradually enabled me to catch the odd fish, but in the mid-fifties I gained membership of the Esk Fishery Association, with water on the little Yorkshire Esk, and then I had access to the water whenever I chose. Now I began to learn something about one of the questions paramount in successful fishing – the height of the water.

Although the bulk of my fishing on the Esk was with spinning and natural baits, and was as much for sea trout as it was for salmon, I learned to think in that third dimension. One of the important things I was to learn from David Cook (the river keeper of that time) was which places it was worth fishing and which it was best to leave alone – priceless knowledge, which must be acquired about any piece of water before it can be exploited to its full potential. In the late fifties I saw an advertisement in a fishing magazine offering water at Upper Hendersyde on the Tweed in March for the princely sum of £30 per week for the two-rod beat. Just think of it, £2.50 per day per rod for prime spring fishing on the Tweed, and all this only thirty years ago! Now I was fishing more with expectation than mere hope. We came back with a good catch of fish and I was to become a regular tenant on that beat of the Tweed for many years.

At about the same time I made my first spring visit to the Spey at Grantown. Initially I was invited there to take photographs for a book, *The Angler's Cast*, to be written jointly by Captain T.L. Edwards and Eric Horsfall Turner. At the end of a long photographic session I found time to ask Tommy Edwards exactly what he thought of my casting. Despite his choice of a few four-letter

adjectives and the odd noun I put my pride in my pocket and begged to be shown more. The outcome was that at the end of the week I was invited back as an assistant instructor on the courses for the following year, and I have been back there every year since.

Being a casting instructor, however, is not without its problems. Sadly, there is a tendency for those of us who have entered the commercial side of angling to indulge in show business razzmatazz and bill ourselves as the greatest. This, of course, is not only very arrogant but is also untrue. It is about as useful or valid as claiming that you are the fastest gun in the west. As soon as you do so you are highly vulnerable and likely at any moment to stumble to the ground with a bullet between your shoulders. I am no better a fisherman or casting instructor than a few others I know, but I have been doing it for longer than many and have learned a little bit about the realities of it all.

For those of more modest means, it is my view that the association water at Grantown-on-Spey makes an ideal starting-

Fly fishing for salmon on the Upper Hendersyde beat of the Tweed, best in early spring and late autumn.

The Lurg pool on the Strathspey Angling Association's water
at Grantown-on-Spey. A superb spring and summer river.

ground. Contrary to the popular opinion that the Spey is principally
a salmon river, I must make the observation that it is also one of the
finest sea-trout rivers in the kingdom and it has a stock of wild
brown trout which will often defy all but the most talented anglers.
However, it is a water which is kinder to those who have served an
apprenticeship on it. You may not catch a salmon on your first visit
to the water, but if you persist and visit it at a time when the records
show good catches are likely the day will come when it will yield its
trophies. At its present price (1985) of £22 for a six-day ticket it is
remarkable value for money. I used to make the idle boast that in the
good old days, when it cost only £1 per week, I could average a fish a
day from its waters. Of course, it was a rather stupid boast and I
would not like to have to stand by it today, but I did spend years
learning the water, which gave me a head start on many other visitors.

Arthur Oglesby fly fishing for salmon on the River Tay, at Kinnaird, in April. Like many of the classic Scottish rivers, it may fish well all through the season.

A party returning from fishing the Sandia beat of the Alta
river in North Norway in July, the prime month.

If association water is not your scene, you may be able to find
good hotel water at the time of your choosing, though usually the
best fishing is fully booked by regular guests. Failing that, it may be
possible to get access to a beat by taking a rod on a one-day-a-week
basis, in which case it pays to live reasonably close to the water and
you must not mind being confined to one day a week. This would
not suit me, for the simple reason that I could just not stand the
frustration of knowing that the fishing was good two days before my
arrival and might be good again two days after my departure. The
chances of ever finding the river in a perfect condition would be too
remote for me to fish the water with any enthusiasm. I am quite
prepared to take water for a week or more on a pot-luck basis, but if
I am going to take a long tenancy I must have the right to go and fish
at any time of my own choosing.

TIME-SHARE

The current trend towards offering beats for sale on a time-share basis presents another alternative. Ownership of property is usually sold in units of one week, to be held in perpetuity. Buyers should ensure that those rivers in Scotland which come under Scottish law do not revert to the estate at the end of a period of 99 or 999 years. This may matter little to an individual of one generation who is prepared to make the purchase, but there is little doubt that it is all merely another method of asset stripping and is designed to be of more immediate benefit to the vendor than to the many lambs who seem to come happily to the slaughter. Even for the vendor all is not what it seems. The best weeks are quickly sold, albeit for the highest prices, to those with enough money. But the lean weeks, at the poorest times of the season, may go unsold for a long time.

At first sight part-ownership of a superb beat may seem an attractive proposition. But I would be worried about the management aspect for the future generations who may only have a remote interest in angling. In my view, time-sharing on salmon and sea-trout rivers will not ultimately be in the best interests of sound river management.

ARTIFICIAL FISHERIES

Yet another alternative for the newcomer, particularly to salmon fishing, is the simple and expedient method of visiting one of the artificial fisheries, such as those at Upton Bishop near Ross-on-Wye and at Lichfield. In a totally artificial environment, the waters have been stocked with salmon from hatcheries. A regular stock is maintained in much the same way as with reservoir trout fisheries and, although the fish are not quite so easy to catch as stillwater trout, they can provide the novice with an inexpensive way of sampling the sport. I don't think many salmon anglers weaned on wild rivers and wild fish will warm much to this style of fishing, but there is little doubt that it will appeal to many newcomers who find it difficult or impossible to make long journeys to the classic rivers. These artificial fisheries would not suit me for more than a casual cast, but that they will have a place in the order of things in the future is undoubted.

Arthur Oglesby about to hand-tail a salmon from the new fishery at Lichfield. Might this be the style of fishing when all our wild-bred salmon have been annihilated?

SEA TROUT

Salmon and sea trout rarely have identical behaviour and running patterns, and it is only the late spring and summertime anglers on such rivers as the Spey who can enjoy both salmon and sea-trout fishing at the same time. Late evening and full darkness will often offer the best chance with sea trout, and it requires a special type of individual to stand the ordeal of fishing all day for salmon and over most of the night for sea trout. In the end many compromises are made to try to get the best from both. Later on, of course, as rivers fall to their low summer level, it may be best to concentrate on fishing into the hours of dusk and darkness when the best opportunities for sea trout can be exploited. Continued low water rarely offers good fly fishing for salmon, but a night attack on the sea trout may provide some phenomenal sport.

Salmon and sea trout are also found together in the lochs of the
west coast of Scotland and in the Hebrides. Here you may find some
quite remarkable fishing for very modest cost. Much of the time
there is no knowing whether sea trout or salmon will be caught. On
some of the lochs where I fish in the Isle of Harris six times as many
sea trout as salmon are caught, but, although we frequently fish with
two or three flies on our leaders and alternate with salmon and sea-
trout patterns, the fish show little concern. We catch many sea
trout on salmon patterns and a lot of salmon on sea-trout patterns.
Much of this fishing is confined to the summer months and it is rare
for these lochs to get worthwhile runs of fish until June is nearly out.
Of course, there is a high annual rainfall on the west coast and in the
Hebrides. This usually ensures some chance of sport, although I

Loch Ulladale, Outer Hebrides. Salmon and sea trout may
often be found together in the lochs of the west coast of
Scotland and the Hebrides. Here you may find some quite
remarkable fishing for reasonable cost.

have been there when a bright sun shone out of a semitropical sky on a parched landscape and virtually bone-dry rivers for days on end. Combined with a virtual lack of wind on the lochs, this does make almost anything other than fishing an attractive alternative.

For most of us the normal choice is to team up with a few friends and rent a beat for at least a week, and then stick to that week each year unless a better week becomes available that we can both afford and be free for. It may, in fact, take several years to acquire the type of fishing we want, at a time when we want it, and at a price we can afford. Many anglers may be prepared to take fishing at inclement times of the season when fishing is best done with some type of artificial or natural bait. The first two weeks of the season and the last ten on the Tweed, however, are confined to a fly-only rule, but they can also be very cold – and not every angler enjoys bad-weather fishing. On the other hand, the best spring fishing is likely to come only on a very few rivers. This may mean an increased rent merely for what some might call fair-weather fishing. I am thinking now of classic beats of the Dee, Spey, Helmsdale or Naver, where there is just not enough fishing to satisfy the demand.

This demand has led to some trends that are not in the best interests of the sport. For example, nowadays more rods are often granted access to water than used to be the case. Many beats which thirty years ago might have been expected to accommodate six rods have now been split up into smaller beats and are fished by three times that number. There is also a growing trend for anglers to share a rod and thus halve their individual expenses. This seems a good arrangement, but it does tend to mean that a piece of water comes in for continuous round-the-clock attention and some of us believe that overfishing is bad for any piece of water.

In deciding just where to go, therefore, you must weigh up a complex jigsaw of information. Faced with the scarcity of good water, how do you set about getting the best fishing available? First you must recognise that, land values being what they are, a growing number of riparian owners will seek to derive some income from whatever water they have. Most put the letting rights into the hands of agents, who then advertise the water on the terms which they think will secure some tenants.

The brochures tend to make the proverbial sow's ear look a bit like a silk purse and you must be ever vigilant in reading the small print. It is one thing to be told that, let us say, the Tweed is the finest

salmon river in the kingdom, but it is an entirely different exercise to decide which part of the Tweed to go to, and when. The Tweed is noted for good spring and autumn runs, but a run of summer fish may only coincide with a flash flood and be all over in hours rather than days. You then soon find out that fish in very cold water tend to run much more slowly than those in warmer water and that it is rare for the early-run fish, in the months of February and March, to run much higher upstream than the town of Kelso. Indeed, in times of mild weather they can get well beyond Kelso, but as a guiding rule it might be better to seek a beat below Kelso for the first two months of the season.

The rent asked is usually a good indication of the sport to be expected. During February and March it may be possible to gain access to lots of water in the upper reaches of the river, and even to well-known beats; but you must realise that they will not come into their own until the main autumn run comes in. You must make it your business to find out these things before you spend your money and precious time on wasted excursions.

If the water below Kelso is good for the early part of the season when the water is cold, it is an equally safe bet that it is not going to be of much consequence as the water warms up, for now the fish that are left – or those that are to come – tend to run straight through these lower beats and into the middle and upper reaches. Usually it is not before autumn and a consequent cooling of the water that the fish start slowing down their running pace and spend more time in the lower beats. Good overnight autumn frosts quickly slow down the running pace of the fish and make angling for them more profitable.

Thus the pattern of salmon and sea-trout behaviour on a specific river must be studied carefully by those who wish to fish at the best times. Not all rivers are the same in this context. The Aberdeenshire Dee, for instance, is essentially a spring river. It too opens on 1 February, a time when the river could be in roaring flood from melting snow or rain or even frozen solid from bank to bank in the grip of a hard winter. Most of the best Dee fishing occurs between February and June, but odd runs of summer fish may creep into the river from time to time and, sadly, there are always some anglers who are content to catch fish that have been in the river for several months and are way past their best – fish which would be better spared to make it to the spawning grounds.

The Spey is another river with a slightly different routine. It opens on 11 February and, although there are always a few fish already in the higher reaches, it is to the lower beats that you must look for the best early sport. By April and May, certainly, salmon and sea trout are well spread out throughout the entire river system and at this time the river may well be producing its best sport to those whose prime interest is fly fishing. Runs of grilse and summer fish usually follow in June, July and August, but – perversely – some of these tend to stay in the lower beats almost until the season is over at the end of September.

It is one thing, therefore, to speculate on the pattern of fish behaviour in any given river system and quite another to have sound knowledge of what usually happens. Great Britain, of course, considering its latitudinal position in the world and due entirely to the Gulf Stream, is almost unique in the generally mild climate it enjoys. This gives us a longer season for migratory fish than almost anywhere else in the world. Here almost every river has a slightly different time for producing its best potential and it is for this reason that the seasons have come to vary so much from river to river. Most spring rivers open on 1 February, but a few open on 15 January and odd ones in Ireland open on 1 January. Again, most rivers close their fishing to anglers by the end of October, but the Spey, rightly, closes at the end of September, while the likes of the Tweed and Nith stay open until the last day of November, and the odd South Country river is open in December. So, by being a bit of a nomad, it is possible to find salmon fishing in Britain or Ireland in open season on any day of the year.

Anglers visiting salmon and sea trout rivers outside Britain usually have to contend with a much shorter season. I am thinking particularly of the rivers of Norway, Iceland and north-east Canada. Here the climate is such that the big thaw does not usually come until late April or May and then the sport is confined to the months of June, July and August. This is due entirely to the fact that the fish just cannot gain access to the rivers until the general thaw comes along. Following this, of course, the sport may come in a fast and furious manner and may account for the fact that some anglers think it all so much better than in Britain. The principal factor is that they usually offer the best fishing at that most desirable time of the season – long, almost endless summer nights, possibly under a midnight sun, and concentrated runs to provide lovely fresh fish at a

Fishing at Bolstadoyri on Norway's Vosso. In terms of cost,
this is possibly one of the most expensive rivers in the world.

time when our spring fishing at home is getting past its best.

PRICES AND VALUE

The best fishing nowadays tends to be fearfully expensive and the
worst almost not worth having at any price. For many years I visited
Norway's Vosso River during mid-June, a time when the really big
fish were just entering the river. I even caught several monsters
weighing over 40 lb. By 1985, however, the syndicate of farmers
who owned that portion of the river were demanding a sum in
excess of £100,000 as rental for the three-month season. This
sum my friend Odd Haraldsen, the previous tenant of the water,
quite rightly refused to pay and the five-year fishing lease passed
to a consortium of British and American anglers who then paid
this stupid price.

In the spring of 1985 fishing on the Bolstad beat of the Vosso was
offered to individual rods for the princely sum of $1,000 a day, or

$7,000 for a full seven-day week. At that time the dollar had near parity with the pound, but converted into any currency it is still an awesome figure. From the catch figures quoted (which, incidentally, seemed to be rather optimistic compared with the ones in the catch book) it was possible to deduce that they claimed a ten-year average of 190 salmon for the three-month season, or an average of 15·83 salmon per week to the six rods entitled to fish there. This gives an average of 2·63 fish per person per week – and another little clause states that all fish under 30 lb are to be retained by the landlords. One remembers the old cliché about one being born every minute, but, at an average of $2,662 per fish (on their figures) and the distinct chance of a blank week, surely takers must be hard to find!

Many other good Norwegian and Icelandic rivers also command high rents which make them much more expensive than most rivers in Britain. At the time of writing (1985) it is rare to hear of any British river costing more than about £200 per day per rod. I once vowed that I would never pay more than £2,000 for a motor car or £50 a week for top-quality salmon fishing, but those days have gone. Even only modestly priced salmon fishing can cost as much as £50 per day.

So the angler who is not too well heeled is best advised to start in a modest manner and serve his apprenticeship. I reckon that it took me the best part of ten years of incidental fishing for salmon and sea trout before I was in a position to tackle them in a more serious and predictable way. The turning-point undoubtedly came when I got regular access to such rivers as the Yorkshire Esk and the Tweed, Lune and Spey, but only in the past ten or fifteen years have I acquired access to those waters which I sought, at a period when I wanted to fish them and at prices I can just about afford.

5

Tackle for Salmon

If your tackle is such that you cannot fish at ease, where lies the sport?
Charles Cotton, The Compleat Angler

RODS

The subject of tackle is a veritable minefield. Much of the tackle
used by our forefathers was heavy and cumbersome, with rods of up
to 20 feet in length. In North America the trend has been towards a
complete reversal of our traditional methods and expert fishermen
such as Lee Wulff declare a preference for diminutive 6-foot rods
weighing little more than two ounces. It has to be stated at the
outset, therefore, that there is more than one way of killing the cat.
Diehard British salmon anglers have been weaned on a diet of long
rods whereas most notable American anglers regard any rod over
nine feet as unnecessarily long.

For many years I was steadfastly in the British camp and firmly
indoctrinated with the notion that only a double-handed fly rod of
over twelve feet was of any use for fly fishing for salmon. It was
some time before I even acknowledged the other point of view and
it was not until meetings with Wulff and McClane, when I was
actually able to watch them fish with their short rods, that I saw any
logic in what they were trying to achieve. The sad thing is that the
traditional British angler is still of the opinion that the average
single-handed rod is far too short for salmon fishing, while the
uninformed North American angler shares an equal prejudice
against anything over ten feet. This is a pity because I am sure that
these doctrinaire views are based on little more than bigotry. Most
certainly they do not seem to be associated with logic.

It is one thing to be able to cast a long line with any type of rod
but quite another exercise maintaining what I call effective water
command. It is one thing to have space to cast overhead all day and
another to be compelled to do a Spey or roll cast from under trees or

with high obstructions behind. In competent hands and by the use of the double-haul technique a single-handed rod can be used to throw a fly over fifty yards (tournament casters are doing it all the time). With a suitably balanced shooting head and a strong double-handed rod, distances of more than seventy yards are not considered spectacular today. But such fantastic distances are just not required in most practical salmon-fishing situations and it is the man who can

Now most notable American salmon anglers regard any rod over 9 feet as unnecessarily long. Here Lee Wulff brings in a fish on the Upper Humber river, N.E. Canada, on a 2oz 6-foot rod.

An advantage of the double-handed rod is that it allows the fisherman to 'mend' the line as it fishes round. This picture shows Sandy Leventon, Editor of *Trout and Salmon*, fishing the River Sand in S.W. Norway.

comfortably cast up to thirty yards of line and then control the action of the fly who will be the most likely to succeed.

Although it can be done, there are not many of us who can throw an entire 30-yard fly line with a single-handed rod shorter than nine feet. The line has to be of a forward-taper design and the elements have to be helpful. It is much better, in my opinion, to rely on a longer double-handed rod and a double-taper line and thus achieve this distance with comparative ease. The other aspect is that of being able to 'mend' the line and keep full control of it while the cast and fly are swinging or 'fishing' round. Another consideration is the space available for an adequate back cast.

Perhaps at this stage it may help to consider the different tactical requirements of the British and North American angler. Fishing for salmon in North America, and indeed in many other countries where *Salmo salar* exists, is largely confined to the months of June, July and August, after the spring thaw has provided enough water for the new run of fish to negotiate the rivers. By the time the floods

In competent hands and with the use of the double-haul
technique, a single-handed rod can be used to throw a line of
over fifty yards.

Under low water conditions in Strathspey, where water
command is easier to achieve, Lee Wulff demonstrates the
obvious advantages of a shorter and lighter rod.

have subsided it is June – a delightful time for fly fishing with a
single-handed rod anywhere. With deep wading or fishing from
canoes there is little need for anything but a single-handed rod and
with ample casting room there is no reason to be overencumbered
with heavy tackle.

In Britain it is possible to do some form of fly fishing from early
February through to the end of November, but tactics vary quite
drastically from the techniques best employed in February or
November and those required for low water in July or August.
While I hold no great brief for the ultra-short rod, as used by Lee
Wulff, I feel that there are times when an ultra-long rod is merely an
encumbrance better avoided. My choice is clear, and in the longer
lengths of rod has been dictated by the advent of carbon fibre, or
graphite, which has provided me with a 15-foot rod which will easily
throw an entire 30-yard fly line with either a Spey or an overhead
cast and also give all the water command I could require. Such a rod
is the 15-foot 'Walker' by Bruce & Walker, of Huntingdon,
England.

Although there will be new and revolutionary designs of these rods on the market by the time this book is in print, it is current Bruce & Walker policy to offer customers a 15-foot rod with two differing actions. Many years ago Jim Bruce decided that he liked a salmon fly rod with a slightly softer action, while his co-director, Ken Walker, opted for one of stiffer or faster action. Their commercial sense told them that there would be a market for both rods and it was not long before we had the option of the 'Bruce' or the 'Walker'. My preference generally is for the 15-foot 'Walker' but I have used the 15-foot 'Bruce' to equally good effect. The 'Walker' feels happier with a no. 11 line while the 'Bruce' seems well exercised with a no. 10. Bear in mind that a Spey cast is best accomplished with a double-taper line or one with a continuous taper. A forward-taper line will not do!

Such a rod is my constant companion when fishing the Spey in April or May. It is also well suited to casting big flies on heavy sinking lines and shooting heads in the early spring and late autumn. Come to June, however, and the Spey may well be shrinking down to its bare bones. It may be easily waded and covered with little more than the 6-foot rod as favoured by Lee Wulff. With such a rod, however, a useful form of Spey cast is virtually impossible and it may require several overhead casts to work out the required length of line to cover the water properly – in other words, to achieve effective water command. It is for this reason that I opt for a single-handed rod of 10 feet. This gives me all the overhead casting power I need and yet will still permit the occasional Spey cast in confined places. My favourites are the 10-foot 'Light Line' or the 10-foot 'Multitrout' by Bruce & Walker. Both directors would hotly deny that either rod is suited for salmon, but I have caught salmon of up to 14 lb on these slender rods and never felt any risk of breakage.

It must be realised that any rod of any length has to perform two tasks. It must act as a spring when you are casting and as a lever when you are playing a fish. Many anglers overencumber themselves with unnecessarily strong rods in the mistaken belief that they will tire a fish more quickly. In some cases it may be true that, provided the leader will stand the strain, a very strong rod will horse in a fish a bit more quickly than a soft, sloppy rod. But more often than not it is the length of the rod that determines the speed with which a fish may be played out. Some anglers who fish on reservoirs also rely on very strong rods to achieve long casting distances. Now that I am

The great duo of rods from the Bruce and Walker stable;
the 15-foot Walker is the powerhouse, while the 15-foot
Bruce has a slightly softer action.

reaching the age of maturity I look for a rod which will be comfortable to use all day and which will play a fish competently. As casting time is likely to represent at least 95 per cent of a fishing day I see little point in fishing with something which is merely going to make my wrists or arms ache. Often the time taken to land a fish on a light rod is only fractionally longer than it is with a heavy, stiff one.

Much confusion has arisen in the minds of some anglers who are diehard traditionalists and who think that split cane epitomises the very best in rod construction and action. At a sporting dinner some few months ago a fellow fisherman turned to me and said that he refused to believe that carbon-fibre rods could be better than his trusted split-cane rods. He was, of course, perfectly entitled to a preference for his rods, but to suggest that split-cane rods are better than carbon-fibre is to neutralise man's achievements through the history of discovery and invention – a bit like suggesting that he would prefer to cross the Atlantic in a DC3 than in Concorde. The conversation then drifted on to some discussion on the merits of carbon fibre, but when it was suggested to me that it is much more difficult to play a fish on a carbon or graphite rod than it is on one of split cane I nearly blew my top. Now that we are faced with such a wide choice of carbon-fibre rods, including cheap, substandard imports, I feel it is important to examine some of these myths and get a bit nearer the truth.

The facts on playing fish with any type of rod are difficult to establish. A great deal depends on circumstances. Are you in contention with your fish in deep water from a boat or are you well away from the river bank and playing it in shallow water? Are you fighting your fish on a long or a short rod? And is the fish directly under the rod point or at an angle of 45°? Very often the last consideration has most bearing on the problem and, although it might not seem logical, I can assure you that, from the pure aspect of playing fish, it is easier to fight a fish on a short rod than it is on a long rod. The fact is, of course, that the lightness of carbon fibre has enabled us to make rods longer than we found comfortable when they were made of cane. It is for this reason alone that some anglers are complaining that playing times with fish are now more pro-longed. This has nothing at all to do with the materials used in rod construction, but everything to do with the length of the rod concerned. I have played and landed salmon of 36½lb and 45lb on a Bruce & Walker 10-foot 'Multispin' carbon spinning rod in under

fifteen minutes, but I can recall playing a fish of only 28 lb on a 16-foot cane rod for over thirty minutes before I could come to terms with it.

In late spring and summer I get great pleasure in salmon and sea-trout fishing with a 10-foot 'Light Line' or 'Multitrout' rod. On most occasions either of these rods will bring a fish to the bank almost as quickly as my big 15-foot 'Walker' – they have easily coped with fish up to 14 lb.

It is important at this stage not to get the impression that long rods are bad news. The modern, longer carbon rods give great water command and you must never overlook the fact that over 90 per cent of your time is going to be spent casting and 'commanding' water and that less than 10 per cent will be spent playing fish. The combination of lightness and water command offers a greater dividend than anything you might achieve from shorter rod lengths.

As I have indicated, one of the greatest advocates of the short rod is Lee Wulff. During the early autumn of 1982 and again in the summer of 1984 it was my pleasure to spend some time with Lee and Joan Wulff, first at their home in the Catskill Mountains of New York State and then again in Strathspey. Aged 81 (1985) Lee is no chicken, but it was a sheer delight to watch both him and Joan as they manipulated their small 6-foot and 7-foot rods with great ease. Indeed, where wading or canoe fishing is possible, as it is on many of the rivers of the north-eastern American seaboard, there is a great deal to commend the short rod. But, where wading is limited and Spey casting becomes highly desirable, if not essential, there is nothing to beat the long rod *for water command.*

It was while discussing rod action that the question arose of the advisability of 'giving a fish the butt'. This is a much-used saying among anglers and one wonders how many there are, like myself, who glibly accept it with little more than casual consideration. On reflection I had to admit that I really did not understand what the expression meant. I had merely presumed that it referred to excessive flexing of the rod down to the butt, in order to exert its full power and influence over a fish in play. To confuse matters, I discovered that other anglers thought differently. For instance, some thought that it meant bending the rod over the shoulder so that the butt end was pointing towards the fish, while others thought that it meant holding the rod high and gaining maximum bend in the tip section. Let us examine some of the facts.

Here the curve on the rod reduces the shock loads to the leader. For maximum effect, the rod should be held at an angle of 45°, while the line to the fish describes a similar angle.

The first thing to consider is that maximum leverage on a fish is achieved simply by pointing the tip of the rod directly towards the fish and playing it straight off the reel. Here the only cushioning effect is provided by the elasticity of the line and leader. Given a sufficiently strong leader it is possible to literally winch in a good fish with little ceremony. I even use this technique myself for quickly horsing in small trout or parr which take my salmon fly. Providing that the leader or terminal tackle will stand the strain, it is the quickest method of bringing fish to the bank – much like handlining a sea fish in from a boat or pier.

It is only when playing a good-sized fish on comparatively slender tackle that you need the bend of the rod to act as a cushion. This curve reduces the shock loads on the delicate line or leader. It gives you the so-called feel of playing a fish and you may adjust the angle of the rod to produce specific effects. Ideally, for maximum effect

Playing a fish with a long rod while seated in a boat can be a problem if it chooses to dive beneath. Here, Ken Walker demonstrates the traditional method of playing a salmon ...

of the bend, the rod should be held at an angle of 45° while the line to the fish describes a similar angle (as shown in the photo). Here the rod is bending down to the butt and the greatest cushioning effect is being produced from all the items of tackle involved. Rod angle may be maintained until the fish is floundering near the bank and there is little doubt that this combination of angles and forces exerts the greatest effect in fighting fish. Some lowering of the rod point might bring greater leverage, but the less the bend in the rod, the more likely is a break in the slender leader through sudden shock loads which the rod cannot now absorb. The expert who tells the novice to keep his rod well up when playing a fish offers good advice.

There are occasions in boat fishing when the fish fights from immediately underneath the boat. Here you may be tempted to hold

... into boatman Jim Hunter's waiting net.

the butt in the vertical position with rod point forming a complete
'U', so that the point faces straight down into the water. In this
situation only the finer tip section of the rod is under load and being
used as a cushion, the butt section is not under any load at all.
Providing that the fish stays under the boat it is possible to maintain
this position for a prolonged period. The fish is hardly likely to
break the line or leader, but there could be a definite risk of
breaking the slender rod point if excess pressure is applied. Long
rods are particularly prone to this problem and I have fought big
Norwegian salmon on a fly rod from a boat without apparent effect
for some long times. Only when I have got back to the bank again
and been able to use the maximum efficiency of the rod have I been
able to bring the fight to a successful conclusion.

For the same reason it is not always easy to play a good fish in still
water from a boat. Following the initial run or two, the fish
frequently make for the shadow of the boat and have to be handled

forcibly to get them to the surface and into the waiting net. It is always better to maintain the 45° angle of the rod, but one sees too many anglers raise the rod point beyond the critical angle, and some even point the butt of the rod towards the fish – thus losing most of the useful leverage. Of course the rod point has to be raised at the final moment in order to get the fish over the net. The only alternative to this would be to get a net with a handle as long as the rod. Whatever the expression means, therefore, I am sure that 'giving it the butt' must involve bending the butt section more than the slender rod point.

Other aspects of playing good fish in a strong stream involve what is often called 'side strain'. This is yet another of angling's ambiguities and it usually only means altering the point of pressure to a lower angle than that applied with the rod held upright. Usually a slight shift of position will achieve the same result. It is important to establish the best fighting ground you can get. It is not a good plan to have your fish floundering downstream. Here the pressure you apply with the rod merely makes it easier for the fish to swim against the current. You are, in effect, giving it a tow. Side strain is most effective with a fish swimming slightly upstream of you, when continually pulling it off balance will shorten proceedings. Even then it may be a mistake to be over-influenced by the advantages of side strain. If you follow a fish downstream all the time, merely to maintain side strain, you might have to face a situation where the fish could run out of the pool and down into the water below. Such tactics may then prolong the period of play it was hoped to reduce.

In times past I used to get some quiet satisfaction from landing or beaching a salmon from the same place where I had hooked it. Initially the fish had to be worked up to my position and then fought as conditions dictated. Of course, things did not always go as I had planned, but there were few times when I had to move and learning to command a fish and get it out as quickly as possible with the minimum of losses was an interesting exercise. Most fish are lost through over-timidity or over-anxiety. Ideally you should sense those subtle moments when to hustle and when to caress.

As already stated, the length of the rod does have some bearing in the playing of a fish. Often the most leverage is exercised with a short and rather stiff rod. But this has nothing at all to do with the *material* used for rod construction, so I have little hesitation in suggesting that modern carbon fibre or graphite – providing it is

from a reputable company – is the best rod-building material available today. The long rod comes into its own in the extra water command we get from it; but it does *command* a fish as well – providing that you know the best angles and attitudes for maximum leverage.

Although they filled a great need and will remain popular for many years the snag with all tubular rods – and one that all manufacturers have been reluctant to concede – is that they all have in-built faults. Almost without exception, they all have a spine, or a portion of their circumference which is thicker than another. This is due to the fact that the 'cloth' or matrix of carbon or glass is rolled on a mandrel before heat treatment and ultimate formation. This spine effect may give a stiffer action in one plane than another and in the practical situation of rod assembly on the river bank it is impossible to get the spines of each section running in line. Another snag with any tubular rod is that when it is flexed beyond a certain and critical curve the tubular section bends into an oval shape, with a consequent loss of power and increased risk of breakage. These faults are in-built in any rod of hollow, tubular construction and this may be why some diehard anglers cling to their old-fashioned and heavy split-cane rods.

In order to marry the merits of carbon fibre as a material and the construction techniques of split cane, the Bruce & Walker company has recently launched a carbon-fibre rod on the tried and tested principles of hexagonal strips cemented together. Gone instantly is

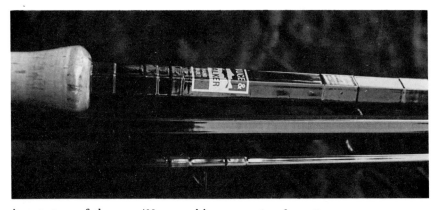

A prototype of the new 'Hexagraph' construction from Bruce and Walker, designed to combine the best of modern and traditional construction techniques.

the problem of the spine and gone too is the tendency of the rod to adopt an oval shape when under stress and strain. At a stroke this rod has silenced all the possible criticisms of carbon fibre and tubular construction and offers a unique opportunity to have light rods with all the traditional feel and action the diehards have demanded. In February 1985 I tested 'Hexagraph' prototypes. While they might not eliminate the tubular rod overnight, and will certainly cost that bit more, there is every possibility that these will become the rods of the future.

REELS

On the question of reels for fly fishing there is not a lot to be said. In most practical situations a rod would cast better without a reel. Some anglers believe that a heavy reel merely balances a heavy rod. The same theory is put forward by those who suggest that it is easier to carry two buckets of water than one. It is a theory which I do not find very convincing. However, I don't much care about how much a reel weighs so long as it is well made, holds the right amount of line and backing and has an adequate check mechanism to offer some resistance to a fast running fish. Although fractionally heavy, the Bruce & Walker 'Expert' range of reels is admirable in every other respect. One of the finest reels ever used by salmon anglers is the American Bogdan reel. I met Stanley Bogdan on Norway's fabulous Alta river in 1985. He is a very fine angler and engineer who will only use the very best in fishing tackle. For those who insist on ultra-light tackle there is some merit in carbon-fibre reels, but it is not a topic about which I am prepared to be too pedantic.

LINES

As to lines, I tend to favour those of American manufacture, with Air Cel and Wel Cel my current favourites. However, Bruce & Walker will shortly be entering this marketplace and I hope that I may be instrumental in influencing design and manufacturing policy. Meanwhile, I find that the Air Cel double-taper no. 11 floating line (DT–11–F) does all and more than I could require of it when used with my 15-foot 'Walker' rod. I use it in conjunction

with a no. 2 wide-drum 'Expert' reel and sufficient 30lb test backing to fill the reel. Usually I also like to use a long leader of about 14lb test. I do not bother with conventional leaders, which one can buy in the shops, but merely settle for about twelve feet of level 14lb test monofilament taken from a spool. I think that it is important not to overencumber yourself when fishing – particularly when deep wading. Apart from breast waders, which are essential on many rivers, all I carry with me into the water is my rod, reel, line and fly, and a box of flies and a spool of nylon in my pocket. A pair of specs is also an essential item for me, as are scissors tied to my fishing coat. I have yet to find it necessary to festoon my body with fishing vests, wading sticks, nets and tackle bags, but I do acknowledge that a wading stick should be regarded as an essential item for those anglers fishing strange water or those who need the security of a third leg.

For fishing with sinking lines I have come to the firm conclusion that a shooting head is used with much more ease than a full 30-yard line. The beauty of the shooting head is that it may be cut from a full line to just the right length that can be comfortably aerialised, and then spliced to oval monofilament backing of about 30lb test. When casting it is important to have the whole of the shooting head outside the rod point. Then with a suitable length of backing pulled off the reel and coiled it will be possible to make 30-yard casts with ease. Initially I merely cut a 30-yard DT–11–S line in half. I then splice the butt section of the line to the monofil backing with a nail knot and give it some trial. Usually I find that 15 yards is fractionally too long for comfort and experience has shown me that 12 yards makes an ideal length for a 15-foot rod while 10 yards cut from a DT–8–S line (the normally accepted length of a standard shooting head) is better for the shorter single-handed rods. However, I rarely use a sinking line when I am fishing with a single handed rod. Usually the single-handed rod comes into use in late spring and summer and at this time a sinking line is rarely required anyway.

To cope with the full range of water conditions at least three densities of sinking shooting head are needed. For those rare occasions when the river is very big, in flood even, I like to have a 550-grain lead-cored shooting head such as the Deep Water Express. This I have used to good effect on the gigantic rivers of Norway, though it has to be admitted that it is used only rarely in Britain, as is the Wet Cel Hi-D. Lines more normally used would be

the Wet Cel II or the Wet Cel Intermediate – the former for a
reasonable height of water in the cold weather of spring or autumn
and the Intermediate for those other occasions when the water may
be low merely due to frost or lack of rain. This latter line just sinks
slowly beneath the surface and is very suitable for many types of
wet-fly fishing.

LEADERS

Leader strength and length is a question which frequently crops up.
My formula is fairly straightforward and is based on such considerations as the strength of the rod I am using, the size of the fly, the
depth and strength of the current and the size of the fish likely to be
encountered. As already indicated, most of my spring fishing on the
Spey is undertaken with a 15-foot rod, a DT–11–F line and about
twelve feet of 14 lb monofilament as a leader. Were the river to fall
towards summer level, I might opt for the 10-foot 'Light Line' rod,
but I would expect the leader strength chosen to be adequate to
match the rod. It is of little use using big flies on slender leaders for
the simple reason that they will quickly crack off on casting. Nor
does it make sense to use small flies on very thick leaders. The fly
does not move in a very animated manner and is restricted by the
thick monofilament.

When fishing with very big tube flies, however, it is important to
have a very strong leader if only so that it can absorb the shock loads
of continuous casting. During the early spring and late autumn on
such a river as the Tweed I frequently use monofilament of 25 lb test
in conjunction with the very heavy tube flies. Even then it pays to
make a periodic examination of the point where the leader joins the
fly. Continued casting can abrade the leader and thus cause an
early break when a fish is in play.

Although I have caught salmon and sea trout accidentally when
fishing for trout with ultra-light leaders, I do not recommend fishing
with leaders of much less than 5 lb test. The play has to be prolonged
and there is always the risk of the fish getting free with the fly stuck
in its mouth. If it really is your intention to *catch* fish then it
demonstrates greater reponsibility to use a leader strong enough to
achieve this easily. For this reason I am totally opposed to the
line/leader strength classes they have in some forms of competitive

fishing. For every fish caught and landed on ultra-light tackle there are scores that go away with hooks festooned around their mouths. In my view this is the antithesis of good sportmanship. We owe the fish some respect.

OTHER EQUIPMENT

Many anglers like to adorn themselves with more tackle and equipment than they need. If you must wear a fishing vest, I suggest that you opt for one of the buoyant types which may just save you from a nasty accident. Of course, there will be times when waterproof clothing is required and it is difficult, even in this day and age, to find totally waterproof garments. Waders are another bone of contention and there are not many marketed today which conform to my specifications for classification as good or even average. The best tend to come from America and, due to a very expensive dollar, they are very costly to buy in Britain. I insist on felt soles or some other composition that has all the qualities of felt. It is bad enough wading over the uneven bottoms of some rivers even in the best of footwear, but to be clad in anything which adds to the hazards makes life very uncomfortable.

To be fully equipped for most salmon fly fishing situations, therefore, you should consider buying the following items: a good double-handed fly rod of carbon-fibre construction and between 14 and 16 feet in length – depending on the size of the river and the time of the year you are to fish it. Two good-quality reels which will comfortably hold 30 yards of fly line and 100 or 150 yards of 30lb test backing. A double-tapered number 10 or 11 floating line (DT–10–F or DT–11–F) to go on one reel and a selection of at least two densities of sinking line to go on the other reel. You may, if you like, also have spare spools for these reels with lines already assembled. You will also need various spools of monofilament nylon to offer leaders ranging in strength from about 10lb to 25lb. A selection of flies will be considered in the next chapter, but it is nice to have a wide selection in size, weight and colouring to complete your inventory for early- and late-season fishing.

For summer fishing, you should consider a single-handed rod of between 9 and 10½ feet, a good-quality intermediate size reel with 30 yards of DT–7–F or WF–7–F line, and leader monofilament of

Extracting fish with bare hands may be difficult at times.
Here Arthur Oglesby is pleased to have a gillie with his net.

between 6 and 10 lb test. Some small, but strong, boxes to carry a wide variety of flies should be added to the list. Other items should include a suitable pair of waders – and it may be that the itinerant angler will need both breast and thigh waders – and suitable rainproof headgear and clothing. If one is thought essential a good wading stick should be constructed so that it does not float and get fouled up with shooting lines. The best have a weight in the base which ensures that they come more readily to hand and rarely get in the way when casting.

Many anglers consider it necessary to carry a gaff, net or tailer. All these appliances, in my opinion, are unnecessary encumbrances. There are times, of course, when it might be highly desirable to have a net, tailer, or even a gaff on hand, but they are not so frequent as some writers would have us believe. It is many years since I last gaffed a fish and about as long a time since I last used a tailer, but there are occasions when I have been glad of a friend's or a gillie's net. Usually, however, I rely on my bare hand to get salmon out onto the bank, though there are special problems with sea trout about which I shall comment in a later chapter.

In most angling situations the only time I have been glad of some contrivance for extracting my fish has been in Norway when I have been playing fish of more than 30 lb. In Britain I used my bare hands to extract the biggest fish I ever caught on this side of the North Sea. It weighed 27½ lb. Of course it is important to find a suitable beaching site and you may sometimes have to move a considerable distance to achieve this. In the Hebrides recently, I should have had great problems on the little Blackwater river near Garynahine if a gillie with his net had not been on hand. The banks were steep and there was no way I could have lifted a fish of 4½ lb out of the water on a slender leader. If you must have some contrivance, the net is the most efficient but also the most bulky. Perhaps a mechanical tailer offers the best compromise.

KNOTS

It would not do to let this chapter on tackle pass without mention of an essential adjunct to tackle – the use of a variety of good knots. Even the best knot will weaken the line or leader in which it is tied, so it is important to use only those knots with a proven record of

reliability for use with modern synthetic materials. Ideally, you should master at least five of these knots and be so adept that you can do them semi-automatically without recourse to diagrams or concentrated thought. The first knot to master is the one which joins the leader to the fly. Many anglers settle for the half-blood knot as the easiest and quickest, but it is not the best knot for this purpose because its tying often leaves an unsightly crinkle in the nylon near the knot. Additionally, the fact that the knot is tied outside the eye of the hook causes the fly to hinge. It is far better to use a knot like the single Turle. This is very easily mastered and makes a much better knot in every respect for small flies. The half-blood is quite acceptable for tying on tube flies and spinners, but it is not the best when small flies are being used.

The next knot to be mastered is the one used to form a loop in the butt of the monofil leader to join it to the fly line. For this, the

Right Fig 1   Knots
1.   The Needle Knot for joining backing and leader to fly line. The nylon does not have to go through a hole in the end of the fly line, it can simply lie alongside.
2.   The Double-loop Knot is the loop for a level nylon fly leader.
3.   The Figure of Eight Knot for attaching line to leader.
4.   An alternative to the above, using two loops.
5.   The Turle Knot for attaching fly to leader.
6.   The Blood Knot for attaching two lengths of nylon (preferably of similar diameter).
7.   The Double-grinner Knot is a useful alternative to the Water Knot.
8.   The Nail Knot, an alternative to the Needle Knot.
9.   The Water Knot for joining two lengths of nylon of differing thicknesses and for producing an effective dropper.
10.   The Half-blood Knot for attaching fly to leader, but not ideal.
11.   The Tucked Half-blood Knot is a slightly more secure version of number 10.
12.   The Grinner Knot for attaching fly to nylon leader.

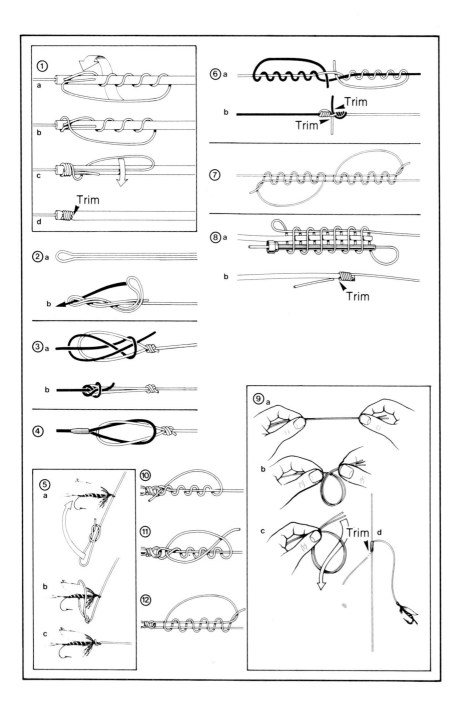

The upper fly is tied to nylon with a Turle Knot. The lower
fly is tied with a Half-blood Knot which causes the nylon to
crinkle and the fly to hinge round the knot.

double loop knot, with the loose end lying parallel with the standing
line, is the most efficient. It is then a simple matter to link this loop
with a similar loop made in a short length of stiff nylon joined
permanently to the fly line with a nail knot. Alternatively you may
join the two ends with a blood or water knot. Both are excellent
knots but this method has the slight disadvantage that over a period
of several outings the fixed piece of nylon will be nibbled away and
require replacement.

To join two pieces of nylon there is little to beat either the blood
or the water knot. Both may be used to form droppers in a leader.
With short lengths I favour the water knot. It is more simple to tie
and more efficient for joining two lengths of monofilament of
different thicknesses. Mastery of the nail knot completes the
repertoire and will give you the confidence to fish in any situation.

6
Artificial Flies
and Lures
for Salmon

There are four leading questions that require answers before the salmon fisherman can embark on his sport with a rational outlook. They are: Why does the salmon take a fly? When does the salmon take a fly? Where does the salmon take a fly? How does the salmon take a fly?
    Richard Waddington, Salmon Fishing: Philosophy and Practice

Salmon and sea trout will occasionally take a wide variety of artificial flies and lures but it has to be admitted that there is very little logic that can be applied to our choice. As I have noted, salmon and sea trout do not feed in fresh water in the accepted sense, but they do have a history of vigorous feeding in fresh water as parr or immature fish, and another, though less known, history of prolific feeding in the sea. In other chapters I examine some of the speculation on freshwater taking habits but reluctantly I have come to the conclusion that I really know very little about it at all. This, for me, is one of the great fascinations of fishing for migratory fish – the knowledge that I do not really know for certain what might induce them to take my lures and flies.

This is why the evolution of artificial lures for salmon and sea trout has been based more on trial and error than on logic. In earlier years the angler watched trout feeding on hatching flies and came to the rather naive conclusion that if trout would take small flies salmon and sea trout might take larger flies. Back in the late nineteenth century George M. Kelson, in his book *The Salmon Fly*, postulated the theory that salmon actually fed on butterflies and that similar garish-looking creations might make suitable artificial flies. Even some of our modern writers on salmon allow themselves the luxury of claiming not only that fish can tell the difference between subtle changes of colour in our flies, but that the difference

really matters and can influence the taking response of the fish. Frankly, I regard this as nothing more than arrogance. It is little short of an inference on the part of these authors that they have some divine information which is denied to ordinary mortals.

In this situation, what are you to do? On what rule, if any, do we base our choice of the size and pattern of the fly or lure? It could well be argued that one man's opinion is just as valid as any other – particularly if that opinion is based on sound and lengthy experience and not merely on whim or fancy. Usually, in any salmon or sea-trout situation, one fishes with a certain pattern and size merely because the word goes round that it does well on such-and-such a water at a particular time of the season. In May 1985, for instance, it was impossible to purchase a size 6 or 8 Munro Killer fly anywhere in Grantown-on-Spey. Local anglers were catching fish on them and the word spread round so quickly that the tackle shops had soon exhausted their stocks. It is my view that the fact that 90 per cent of the fish at that time were caught on Munro Killers had nothing at all to do with the pattern of the fly, but everything to do with the fact that the taking fish in the area were being offered little other choice. Against all the dogma I had a brief cast at that time with a 10-foot trout rod, a 6lb test leader and a small size 12 Greenwell's Glory and caught a lovely fresh salmon of 7½lb.

It is again my view that the choice of pattern of an artificial fly is possibly the least important factor in any tactical appreciation of the game. The size of the offering at any one time might be worthy of study, but it is not so paramount as the question of getting on that collision course with a fish which might be in a taking mood – a subject I shall continue to examine from time to time.

With this firmly in mind, therefore, I shall simply relate what prompts me to use certain patterns and sizes at different times of the season. If other writers suggest differently, who am I to suggest that they are wrong? Their choice of flies may be just as successful on their day as mine, just so long as they don't pretend that their choice is dictated by some superior knowledge denied to the rest of us!

Over the years many angling writers have sought to demonstrate that salmon in cold water require a much larger offering than salmon in relatively warm water. A figure of 48° F has been offered as a base for the water temperature at which a change in behaviour occurs. It has been assessed on the experience and observations of many practical anglers and may be said to be good enough to bear

Arthur Oglesby with his best ever day's catch of salmon
taken on a fly. The best fish weighed 22lb and they averaged
$14\frac{1}{2}$lb.

Left: It may look untidy, but the double Spey cast is very effective for casting long distance when a good back cast is not possible.

Below: The late Captain T.L. Edwards demonstrating impeccable style with a double-handed fly rod.

Top right: Spring salmon in the St Marys River, Nova Scotia, Canada.

Gilbert van Rijckevorsel

Centre right: Two salmon from the Spey. The top fish showing the first signs of coloration due to a longer spell in fresh water.

Centre far right: Fresh salmon suffering seal bite damage.

Below right: A tragic sight on the Tweed in 1967 when the disease UDN broke out with dire consequences.

Ed Zern, associate editor of
Field and Stream, brings a Spey
fish to gillie George Smith.

Odd Haraldsen playing a sea
trout on Norway's Vosso river.

A fresh-run Spey salmon
nearly ready for beaching.

Two fresh-run Spey salmon.
The top fish, which weighed
in at 19½lb, is untypical of
the Spey because of its shape;
incidentally, the lower, more
typical fish is less than half its
weight.

Late summer salmon fishing on the Spey at Castle Grant.

Alastair Perry hand-tails a fine 10 lb Spey salmon for Richard
Wilkinson.

Arthur Oglesby with a 29lb Vosso salmon, taken on a tube fly.

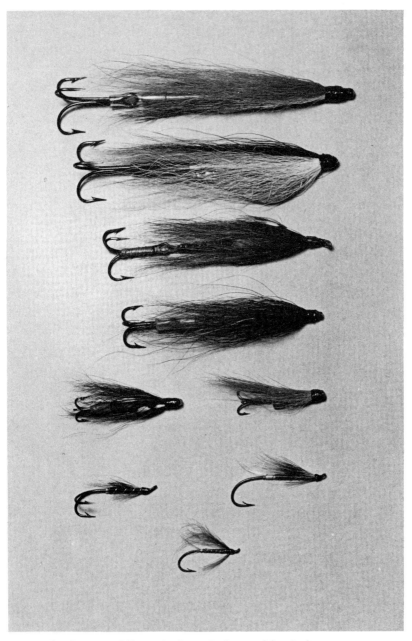

A varied selection of flies which might be used by Arthur throughout a season. The choice of pattern fly is not as important as getting it on a collision course with a taking fish.

in mind. The fact that salmon may be caught on small flies in water of 42°F or that they will take a 3-inch tube fly when the water is in the sixties does not alter the basic premise, which seems about right.

It was quite early on in my days as a salmon fisherman that I began to experiment with different types of fly. Eventually I constructed a glass-sided tank which, with a flow of water passing through it, provided an ideal test-bed. Various types of flies were suspended in the running water and I filmed many of them with my movie camera. What quickly becomes apparent is that practically all the old-fashioned flies with feather dressing appeared much more inanimate than the modern type of flies with hair dressing. Indeed, some of the larger single-hooked patterns, as used by our grand-fathers and great-grandfathers, had little animation at all. Flies constructed on the Waddington or tube principle, on the other hand, with long flowing fibres of heron or squirrel tail, took on the appearance of something alive and vibrant, and the treble hook at

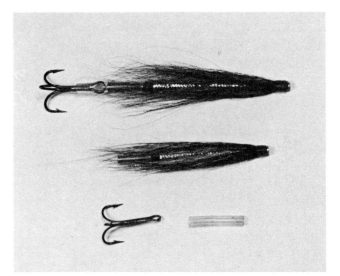

Tube flies, with their long fibres of heron or squirrel tail and triple hooks, look alive and vibrant in flowing water and are considered to be more effective than the larger single-hooked patterns used by our grandfathers.

the tail bore a strong resemblance to the tail of a small fish.

Certainly in their time the old-fashioned flies were just as successful as the modern ones, but if we are seeking some thread of logic it must make sense to assume that the more lifelike flies should have more appeal to the fish. In the construction of my flies, therefore, I look for those materials which are likely to cause a greater degree of animation when the flies are tethered in running water. This means that I like to use heron fibres, soft squirrel tails, and goat or yak hair. Bucktail works quite well in the larger sizes but is a bit inanimate in the smaller patterns. Squirrel tails offer the most-used materials and these may be dyed in a wide variety of colours to suit your whims and fancies.

If it is generally agreed that in salmon and sea-trout fishing we cannot make exact imitations of flies or small fish as we aim to do in trout fishing, we must seek some peg on which to hang our piscatorial hat. I think that it is dangerous to assume that salmon or sea trout take our offerings merely because they might represent food upon which they have fed in the past. The entire history of the genus *Salmo* demonstrates a highly developed predatory nature, so we might assume that salmon on their return to fresh water need only have their predatory instinct triggered for them to attack anything that suggests lifelike behaviour. Whether in the past they have actually fed on anything similar to what we are offering is not important – we know that they do not attack our flies with the intention of serious feeding. Are we safe in assuming that there will be occasions when they might take anything that merely suggests some form of prey? If so, can we make the corollary assumption that anything we care to construct, within the broad definition of what has become known as a salmon or sea-trout fly, in whatever bizarre colours we care to choose, will occasionally be attractive to the fish provided that it has some semblance of life?

Sadly, this seems to be too vague and too simple a solution. Whatever offering a fish might be induced to take, it does not make aesthetic sense to construct flies which do not vaguely resemble something in nature. Every live object, other than man, is endowed with a way of protecting itself and it does this by what you might call its natural camouflage, colour or pattern. This being so, is it not reasonable to expect the most rapacious animal or fish to be slightly perturbed by the sight of some prey which is so garish-looking that it could not exist in nature?

I think that we can assume that the stronger the current and the colder the water, the larger and heavier the fly or lure should be. Salmon in cold water do not seem to want to move far or fast to intercept a lure. The lure needs to be brought into close proximity with the fish – and this usually means the biggest and heaviest flies, offered on heavy sinking lines. So, how do we construct these lures or flies and in what colour or pattern?

Having noted that it makes sense to be aware of the colours of nature, we have now to consider another aspect of fly selection – that of making sure that our offerings are visible in differing situations of water clarity. In perfectly clear water obviously little more is needed than a fly or lure that looks as though it belongs there. It should not stand out like a sore thumb and should take on a similar appearance to many other forms of natural life which rely on their colour to protect them from predators. It might help to consider the overall colour of the particular river we are going to fish. On the Spey, for instance, particularly following a snow melt or recent rain, there tends to be a slight coffee or peaty tinge to the water. This may suggest the use of darker flies, with those containing a smudge of black or brown the most popular. Perhaps this is why such patterns as the Munro Killer, the Stoat's Tail and the Thunder and Lightning find great favour – they look totally natural in that environment.

The Aberdeenshire Dee, on the other hand, tends to have a more clear, sandy colour and this may account for the continuing popularity of the Blue Charm, along with the Logie and the Hairy Mary. One of the four classic rivers, the Tweed, tends to get more suspended matter in it from time to time – particularly in the high water of early spring and late autumn. In these circumstances it may be desirable to overcome some of the loss of visibility by the use of more garish-looking flies, such as the Garry Dog or Tosh.

In the absence of rigid guidelines, let us start by considering what we might need on the Spey, Dee or Tay in the months of February or March. Over most of this period there will still be a deal of melting snow from the higher mountain slopes. This should keep the rivers well topped up and it may well be that the snow-melt is augmented by fill-dyke rain. With the winter floods having got rid of much of the autumnal debris, most rivers will be running big and fairly clear over well polished stones. Other than at times of flood it may be safe to presume that there will be little suspended matter and that the

water temperature is still in the low forties. Few fish may be showing and we might well have to rely on little more than an assumption that there are any there at all. Most will be well down near the bottom of the river and in those deeper pools where their workload is at a minimum. It may need a good-sized lure in an eye-ball-to-eyeball confrontation to spur the fish into taking mood. In these circumstances I would opt for a 2-inch or 2½-inch tube fly on a sinking shooting head such as one of those described in the last chapter. I might not want the fly to look too subdued in colour and particularly on those short, grey, overcast days. I might opt for something with a bit of yellow or hot orange in it to make it fairly easily seen. Dyed bucktail is an excellent material for the construction of these large tube flies and there are several examples shown in the photographs.

Tube flies may be used right through to the end of April if it is thought desirable, but it is usually about the middle of that month that water temperatures start to rise towards the critical level of 50° F. From long experiences of the Spey at this time I know that water temperatures may vary by as much as ten degrees in a week. I have known times when the water may be up at 52° and a week later back down to 42°. Alternatively, I have known temperatures to rise by ten degrees just as quickly. It is at such a time that many of us are faced with a dilemma on the size of fly to choose. Some anglers may be reporting great success on size 6 flies on floating lines, while others may insist that the large fly on the sinking line or the spinning bait does best for them. The reality is that the rise and fall of temperature is equally confusing to the fish and the question is not so much one of the choice of fly or lure but of the sheer luck of presenting the offering close to a resting fish.

It helps to remember that providing the water is fairly clear a fly moving near to the surface is usually more easily seen by the fish than one fishing close to the bottom. In the first instance we rely on a positive move by the fish to intercept the lure or fly; in the latter instance we attempt to move the lure into a position where it prompts the fish into an attack. Indeed, it is amazing just how fish will sometimes move out of the way of an intimidating lure and not be provoked into taking it. Fortunately, of course, there are other occasional times when the provocation proves too much for it and then a springer is on!

My box of flies contains a wide variety of tube flies for use in the

early spring and late autumn. I like to have a selection in a wide
variety of colours, from subdued to garish, and in different sizes and
weights. Usually I tie them on polythene-lined brass tubes. But it is
wise to have a selection on the much lighter aluminium or plastic
tubes for when you don't want the fly to fish quite so deep. I think
that the length and colour of the fly must be chosen according to
clarity and temperature of the water, while the weight should be
decided on the volume of water the river is carrying at any one time.
Such decisions are not made without experience of the water being
fished and, until you know the form, it might pay best dividends to
be advised by the gillie or the local tackle shop.

In a normal year it is usually about mid-April when such rivers as
the Spey and Dee come down to what might be termed a good fly
height – that is, they begin to look promising for a trial with a full
floating line and slightly smaller flies than we might have been using
with the sinking line. Here again the choice may be based on little
more than fancy or knowledge of the popular patterns being bought
at the local tackle shop. Providing the water is clear and the fly does
not seem out of place colour-wise, when suspended in the current,
it may be that one choice is as good as any other. I have a great liking
for my early-season flies to be tied on treble hooks. Those marketed

Salmon flies, as tied by Esmond Drury using 'Lureflash'.

by Esmond Drury are superb. In sizes from 2 to 8, they offer a wide permutation of patterns for every conceivable occasion. Often I fish on through April with a well dressed size 4, but if the water gets low and slightly warmer than normal I might well use a lightly dressed size 8 during the early part of May.

Many writers have suggested a size/temperature chart for the estimation of the size of fly to be used at any given time – usually a steady graph indicating that fly sizes diminish as the water gets warmer. One suggestion is that in water temperatures of from 35° to 40° you should use a fly of over 2½ inches in length in yellow or with a bright-coloured wing or body, or a gold body ribbed with black. Between 40° and 45° the fly should be a size 2 or 4 of almost any colour you care to choose. Between 45° and 50° it is suggested that fly sizes may alternate between 2 and 7 and again be of any colour, while temperatures of between 50° and 55° might call for a dull-looking fly from size 4 to 8. The final temperature range given, between 55° and 60°, calls for dirty-grey or brown-coloured flies from size 6 to 10.

As a rough guide I do not find too much to quarrel with in this little package. It makes a basis for trial, but it presupposes that the water is always slightly colder than the air and that the river is running at a normal height without any suspended matter to decrease fish vision. Bear in mind that with any fly fished on a floating line, and providing that the water is clear, the fish are going to have little difficulty seeing it no matter what its size. In most situations in the early season, however, I am sure that it is a mistake to choose too small a fly. There are times when salmon and sea trout will take exceptionally small flies – trout flies even – but I would rather offer them something more substantial until later in the season.

The choice of treble-, double- or single-hooked flies is one which exercises much space in the correspondence columns of our angling magazines. I like to have all three on hand, and it is worth considering their relative merits. The advocates of the treble hook rightly claim that it offers wonderful hooking potential. It does not seem possible for a fish to take a treble hook into its mouth and then pull against the rod and line without being hooked. Of course, we know that fish can and do fail to become hooked in such situations, but it may be reasonable to suppose that they do so less frequently than when double or single hooks are used. The snag with the treble,

and one of which you might not be fully aware, is that, size for size, it offers much more drag or water resistance when dangling in a current. The smaller treble-hooked flies tend to rise well up in the water and in a strong current they may skate on or too near the surface to be fully effective. A single-hooked fly of the same size, however, may offer less drag and thus swim slightly deeper, offering a more attractive proposition to the fish. On the other hand, a big treble – merely because of its weight and irrespective of its extra drag – may well fish at a greater depth than a lighter single-hooked fly which offers less drag.

This raises the question of the ideal depth at which a fly should swim or move when it is being fished on a floating line. Some writers have attempted dogmatic statements on this score, but I find it all too speculative to be able to deduce anything of meaning. A lot obviously depends on the strength of the current, the weight/drag effect of the fly and the length of the leader in use. Another factor is the buoyancy of the front section of the fly line. Old lines get frayed and the point tends to sink slightly. Most certainly I regard the question as too academic to be worth much practical consideration. Many writers argue, and I am certainly one of them, that in most situations of fishing with a floating line it is desirable to have the fly as near to the surface as possible without it actually cutting the surface and creating visible drag. Lee Wulff, on the other hand, pleads with us to try his method of the 'riffling hitch' when salmon become difficult: the fly is tied on at right angles and is allowed to skate over the fish lies with a pronounced V wake coming from it as it moves.

When fishing with a sinking line, on the other hand, I like to know that my fly is well down. If I feel it scrape the bottom on odd occasions, without continually getting hooked on some obstruction, I have that confident feeling that it may be at or near to an eyeball-to-eyeball confrontation with the fish I am seeking to catch.

Although I have caught fish on very small flies I tend not to fish deliberately for salmon with anything smaller than a size 12 hook. Many times while fishing during the late dusk of a June evening I have caught salmon on size 12 and 14 flies intended for sea trout. There were several years when, during May on the Spey, I would fish for the resident brown trout with size 14 and 16 flies and not be surprised to catch salmon. With such small flies, however, there is a danger of the fish merely mouthing them without being hooked, but

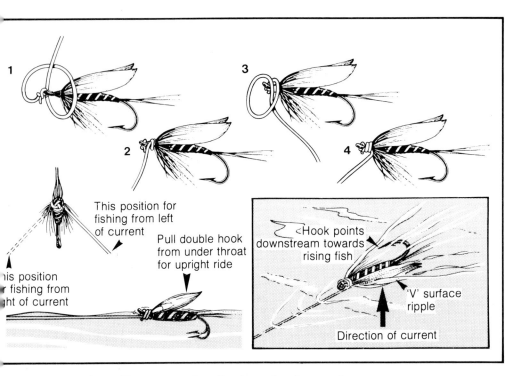

Fig 2   The Riffling or Newfoundland Hitch. The two lower
illustrations demonstrate how the position of the hitch may
be varied to give a high or low swim in the water.

when those small singles do go in over the barb, into somewhere like
the tongue of the fish, they may need to be prised out with pliers.

My stock of salmon and sea trout flies, therefore, tends to be
rather large. When fishing with a floating line, I usually have a
specific pattern in sizes from 2 to 12, with some flies lightly dressed
and others more heavily dressed. Some will be tied on trebles and
others on doubles and singles. Outpoint hooks are preferred,
although I do like a sneck-bend for singles. All in all I should have at
least half a dozen size variations in one pattern, with a similar
number of flies with more or less dressing than is standard.

A glance at the photographs will give some idea of the wide
selection I carry. A useful addition to any tube fly is a piece of valve
rubber or polythene tubing, which fits over the base of the tube and
prevents the treble curling round and snagging on the leader. This
can occur with tubes and all treble-hooked flies and constant
vigilance is needed to be sure that the fly is not in fact snagged round
the leader and facing the wrong way in the water.

Grace Oglesby playing a Tweed salmon, caught on a sinking
line and a large tube fly.

Large tube flies are most often used with sinking lines during the
early spring and late autumn. Just occasionally I might try one on a
floating line in the low water which follows a freeze-up. At best they
are not nice to cast and the very heavy ones may require modified
casting techniques to get them any appreciable distance. I have these
tubes or lures in many different colours from all-black, for clear
water conditions, to garish red, yellow or hot orange for water
which is very cold or contains a lot of suspended matter after a
flood.

Most of my flies for fishing with the floating line, on the other
hand, are of more subdued colour. I like browns and blacks with an
occasional flash of red when fish have seen regular patterns or when
exceptional circumstances obtain – times of unusual water height or
temperature. Red often seems to attract migratory fish and one
wonders if there is a link with the colour of natural ova. On rivers,
such as those in Alaska, where some fish are feeding on salmon eggs,
a touch of red in the dressing of a fly seems to add to its appeal. One

fly that has caught me a few fish – one which I have christened the 'Oglebug' – is constructed of nothing more than a black body with mixed black and red goat hair for winging. I tie them on trebles, doubles and singles, but I do not pretend that they are any better (or worse for that matter) than many other fly patterns.

If I have to name some of the long-established patterns that I find I use most, I would opt for the Blue Charm, the Munro Killer, the Thunder and Lightning, Jeannie, Logie and the Stoat's Tail. But if you tell me that you prefer the Jock Scott, the Durham Ranger, the Green Highlander or the Black Doctor, I should not and indeed could not offer any argument at all.

As we have seen, the old theory that you offer smaller flies as the water gets warmer and lower seems to be acceptable to most of us. There is also that other cliché about 'dull for a dull day and bright for a bright day'. If I adhere to any tenet on bright and dull flies, I tend to think of bright flies for cold water and dull flies for warm water, but it is unwise to adopt any firm notions.

I recall fishing the Spey during the month of July. The best of the spring fishing was past and the water temperature was in the sixties, but I was on a beat known as Castle Grant No. 3 where that well-known pool, Pollowick, was literally full of fish – old and new. On the Monday morning I went down to Pollowick and took the boat over to the right bank. My wife and a friend stayed on the left bank and by lunch time they had three fish between them to my two. It rained heavily that afternoon and we did not bother to go back to the river until the Tuesday morning. By then it had risen an inch or two and was the colour of clear, though dark, coffee. There was a foam on the water which suggested an excess of acidity from the peat in the hills and no amount of fishing with a floating line and a normal-size fly would bring the slightest response from a fish. It was the same all day on the Wednesday and Thursday morning, but by lunch time I was totally fed up of my fruitless casting.

I talked the situation over with my wife, she asked me what I thought was the best course of action. 'In my book', I said, 'in circumstances like these I suggested trying the large fly on a sinking line!' 'Good heavens!' exclaimed my wife, 'why aren't you trying that now?' I had to admit that it did seem an appropriate moment to take a bit of my own advice and it was not long before I had tackled up with a sinking shooting head and the same garish-looking 2-inch fly I would use on the Tweed in February or November.

I had not been fishing for more than a few moments before a salmon was on, firmly hooked well down in the mouth. Of course, there is a danger of foul-hooking fish when using this technique in the comparatively low water of summer, but I went on to catch a total of five salmon that afternoon and all were firmly hooked in the mouth. By tea time I made way for a companion who had joined me. Seeing my notable catch he tackled up with a similar line and fly and within five minutes he was playing a fish. It fought well in the strong central current of Pollowick and it did not take us long to deduce that it was a bigger than average fish for the river. Twenty minutes later I sank the gaff into a monster of 36lb to give my friend his biggest ever fish.

It was not until the Saturday of that week, and our final day on the water, that I got any more response to smaller flies on the floating line. Fishing with a fly on a floating line is certainly one of the most enjoyable styles of salmon fishing I know, but the days when conditions are perfect are not so frequent as some writers would have us believe. Let us, therefore, move on to examine some aspects of practical fishing tactics and casting which might help us get a fish or two in differing circumstances.

7
Casting
and
Presentation

The quality of a cast is the measure of its capacity to catch fish. Good casting is a joy to the angler; bad casting is a depressing affliction.
  Captain T. L. Edwards and Eric Horsfall Turner, The Angler's Cast

Throughout this book you will note that I tend to talk at length about effective water command. *Total* water command comes from the correct use of proper tackle and a full knowledge of all the casting techniques. *Effective* water command, on the other hand, comes from a knowledge of the water, knowing where to wade – or be boated into the correct positions, and superb tackle handling to get the distance and angle required. In any event, it means that you have to be thoroughly competent with your tackle and this necessitates the acquisition of all the casting skills you can muster.

CASTING

I have always claimed that it is very difficult to teach casting in a book; that it is a little easier to do it with a film or video, but that the most satisfactory way of teaching anyone to cast is to get him or her on the water and literally spend as long as it takes to get the desired result. Of course, a lot depends on your aptitude and enthusiasm but provided you are enthusiastic – totally dedicated, in fact – and not seriously disabled or one of those rare people who are totally uncoordinated, it should be possible to make you into a competent caster fairly quickly. For the time being I shall attempt to give some instruction through the printed word with the assistance of some drawings and photographs.
  Good casting is not an art; it is merely a craft, and can soon be

Arthur Oglesby and his fishing course at Grantown-on-Spey,
spring 1972.

learned by most able-bodied people provided that they maintain
sufficient enthusiasm. But in order to fish properly, superb casting
has to be allied with proper presentation and, providing you have
good tackle, once these two simple techniques are mastered you
will soon be on the way to being a better-than-average salmon and
sea-trout fisherman. Indeed, there are some rivers and places where
the ability to make exceptionally long casts will give you a head start
over lesser mortals who have not taken the pains to learn. In this
respect it is a source of great amazement to me that a person will
spend several hundred pounds buying the best tackle, a similar sum
on renting the best fishing beat and hotel, and then resent the time
and money spent in learning to fish properly. A few pounds spent
with a top professional instructor, preferably a member of the
Association of Professional Game Angling Instructors, will frequently do more good than the reading of 100,000 words in print on
the subject. Beware of incompetent casting instructors – the blind
leading the blind. These self-styled experts abound!

Following my apprenticeship with the late Tommy Edwards, it

did not take me long to learn just how important good casting is in order to fly-fish for salmon and sea trout to full potential. But general standards are abysmally low and it was for this reason that, under the leadership of Esmond Drury, a few of us formed the Association of Professional Game Angling Instructors back in the seventies. Other organisations have tried to set the same high standards upon which we insist, but in my experience – and as I am currently the chairman I try not to be prejudiced – comparatively few instructors are fully competent to teach all the casts a complete game fisherman might require. Even some expert anglers find it difficult to translate what they do so effectively when fishing into useful tuition. In the final analysis we may not be able to make you into the expert fisherman you might like to be, but we surely can make the average novice into a reasonably competent caster.

Let us assume that you have equipped yourself with two outfits –

The Arthur Oglesby fishing course at Grantown-on-Spey. Tuition may not turn the novice angler into the successful angler he might dream of becoming, but it will make him a more proficient caster and improve his chance of success.

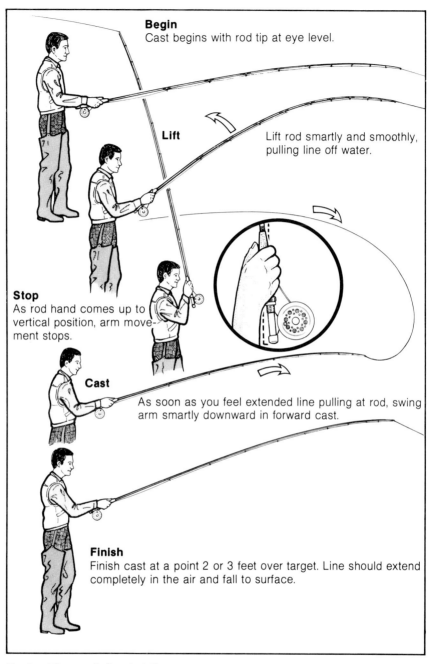

Begin
Cast begins with rod tip at eye level.

Lift
Lift rod smartly and smoothly, pulling line off water.

Stop
As rod hand comes up to vertical position, arm movement stops.

Cast
As soon as you feel extended line pulling at rod, swing arm smartly downward in forward cast.

Finish
Finish cast at a point 2 or 3 feet over target. Line should extend completely in the air and fall to surface.

Fig 3   The single-handed fly cast. Points to note are that the angler does not bring his rod much past the vertical in the back cast, and that there is slight movement to the wrist to obtain the 'hammer' action.

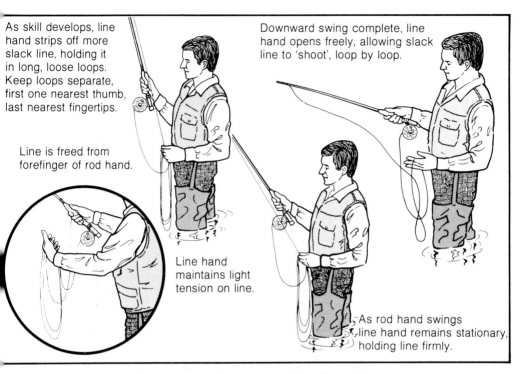

As skill develops, line hand strips off more slack line, holding it in long, loose loops. Keep loops separate, first one nearest thumb, last nearest fingertips.

Line is freed from forefinger of rod hand.

Downward swing complete, line hand opens freely, allowing slack line to 'shoot', loop by loop.

Line hand maintains light tension on line.

As rod hand swings line hand remains stationary, holding line firmly.

Fig 4   Shooting a line. Greater distances may be achieved by shooting hand-held coils of line at a precise moment, following application of power in the forward cast.

a substantial double-handed fly rod, such as the 15-foot 'Bruce' or the 15-foot 'Walker' and a 10-foot single-handed fly rod such as the 'Light Line' or 'Multitrout' or, if you like a stiff-actioned rod, the 10½-foot 'Salmon and Sea Trout' rod by the same maker. To match the 15-foot rod you should have a double taper no. 10 or no. 11 floating line (DT–10–F for the 'Bruce' and DT–11–F for the 'Walker'). Cut portions of two densities of DT–10–S, or DT–11–S will do for the sinking shooting-head lines, and these should be spliced to oval monofilament backing of about 30 lb test. Almost any old reel will suffice, but I like the 'Expert' range marketed by Bruce & Walker, or the Hardy Marquis series. For the single-handed rod I usually opt for a forward-taper line (WF–7–F) spliced to backing of about 20 lb test, while for the stiffer 10½-foot rod a no. 8 (WF–8–F) might work better.

If you have no experience of casting at all, it máy be better to start practising with a single-handed fly rod and a floating line. Line size has direct bearing on the thickness or the weight of the line. The

AFTM (Association of Fishing Tackle Manufacturers) rating is assessed on the 30 feet of line which are to be aerialised outside the rod point and it is the weight of this line, and its effect in loading the spring of the rod, that determines the rating of a given rod. Most single-handed trout rods up to about 9 feet require no. 6 lines and will hence have the symbol # 6 stamped on them. Rods above this length, or with a stiff reservoir action, may require a 7, 8 or even a no. 9 line. Double-handed salmon fly rods, on the other hand, usually call for a no. 9 in the smaller sizes, working up to a 10 or 11 for the longer and more powerful rods.

Your initial lesson, therefore, will begin with a 10-foot carbon-fibre fly rod such as the 'Light Line' and a no. 7 forward-taper (WF–7–F) floating line. If you are right-handed, take the rod in your right hand and stand with your right foot slightly forward of the left foot. Pull off six or seven yards of line and lay it down in front of you. Now, starting at the horizontal and with a snappy flick, raise the rod until it is just past the vertical in order to drive the line and leader up into the air behind you. To achieve this, many instructors suggest that you maintain a stiff wrist. It has become fashionable to teach casting in this style, but I find that novices respond much better to the use of a slightly articulated wrist action and the late Tommy Edwards and Eric Horsfall Turner were so adamant that this was the right technique that they wrote the following in their book *The Angler's Cast*:

The point we stress, heterodox though it may be to accepted opinion, is that wrist action is by far the *most important factor* in any single-handed cast. If the sceptic has any doubt on this point, let him pick up a hammer and drive a nail into a piece of wood. Does he hold the hammer with stiff wrist and forearm? Of course not; he breaks the stroke at the wrist and causes acceleration of the hammer head by a sort of flick. That, precisely, is the action of the single-handed cast.

Returning later to the hammer and nail analogy, they write:

The essential feature of striking a nail so that it penetrates wood is that the hammer head reaches its peak of power at the moment of impact with the head of the nail. The moment of impact, translated into terms of the fly cast, is when the rod point stops to allow the

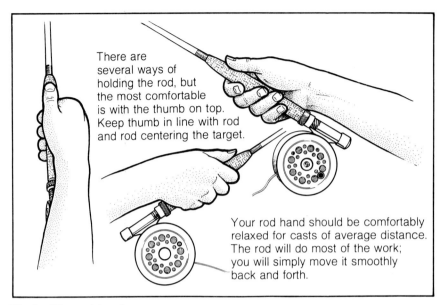

There are several ways of holding the rod, but the most comfortable is with the thumb on top. Keep thumb in line with rod and rod centering the target.

Your rod hand should be comfortably relaxed for casts of average distance. The rod will do most of the work; you will simply move it smoothly back and forth.

Fig 5   The rod hand.

line to travel over the track on which it has been impelled or, in our jargon, allows the line to 'turn over'.

It may help initially to sit on a small stool; place the right elbow on the right knee and merely flick the line back and forth to get the right rhythm. Always assuming that you are right-handed, the rod should be flicked with the thumb coming up to your right eye. But if there is any tendency to go too far back then the rod should be raised and flicked with the thumb coming up to your nose, when, if you are doing it wrong, the rod will bang you on the forehead at the precise point where it should be stopped anyway. A good forward cast requires an equally good and powerful back cast. After some practice casting a modest length of line becomes relatively easy, but you should avoid trying to aerialise too much line as this may cause faults to creep in. You may let the rod and the line go too far back and catch in the ground behind. You may also develop a tendency to 'push' in the final cast. This push will do nothing to achieve more power (and thus greater distance), for it merely kills the spring of the rod you have been at such pains to 'load'. Remember that the rod must act as a *spring* when you are casting and as a *lever* when you are playing a fish.

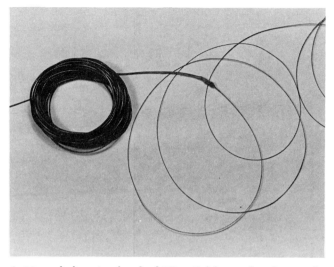

A 12-yard shooting head of Wet Cel line spliced to oval monofilament of 30lb test.

Pushing and waving the rod too far back are the common faults in the early days of casting. Once these have been avoided and extra line is required to be cast, this is best achieved by what is termed 'shooting' a line. Here the maximum length of line that can be comfortably aerialised is augmented by coils of spare line held in the left hand and released at the right moment in the forward cast – fractionally after the application of full power. Any tendency to let the coils go before the correct moment will cause the line to collapse in an untidy heap. When precise timing has been attained it is possible to shoot remarkable lengths of additional line. Indeed, if you replace your forward-taper line with a 30-foot shooting head spliced to oval monofilament backing you will, by the use of the double-haul technique, be able to cast thirty yards with ease.

As soon as you are competent in the normal overhead mode you will invariably modify your casting technique to give you a combination of the precise dry-fly action, just described, and the double-haul technique. This will enable wider movements of the casting arm to achieve greater distances with less apparent effort. Other modifications may include altering the plane in which the cast is made. Bear in mind, however, that any variation of the plane from back cast to forward cast will involve circling with the line – a bad

practice, which will restrict potential distance as well as causing a crooked lay-down of the line.

Although the forward-taper (FT) or weight-forward (WF) line is best suited to the shooting of line, you may find if you are fishing a river which is overgrown with trees and bushes that a double-taper line is preferable. With this line it will just be possible to do some roll and Spey casts. As the longer rod offers an advantage in this respect, I will defer further comment on Spey casting until I deal with the double-handed rod.

In any event it may take a lot of practice before you are fully competent with the single-handed fly rod. Care must now be taken not to develop too much wrist action. I know of one or two eminent anglers who have a fearful wrist action. They would be horrified if I named them here, but their casting looks bad and their style severely restricts potential distance. Once competence has been attained by the use of modest wrist action it may pay to seek to minimise it and develop more power in the wrist in a shorter stroke. It cannot be overemphasised that it is the flexing or loading of the rod that propels the line. Wafting your arms about in wild gyrations and pushing the rod will give *you* all the work the rod should be doing.

THE DOUBLE HAUL

Exceptional casting distances with a single-handed rod may be achieved only by the use of the double-haul technique. This was developed in America some years ago for tournament casting, but it is a cast which is now widely used on our reservoirs and stillwaters when maximum distance is required to get out to cruising fish. Sadly, there are very few anglers who can do it properly. Some do a modified type of single-haul cast, but I see very few anglers who can do the double-haul as it was intended to be done. The whole idea of the haul is to tighten the loop in both the back and forward casts. This increases line speed and thus the potential distance to be cast.

One snag is that a tight loop in the casting line may result in what has loosely been termed a wind knot – a single overhand knot caused by the leader catching on itself. When tightened, this knot reduces leader strength by at least 50 per cent. It might be all right for tournament casters to come off the platform with a highly knotted leader, but it does not do for a practical angler to have them when he

is out to catch fish. There are ways of eliminating the possibility of wind knots in normal casting, but there is still every possibility of their being induced when using the double-haul technique.

Like the Spey cast, the double-haul is yet another cast best learned on the water under competent instruction. It needs constant practice to acquire even modest proficiency. It pays to start with a comparatively short shooting head and with all the line, and the knot joining it to the backing, outside the rod point. The stance should also be entirely different from that adopted with the dry-fly cast. Now you should stand with your left foot firmly forward and with your body facing right-angles to the intended direction of the cast. As you initiate the back cast, pull line down between the reel and the butt ring at the same time as the back cast is being flicked out behind you. This tightens the loop and also produces a bigger load on the rod tip. Some slight drift back of the line may then be permitted fractionally before the forward cast is initiated with the same pull-down action with the left hand. This rhythm is maintained until you feel confident that you are doing it well. Then, with suitable coils of backing already laid out on the ground in front of you, or in a line tray on the water, release the line with your left

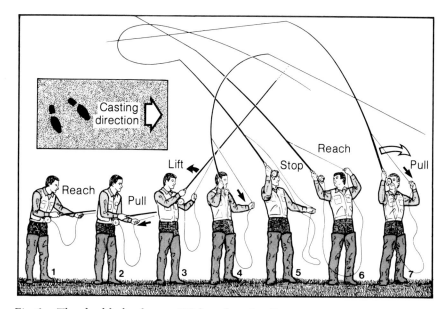

Fig 6   The double-haul cast. With a shooting line, considerable distances may be achieved.

hand while aiming as high as possible in the final forward cast. This high delivery point of the cast will leave ample time for the backing to shoot before gravity exerts its final influence and brings it all down on the water. With practice and development of the correct technique it is possible to achieve some remarkable distances. In the world of tournament casting it is barely worth competing until you can achieve a distance of sixty yards or more with a single-handed rod.

Much practice will be required before you acquire a complete marriage of the action of both hands. When properly done, the double-haul looks like poetry in motion, with an apparent minimum of effort. When done by the average reservoir fisherman, on the other hand, it frequently looks clumsy and inept. Many would do far better to forget all about double-hauling and merely rely on their old style. Sadly, there are so few anglers and instructors who can perform this cast competently that most would be better not bothering with it. I don't think that I have seen more than a dozen anglers who can use this cast to full advantage.

Fig 7   The basic principle of this method of casting is to increase line speed by tightening the loop (as in Fig 5).

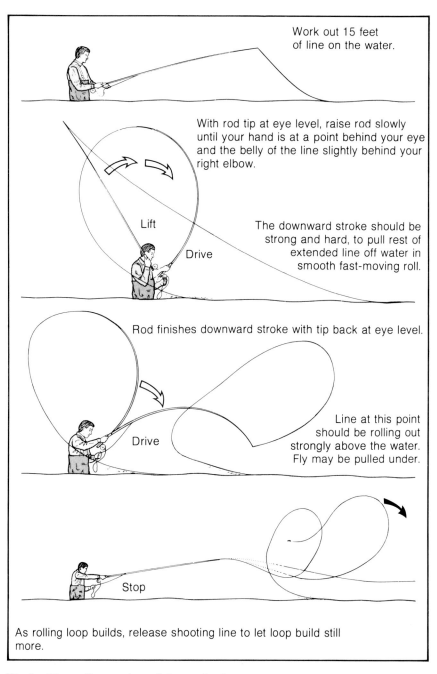

Work out 15 feet of line on the water.

With rod tip at eye level, raise rod slowly until your hand is at a point behind your eye and the belly of the line slightly behind your right elbow.

Lift

Drive

The downward stroke should be strong and hard, to pull rest of extended line off water in smooth fast-moving roll.

Rod finishes downward stroke with tip back at eye level.

Drive

Line at this point should be rolling out strongly above the water. Fly may be pulled under.

Stop

As rolling loop builds, release shooting line to let loop build still more.

Fig 8   The roll cast. A useful cast for laying out line under trees when a change of direction is not involved.

THE DOUBLE-HANDED ROD

In using the double-handed rod it is important to bear in mind that your right hand, again presuming that you are right-handed, will dominate the casting action and the loading of the power. Initially you should stand with the right foot forward so that you can comfortably pivot onto the left foot as you swing back and then onto the right foot as you swing forward. This pivoting of the body from the waist upwards will itself impart a short lifting action to the rod. The right hand should be placed well up the cork grip with the left hand merely taking a loose hold at the butt, just sufficient to share the weight load. Then, with a similar backward flick to the one used with the single-handed rod, make the back cast by a combination of transferring the weight onto the left foot and at the same time flicking the line back high into the air behind you. There must be no attempt simply to wave the rod about. This will merely make you do the work the rod should be doing.

With practice and the adoption of a similar technique to that used with the single-handed rod, you will soon find that you are casting a modest distance. In some respects it is easier to learn casting with a double-handed rod than it is with a single-hander. If, in fact, you have had problems with your single-handed casting – and many ladies do if the rod is too stiff for them – it pays to put two hands on the rod initially until the proper action is acquired.

As soon as modest competence has been achieved with the double-handed rod you must be ever-watchful for the same faults as afflict the unwary in single-handed casting. These include pushing, bringing the rod too far back, or merely waving the rod and not getting that essential loading of the spring. Bear in mind that all casts are best executed in the same plane and that any form of circling with the back cast severely restricts distance and a straight lay-down of the line. This is a particular problem for the salmon angler who has to make his cast across the current and then let the line swing round until it is on the dangle. The initiation of a new cast from immediately downstream automatically entails a circular motion, which means that the next cast will not be as good as it might be.

There are two ways of overcoming this problem. First, with a comparatively short line, it is easily eliminated if you move the rod point from the dangle and point it in the direction where the new cast is to be delivered. Make a back cast from this position, and

Fig 9   The double-handed overhead cast. As with the single-handed rod, avoid taking the rod too far back in the back cast.

deliver to its new position in the fore cast, and it will go out with ease. The second solution, effective when a longer line is being fished, is to pull in some coils of line, with the left hand as the line and leader swing into the side and on to the dangle, and then to make a preliminary circling (bad) cast in the direction where the final cast is intended to go. The final delivery can then be made without circling and a considerable length of backing or shooting line can be shot. Some argue that this double casting disturbs the water and this may sometimes be true, but the extra distance achieved by shooting line with this technique usually ensures that the initial commotion caused by the lay-down of the line is nowhere near the fish or the intended final destination of the line, leader and fly.

For really long-distance casting with a double-handed rod it is essential to master the technique of shooting the line. Under normal conditions of wind and weather it will soon be possible to cast an

entire 30-yard fly line with a 15-foot rod. Great care must be taken not to lift too much line in the initial back cast. A little may be shot during one false delivery before the balance is shot in the final cast.

SPEY CASTING

Long overhead casting with a double-handed rod presupposes that you are wading sufficiently far out or that the banks are so low that the fly and leader do not catch in bankside shrubbery or on rocks in the back cast. It does not take much of a brush with the bank or a rock to crack off a fly or, worse still, remove the sharp point of the hook. While the cracking whiplash sound will soon let you know you have lost your fly, you may fish for a long time and be totally unaware of hook damage. It may not be until you have hooked and lost a fish that you think of looking at the state of the fly. In almost all salmon fly-fishing circumstances and certainly with a double-handed rod, you would be much better advised to adopt some form of Spey cast. Nowadays there is barely a fishing situation I can bring to mind where I do not use the Spey cast exclusively.

Much of my fishing on the Spey in the springtime is done on water where I have a full quota of paying guests. Naturally they get the best pools and I am left with those places which are difficult to fish or which are overgrown and not very noted holding places anyway. By resorting entirely to Spey-casting techniques I do not have to give a thought to bankside vegetation. I can merely wade down wherever it pleases me and then cast the best part of thirty yards of line without a thought for a back cast. This means that while I am often denied access to the best fish-holding lies I do get opportunities of showing my fly to fish which might not have seen one before. I get to cover water that may have been unfished for weeks. On one occasion I recall going to a short stretch of water under a high overhanging bank. Within half an hour I took two fish out of it and all in full view of another member of my party who was fishing the main pool higher upstream. In the bar that evening I overheard an indignant conversation to the effect that 'Oglesby came down at midday and marched straight in to a place which the gillie had been saving for him all that week. He quickly caught two fish while I did not have so much as a touch.'

The single and the double Spey casts, therefore, are essential

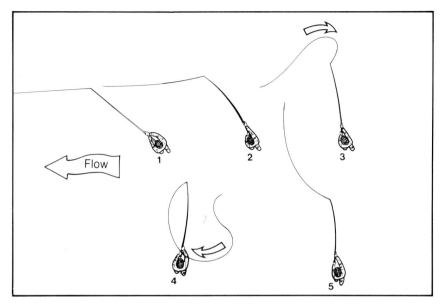

Fig 10　Making a new cast after the fly has come to the dangle involves making a technically bad cast; this may be overcome by making a false cast and then shooting line on the following cast.

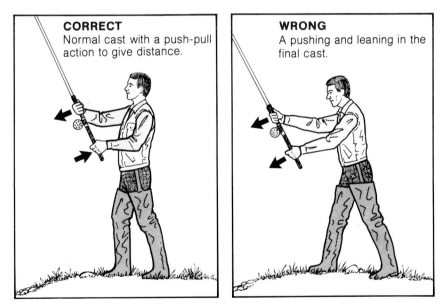

Fig 11　The angler should develop a nice pendulum action when casting. Any form of 'push' (see example on right) will merely kill the spring of the rod.

techniques if you are to fish to your full potential and hold your head up in any angling company. It pays to spend a large slice of your time mastering these casts for they will surely open up an entire new fishing horizon for you. A friend who is a superb overhead caster and a very fine salmon fisherman came to Grantown some years ago to help me with some tuition. He is a fine caster in every sense and a natural fisherman. I spent a little time showing him the Spey casts and he was not long in mastering them completely, but he went away muttering to himself that having spent a virtual lifetime without knowledge of the Spey casts he now realised how much sport he had missed out on. Although he is now fully competent at Spey casting he is still occasionally to be heard muttering and shaking his head sadly that Spey casting only came to him in the autumn of his life. 'Why did no one show me all those years ago?' he pleads.

One of the snags with Spey casting is that although once the technique is acquired it is simple, gaining the initial competence is not easy. Some instructors insist that a Spey cast is merely a roll cast with a change of direction. As I shall attempt to demonstrate, it is no such thing, but it will help to develop some mastery of the roll cast before proceeding further.

A roll cast is the cast you might perform to straighten your line as it lies on the water. This cast should only be attempted on water for it is virtually impossible to do it properly on grass. (In fact all casting practice is better done over water because its 'clinging' effect – especially that of running water – helps to load the spring of the rod before the initial back cast. Water is also kinder to fly lines.) Initially the line should be brought feathering back as the rod is raised slowly. There must be no attempt to initiate a back cast. This will ruin a roll cast, for the power is only to be applied in the forward direction once the rod is in a position to be flicked forwards. The greatest difficulty I have with novices is to restrain them from applying any power in the backward movement. This must be a slow, deliberate raising of the rod and arm as the line and leader are maintained on the surface of the water. When the rod reaches a position just backward of vertical, hold it there for some moments while you slowly raise your arm a little more. Then, with a short but snappy flick drive the rod forwards and downwards as though you were trying to break it. This causes the line to snake back out to its original position and it may be a very useful cast to work your fly

under trees or into little pockets where an overhead cast would get hung up. One of the main snags with the roll cast, however, is that any attempt to change direction usually ensures that the line fouls up on itself and the cast goes nowhere. This is where the ability to do the Spey casts will transform your performance in any location. A word of caution. Do not try to roll cast too long a length of *sunk* line. The rod might not stand the strain. Nor should you attempt to heave too much sunk line from the water in a normal back cast, for the same reason.

One of the greatest criticisms of Spey casting frequently comes from those who either don't know how to do it properly or who have only seen others doing it incorrectly. A roll cast does tend to disturb the water over which it is being deployed and if you were to learn Spey casting on this basis you would soon cause the same water disturbance that gives Spey casting its bad name. In the roll cast you initiate the power stroke slightly downwards towards the water, while in the final movement of the Spey cast the power should be applied upwards so that the line and fly are propelled well out over the water before alighting in much the same manner as in a normal overhead cast.

For all practical purposes I find it easier to teach a novice the double Spey cast before I take him on to the single Spey. The words 'double' and 'single' in this context, in fact, are slightly misleading – the inference being that the double Spey is more difficult to do. Normally the angler who is totally right-handed will seek to do the single Spey from the left bank and the double Spey cast from the right bank (left and right looking downstream, of course). It is perfectly permissible and highly desirable to be able to fish on occasions with the left hand up the rod. In this instance you would do the double Spey cast from the left bank and the single Spey cast from the right bank. Much confusion seems to exist on the whole question of Spey casting and I have seen some videotapes, from supposed teaching authorities, which are little short of a joke.

For the purposes of this chapter, therefore, let us consider how you are to modify your roll casting into a double Spey cast. Initially

Left It is essential to master the Spey cast if you want to fish to your full potential. Here illustrated are two different styles: top – the double Spey cast; bottom – the single Spey cast with the left hand up the rod.

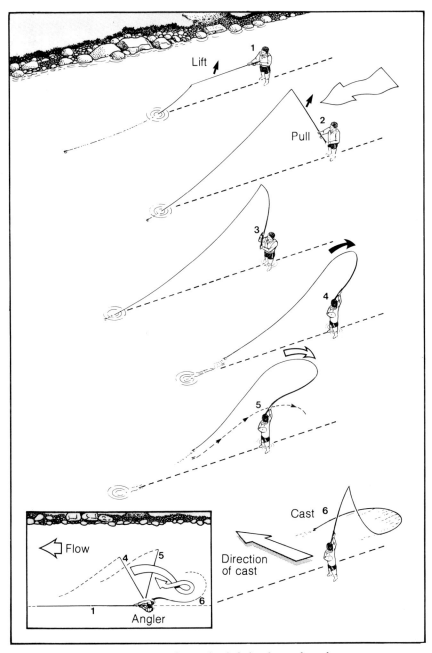

Fig 12   The single Spey cast from the left bank, with right hand up the rod. Achieving the effects of examples 5 and 6 seems to provide the most difficulty for novices. The final cast, following example 6, should be aimed high and not like a roll cast.

David Hield double Spey casting from the right bank of the
Dunbar Pool on the Spey at Castle Grant.

it is important to position yourself on a bit of flowing water and on
the bank appropriate to your style (left or right hand up the rod).
Being predominantly right-handed, I do the single Spey best from
the left bank and the double Spey from the right – although
obviously I occasionally have to teach and demonstrate both styles.
Let us imagine, therefore, that you are on the right bank of a river
like the Spey and that you are wading up to your knees in smooth but
easily flowing water. The fly has come round on to the dangle and
you now need to get it back across the current for its new swing.
There is a high bank behind you and overhead casting is impossible.
Of course, it is just possible from this bank that you could fudge a
type of roll cast which would get your fly out somewhere near
where you want it but with a proper double Spey cast it will go a lot
further and with much less fuss and water disturbance.

Initially, the line should be led upstream slightly so that the bulk of what was originally on the dangle is now in a position in front of you, floating on the water. If too much line is led upstream it will be difficult to cast across the water without the line catching on itself. Some prolonged practice will be required in order to lead just the right amount of line into the right spot before the rod is reversed from the left to the right of your body for the final roll or shoot. This last movement has to be performed with a lot of energy and the final punch must be made upwards and not down at the water. This final hit should be a short, sharp, upward jab delivered with such power that again you appear to be trying to break your rod.

In all instances of good Spey casting it is essential to be wading. This enables subtle little movements to be induced which will enable you to cast just that bit further than Mr Average. Ask a casting instructor if he can Spey-cast an entire 30-yard fly line and he will invariably make noises to the effect that the wind is wrong or that his arm aches – any excuse to avoid the crunch confrontation. Of course, it may be impossible to throw even twenty yards if there is a contrary wind or if the tackle is mismatched. Even in ordinary fishing conditions only rarely is it possible to cast more than thirty yards with the double Spey cast, but this *is* frequently possible with the single Spey. When I was testing a prototype of the new 'Hexagraph' carbon rods in the spring of 1985 I managed a measured Spey cast of 40 yards – albeit in a helpful wind. This is not a distance which is easily achieved and certainly not with a normal double-tapered line in the overhead mode.

The single Spey cast, therefore, is, in my opinion, the most useful cast throughout a season on a salmon river with a double-handed salmon fly rod. Being more powerful with my right hand up the rod, I tend to use it more on the left bank than on the right. I like to be wading slightly out from the bank so that the first and second movements may be made without any risk of the line catching on the bank behind me.

Let us now assume that I have the entire 30 yards of line outside my rod point and that I am using my 15-foot 'Walker' and a double-taper no. 11 floating line in a slightly favourable wind – that is, one coming from left to right over my shoulders as I face downstream. With the rod parallel to the river bank, the fly comes onto the dangle, at which point I lower the rod point down near the water surface. I then handline back the reverse-tapered portion of the line

until the thick belly portion is just outside the rod point and the rest is neatly coiled in my left hand. I then raise the rod point slowly with just the suggestion of a slight inclination towards my own bank as I do so. At a position where the rod is nearly vertical I pause momentarily and then make a purposeful movement, just like describing a large crescent moon in the sky with my rod point, so that the line which was originally all laid downstream of me is suddenly removed to a position on the water in a large semicircle slightly upstream of where I am standing. This is the crucial movement and it is not achieved without constant practice. With insufficient switch some portion of the line will remain on the water downstream below me and obstruct an effective final cast. If it is all switched too far upstream, on the other hand, it is not sufficiently near to be punched out properly in the final cast. The fly must be just upstream of the angler.

Presuming that the miracle happens for you the first time you make the 'U' movement, you should then let the rod point come a little further back before making the final and important punch out, shooting the hand-held tapered portion of the line as you do so. This final cast is to be likened more to a bait cast than a roll cast. All the force must be directed upwards towards the top of the clouds on the far horizon. Imagine, if you like, that you are immersed up to your neck in water and then try to throw the line upwards at an angle of 45° so that it can all alight as softly as a normal overhead cast. Remember that, with both the single and double Spey casts, force or power is only required in the final movement. The initial movements merely involve a form of carefully caressing the rod and line, coaxing them into a position where the power can best be applied to full effect.

Although distinct pauses must be made between each movement, in a strong current of water only a little time elapses before the position of the line in relation to the water surface changes. In practice it is helpful to try and do the three movements to waltz time, saying to yourself one-two-three, one-two-three, *wham*! In the case of the single Spey cast the first 'one-two-three' will cover the period when the line is being lifted to the near vertical; the second 'one-two-three' to the all-important period when the 'U' movement or the crescent moon is being drawn in the sky; while the wham! describes the power needed to drive the line out and upwards to its new position.

In the double Spey cast, of course, the first 'one-two-three' covers the lift of line horizontally and slightly upstream to get the bulk of the line on the water immediately in front of you. The next 'one-two-three' will relate to the time taken to switch the rod point back to your right-hand side before the final wham! to send it out to its intended destination. Both casts will need a lot of practice before full competence is attained.

At no time will Spey casting be easy in a contrary wind. Single Spey casting in a downstream wind is not only difficult, it is highly hazardous. Unless great care is taken there is every chance that the fly will catch you in the shoulder or in the ear or neck. A much better idea is to change hands and do a double Spey cast with the left hand up the rod. Similarly with an upstream wind on the right bank. Again, in this instance, it is much easier to change hands and merely do a single Spey cast with the left hand up the rod.

In all salmon casting situations with a double-handed rod it is important to initiate the cast with the rod point down near the water surface. In the overhead mode this allows a slow but purposeful acceleration of the rod point to a position where the flick is initiated to develop full power on the back cast. When you are competent in this mode, but only then, it will be found permissible to allow some slight drift back of the rod point as the line moves behind you. Then, when it is felt – and not imagined – that the line is fully unfurled, the new power stroke may be initiated in the forward direction, followed by a slow movement of the rod point back down towards the water. This forward movement of the rod point following the application of power serves two purposes. First, it eliminates any tendency to stop the power stroke with the rod point still in a high position. It is in this high position that the forward-moving line, travelling as it should do in a fairly tight loop, may switch over itself and thus put a wind knot into line or leader. Any tendency to put wind knots in the leader at this stage of the cast, therefore, is easily remedied by lowering the rod point immediately after the power stroke has been completed.

As soon as the cast has been completed, however, it pays to lift the rod point slightly so that it is in what I shall call the *expectant erection* attitude, which I shall mention again when commenting on tactics. The higher the rod point and the more it is held at right angles to the river bank, the more line will be kept free of the belly-forming central current. Although an initial 'mend' may be needed

after the cast, the high-held rod will enable your fly to come round more slowly than it would do if you merely kept the rod point in the *despondent droop* attitude or moved the point of the rod in line with the river bank. This latter tactic may be useful in a very slack current, but in a normal flow of water it is more likely to drag your fly round too quickly for it to be of interest to the fish. In later chapters I shall deal at length with effective water command but it cannot be overemphasised that most times you are seeking to achieve a slow movement of the fly over the fish lies.

Good casting will not come without expert tuition, thorough practice and prolonged practical experience. Some will have a natural flair for it while others will need time before competence is developed. Some anglers never seem to reach full potential and there are those who feel that it is not too important anyway. In a boat-fishing situation, of course, the boatman may easily compensate for any lack of skill, but if you are to wade and fish without a gillie at your side it is impossible to be too good at casting. In such fishing conditions it will often be the best caster who will most frequently win the day.

8
Fishing with
the Double-handed
Fly Rod

Many of the best fishermen in Scotland are Spey casters. Spey casting is the technique of casting a fly off the water without it travelling behind or above the fisherman, a way of casting that is necessary on many rivers, not just the Spey. A Spey caster can fish anywhere, among trees or with sheer cliffs rising behind him. It is a very easy cast to perfect, provided, of course, that you have been expertly and painstakingly taught and have spent days and weeks determinedly perfecting the skill and fighting the temptation to cast the way you know.

David Barr, The Haig Guide to Salmon Fishing in Scotland

I think that you will have already realised that the bulk of your salmon fishing, certainly on the classic rivers of Britain and in the early spring and autumn, is likely to be undertaken with a double-handed fly rod. It is the traditional tool of British salmon fishermen and with the advent of carbon fibre it is likely to remain so for many years. The double-handed fly rod gives a greater degree of water command than is possible with short, single-handed rods and it makes possible casts by means of the single Spey cast or with minimum false casting in the overhead mode.

One well-known American writer, Leonard M. Wright Jr, recently stuck his head out for a swipe from short-rod fellow Americans when, in his book *Fly Fishing Heresies*, he declared: 'I'm convinced that the most overrated thing in America today (with the possible exception of Home Movies) is the short fly rod. It is the least effective, least comfortable, least "sporting" fly-fishing tool ever invented for fishing running water.'

To be fair to Wright and his fellow Americans, I must make it plain that Wright was only referring to what we term ultra-short rods. His idea of a long rod, believe it or not, is around ten feet. He

might be just as scornful of my double-handed rods as he seems to be of his fellow Americans and their ultra-short rods.

I have already recorded my preference for the 15-foot 'Walker' for general double-handed work in the early and mid-spring and the late autumn, and I shall doubtless opt for a similar-actioned rod when the new 'Hexagraph' rods are available on the market. Meanwhile, I have little hesitation in suggesting that, back in the early seventies when it first came out, the 15-foot 'Walker' quickly established itself as the market leader in double-handed salmon fly rods.

On the Tweed in the first two weeks of February anglers are restricted to some form of fly fishing, but the sunk line may be used on all rivers where other anglers may prefer to spin. This is the time, therefore, for a rod such as the 15-foot 'Walker', a shooting head of DT–11–S Wet Cel II sinking line and one of the large tube flies discussed in Chapter 6. You may well be on such a beat as Upper Hendersyde (a beat where I have had considerable experience in the past) or one of the beats immediately downstream of the town of Kelso. The famous Junction Pool at Kelso will doubtless be one of the first major resting-places for the early-run spring fish and you may expect all the beats downstream from there to be worth fishing at this time. Some of your fishing may be done from a boat, while casting from the bank may be possible in certain locations. It may even be possible to wade over certain pools and you must be fully prepared for any eventuality. It is not quite so easy when wading to cast a shooting head any meaningful distance, the snag being that the shooting line or backing may drift away in the current and not shoot so well as backing line neatly coiled on the bank or in the bottom of a boat. Ideally, if you are wading you should pick up a few loops of backing in your hands – they are more easily shot when the final cast is made. Alternatively you could use a portable line tray, as in reservoir fishing.

For your first exercise let us assume that you are on the Tweed in February. You are intending to fish from a boat and the boatman is going to hold the boat by rowing over his selected area. In this instance the choice of where you are to fish will be dictated entirely by the boatman. He can quickly measure your competence at casting and may well position the boat so that your fly will best cover the water where he knows the fish to be. Many boatmen of my experience do not like me to cast to my full potential distance and

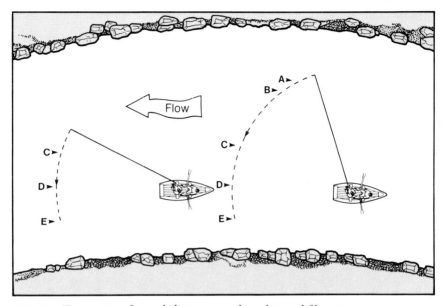

Fig 13   Two casts of equal distance might achieve different
results. In cold, high water the boat on the left would
present the fly more slowly. In lower, warmer water the boat
on the right would search more slowly and still present the
fly at a reasonable pace.

they often urge me to fish with a shorter line. Usually I do as I am
told, but I do know from long experience that it is the longer cast
that permits the fly to go down to greater depths.

Let us assume, however, that the water is about two feet above
normal summer level and that it is about 38°F (3·3°C), with the air
temperature only fractionally higher. The river is running clear and
there has been little recent precipitation other than light snow on
the hills. The bulk of the water will be coming from the run-off of
winter rain in the ground and possibly a little melting snow as the
day warms fractionally. This warmth may induce a slight rise in the
river, but it may take several hours to be noted and in this instance it
may be regarded as of little account.

Your choice of line weight or density may be decided as a result
of your own experience of the piece of water or on your boatman's
advice. As already indicated, I rarely have any use for a lead-cored
line in Britain. Usually I will use the Hi-D, the Wet Cel II or the
Intermediate Wet Cel. In some situations of fishing in a high water

on the Tweed, however, it is occasional practice to place a spiral lead on the leader and just above the fly. This makes the entire contraption the very devil to cast properly. Frankly, in a situation like this, I would either resort to the lead-cored or Hi-D line, where it is permitted, or else I go home! In very cold and deep water it is important to know at just what depth your fly is moving. Fish will not travel far or fast in order to intercept a lure so it pays to have a wide variety of weights of fly on hand. Usually the desired depth is achieved merely by the density of the line chosen, but brass tubes weigh considerably more than those of aluminium so I like to have both on hand, and some even on plastic tubes, in order that I can make minor adjustments to fly depth.

With a 2½-inch garishly-coloured tube fly you begin your operations at the head of the stream or run where the boatman has positioned you. You make a few short casts as you work the shooting-head portion of the line out beyond the rod point and you

Veteran boatman, Bob Paterson, 'ropes' an angler down a
pool on the Tweed.

continue to lengthen your casts until your experience of that piece of water or your boatman tells you that you have enough to cover the lies. The casts should be made at an angle of about 50° or 60° downstream from the line of the boat and the fly should be allowed to swing round slowly and then to hang on the dangle for a few moments before the backing is slowly retrieved and coiled on the floor ready for the next cast. In very cold water it is possible that the fish will follow the fly but make no firm response to it until the retrieve has started. It is important, therefore, to make the first few pulls as slowly as possible and only speed up the retrieve as the knot joining the backing to the fly line comes up near the rod point. Then, with a firm back cast, the entire fly line may be easily lifted out of the water and the backing re-shot in the next cast.

Sometimes, in order to extend an exceptionally long cast, it might pay to double-cast the shooting head in the direction in which the cast is to be made. All casts from the dangle to the new position involve a change of direction and, as we have seen in the last chapter when fishing a long line, it is not possible to get the best cast without double-casting when a change of direction is involved. Normally you try to avoid double-casting because of the disturbance it might cause, but in this instance the commotion created by the short shooting-head is not likely to be anywhere near the fish or the ultimate destination of the fly when a lot of backing is being shot.

In certain circumstances the boatman may prefer to let you down on a rope. That is to say, he will position one of the oars to act as a type of rudder or paravane, tether the boat to his rope, and hold it in the current while he is standing on the bank. As you make each cast the boatman takes a pace or two downstream to ensure adequate coverage of the lies.

My greatest angling pleasure comes when I am fishing entirely on my own and am in a position to wade deep so that I can adequately cover the lies. Here I often require a longer cast than may be needed when in the boat and throughout this book I shall continue to emphasise the necessity of long and accurate casting if you are to achieve complete and effective water command. There is barely a river in Britain which cannot be adequately covered with a 15-foot rod such as the one described and a suitable shooting-head sinking line with suitable backing. There may occasionally be advantage in a slightly longer rod, such as the 16½-foot or the 17½-foot 'Walker', but you have to carefully balance the slight advantage in casting and

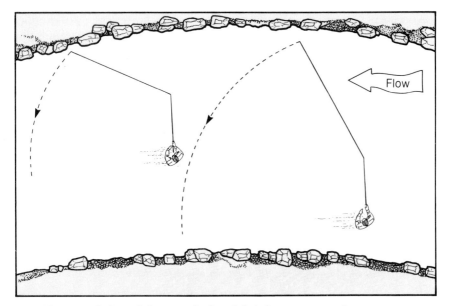

Fig 14   Knowledge of the river bed and fish lies is essential
to achieve effective casting range. Deep wading may
frequently be essential to get the best water coverage.

water command against the weight penalty which has to be carried,
literally, all day. I do occasionally use both the 16½-foot and 17½-
foot rods, but by far my most-used spring and autumn rod is the
15-foot 'Walker'.

In the cold water of early spring you must expect the fish to be
lying in the deep water at the edge of the main runs or in the deeper
dub sections. Fish seen in strong water are more likely to be runners
than potential takers and if the river is carrying much extra water it
may be that the bulk of the resting and potentially taking fish are not
all that far from the banks anyway.

I cannot overemphasise the importance of effective water command. It has little to do with the total distance you cast, but
everything to do with the correct placement of the fly so that it
covers the fish in a provoking manner – sufficiently provoking to
induce the fish to take it. It is the same with both salmon and sea
trout and applies particularly to deep pockets of fast water later in
the season, where fish lie in confined spaces and seem reluctant to
move very far from their lie, and possibly into an uncomfortable
position, to take a fly.

A morning's catch of salmon for Arthur and his wife, Grace, from the Tweed at Upper Hendersyde. These fish were taken before lunch on a Monday. (Not another fish was caught on this beat until the following Saturday afternoon.)

I recall fishing the Tweed one very cold February day many years ago. I started at the head of a pool called the Wintercast on the Upper Hendersyde beat and immediately made long casts towards the point of an island. I fished the pool down for nothing and then decided to go back to the top and try again. This time I waded a little further out, but did not immediately cast as far as I had been doing before. Within minutes I was playing a salmon and it was not long before I had number two safely on the bank. Of course, it may be that those fish had moved into the lie after I had moved out of it on my first time down. Alternatively, it could be that by a better appreciation of the effective water command required on my second try I had covered the fish more tantalisingly. I will never know for certain, but it is an incident that, added to several others, seems to me to be significant.

Casting with the very heavy tube flies frequently used in the early spring and late autumn is not easy. Some of the flies might weigh as much as $\frac{1}{2}$ oz, and with such heavy weights there is a tendency for the weight of the fly to compete with the weight of the line. Bear in

In strong currents, the angler should direct his cast further
downstream. He will cover less water as a result, but will
fish with greater effect.

mind the elementary fact that the rod has to have a weight outside the rod point for it to be able to flex and cast at all. This is why our lines are as thick and as heavy as they are. But with the additional terminal weight of a heavy fly casting techniques have to be modified considerably from those normally practised and taught. For instance, with very heavy flies on sinking shooting heads I find that it pays to pause noticeably in the back cast until the fly is felt tugging at the rod point. Then the forward cast may be initiated, with all the power directed upwards and not down towards the water. This upward power motion is essential if a large quantity of the backing is to be shot in the final forward cast. Tournament casters have developed this technique to extremes and it is essential if extra distance is to be achieved. It may take some time for the salmon fly fisherman who is normally accustomed to the floating line and a small fly to adjust to the new requirement, but it is a very effective method of catching fish in the colder waters of early spring and autumn.

This brings me to another interesting and highly important topic, that of the angle at which the cast should be made. In general terms, the faster the current the greater the angle downstream the fly should be cast. A long downstream cast, of course, will reduce quite appreciably the arc over which your fly moves. In terms of total river width, this arc might represent only a very small section, but it will be the section in which you or your boatman will want your casting to be the most effective. In a fast current there is little point in casting your fly to the other side of the river if the current is going to snatch it quickly away before a fish can see it or take it. Far better that you concentrate on your effective water command, even though it involves casting the same distance as when you cover more water. In any event, always make sure that your fly is fishing at the right speed and depth for it to be acceptable to the fish.

As the water warms, or there is a reduction in the strength of the current, some alteration in your casting angle may be permitted (*see* diagram). This will let your fly search more water, but it will only do this effectively if the depth and the pace at which it moves are suited to the mood of the fish. These tactics are not learned quickly and you will spend much time relying on your boatman or gillie for advice.

When you come to fish with the floating line there is room for continued experiment. In very sluggish water you may even find

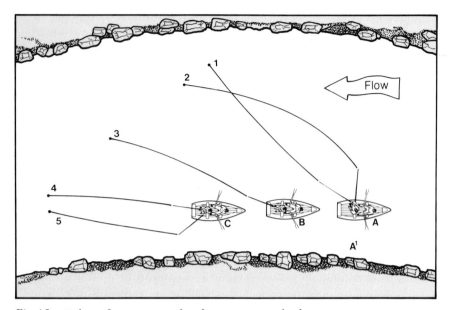

Fig 15   Fishing fast water with a boat requires the boat to
drop downstream slightly as the cast is being fished out.

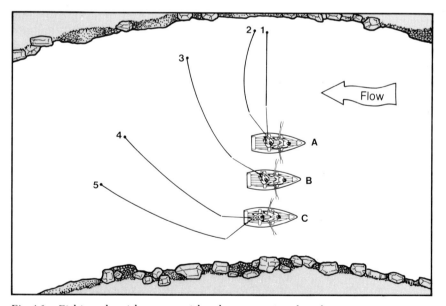

Fig 16   Fishing sluggish water with a boat may involve the
boatman manoeuvring the boat back towards the bank as a
square cast is fished out.

yourself casting slightly upstream and handlining the line back quickly to give extra pace to the fly.

I tend to use the sinking line for much of my salmon fishing until the end of April. As recorded, I have a variety of line sizes and weights, but all are shooting heads of between 10 and 12 yards and all are spliced to non-curl oval monofilament backing of about 30 lb test. The choice of size and colour of the fly will be conditioned largely by the temperature and clarity of the water, while fly weight has to be related to water depth and strength of current. There are many and varied permutations and you may never know what to do for the best until you have long experience of one piece of water.

Much of my April fishing on the Spey is done with a slow-sinking shooting head and flies tied on aluminium-bodied tubes. Nowhere is the Spey a very deep river and the use of a fast-sinking line and brass tubes would invariably cause my fly to get stuck in the bottom at almost every cast. Sometimes I find it pays to be in a position to change tactics as I move down a pool. In my more enthusiastic youth I would frequently start fishing at the head of a pool with a brass-tubed fly and then change to a lighter one as the water got thinner and quieter. This assessment of what might be required can be obtained only from long experience of one piece of water at differing times of the year and in vastly differing conditions. I therefore urge you to give as much time as you can to one piece of water. It may seem more exciting to try a new venue every year, but the angler who takes time to get to know one beat of one river as intimately as he can will be the one to get the most sport from it.

Most of your fishing with sinking lines and large flies will be confined to the colder months of the season when water temperatures are below 45°F, but never go fishing without having them in your tackle bag. Even in midsummer there may be an incident, such as that mentioned in Chapter 6, when their use may save an otherwise dull week. Usually when I decide to put the sinking line to one side and go over to the full floating line I do so in the fairly certain knowledge that I might have to resort to the sinker again if and when the weather changes. This can happen at any time in late April or early May on the Spey, but I do tend to use the full floating line as soon as I think that the method has half a chance. I see little sense in continuing with heavy lines and flies if there is the slightest chance of getting fish on a smaller fly and a floating line. In all circumstances the fully floating line is much more pleasant to use

than the sinker and by an adjustment of fly sizes and weights it is usually possible to get your fly down to an adequate depth anyway.

Also, I like the tremendous advantage I get from being able to Spey-cast, which can only be done with the floater. Combined with the ability to wade deep it is the one thing that gives complete water command anywhere on the river. I don't have to worry about overhanging trees, bridges or high banks behind me. There is no risk of my fly getting caught on the back cast or of the hook point being broken off on a stone or rock. I can fish down any pool no matter what obstructions there are behind and, unless the wind is frightfully contrary, I can throw an entire 30-yard fly line with comparative ease. Coupled with the ability to wade deep while unencumbered with other tackle, I can thus achieve wide water command as required.

In its basic form all double-handed fly fishing, whether with floating or sinking lines, merely involves casting the line and fly out as far as you think desirable and then letting the fly swing round in the current until it comes on the dangle immediately downstream. Then you take a pace or two downstream and repeat the process. It can for some become an almost mechanical exercise, with the guide or gillie providing brief guidelines on where and when to start and where and when to stop. Under good conditions such tactics will undoubtedly be rewarded with a fish or two. I should certainly urge the novice to master not only the overhead casts but the single and double Spey casts as well, so that maximum water command can generally be achieved. You may not always need a long cast, but the ability to perform one in any mode puts you in with a special class of fishermen.

However, it will not do to assume that perfect casting techniques will automatically make you a good fisherman. You have to develop all your natural hunting skills so that you can best attune with nature. Caution and concealment may not play as big a role in salmon fishing as they do, for instance, in dry-fly fishing for trout, but the angler who can move like a natural hunter, instead of bulldozing his way into a pool and then spreading tumult as he attempts to cast to distances which exceed his ability, will be the one to succeed over a season. One angler I know is a superb caster and very pretty to watch. But, sadly, he is not a very good fisherman. He spends the bulk of his fishing time just casting the longest line he can manage. His whole attention is directed to his casting techniques

and he does not seem to have a thought for the tactical requirements. He does catch a few fish, but he would be mortally hurt if I
were to suggest to him that he may never make the natural
fisherman he would so like to be.

WADING

I shall say more about wading in a later chapter, but it is very
important from the outset to be unafraid of deep wading. Unless
you are able to confine your efforts to those rivers and beats where
boats are available or fishing is possible from the bank, you will have
to wade to get the best effective water command. One thing to be
careful about is over-wading the lies. This can be a problem in the
low water of summer when wading is much easier. Normally you are
not likely to over-wade nor, in my opinion, does it often matter all
that much if you do. Salmon are not so easily disturbed by a deep-
wading angler as they are by one who has the bulk of his body
exposed above the water line. Fish get accustomed to bits of rubbish
floating down semi-submerged – old plastic bags and the general
dross often found littering the river banks. In such circumstances a
pair of slow moving legs and feet do not trigger off the alarm bells as
do waving arms above the water line.

I recall some years ago fishing a pool on the Spey behind Hugh
Falkus. We were trying to catch a fish for the BBC TV cameras and
he had started with a floating line while I followed on down with a
larger fly on my sinking line. At the end of a swing of my fly line I
noticed that it was very close to where Hugh was wading and the
thought occurred to me that I had better take care to prevent my
hook catching in his waders. Then, as I was handlining in the
backing line for another cast, I felt the unmistakable tug of a taking
fish. It had taken my fly within inches of Hugh's feet and as the fish
came to the surface the resultant spray actually splashed Hugh on
the face. He was just as amazed as myself that the fish had taken so
close to where he was standing. But I think that it demonstrates two
distinct possibilities. First, that the fish had followed my fly until it
was on the dangle, and, second, that it was then totally unconcerned
about the close proximity of two human legs and feet. We got the
fish and the catching sequence was eventually shown on TV, but it
was not always so easy.

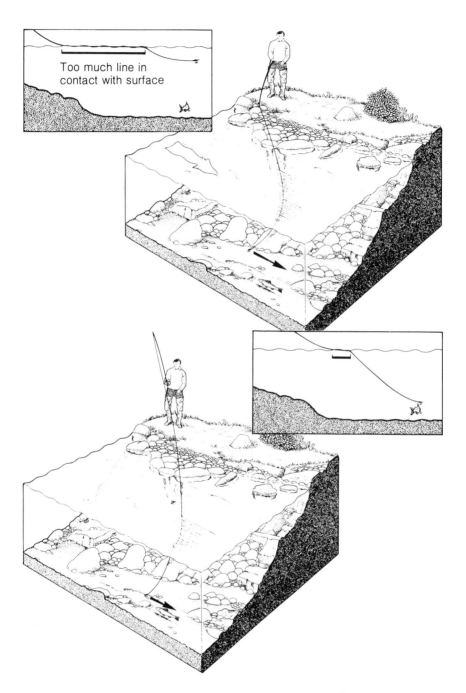

Too much line in
contact with surface

Fig 17   Sunk line fishing. The high-held rod enables the fly
to sink better than the low-held rod.

MENDING AND BACKING UP

One of the first lessons the salmon fly fisherman should learn – and particularly if he is to fish principally with the floating line – is the technique of 'mending' the line. Of course this has nothing to do with mending in the literal sense, but refers to the movement you impart to your line after it has alighted on the water. Normally it will be virtually impossible to make any meaningful mend with a sinking line, and it is important to make a good, straight initial cast so that the central current has the least influence on it. In all situations with a floating line, of course, you will be casting across flowing water and the strength of the current will vary from one side to the other. In many situations the stronger, central, current causes a belly to form in the line, which – as can be seen from the illustrations – produces an unnatural movement of the fly. A powerful central current sometimes causes so much belly that the fly is whipped round in a fast-moving arc, which makes it very unattractive to a fish. By switching or mending the belly formation upstream as it forms, however, you can slow down the pace of the fly and permit it to come round much more slowly than it might do otherwise. Sometimes you will encounter a wide variation in current speeds and the angler who can continually read the situation and 'mend' or modify the curves in his line will have greater success than the one who merely casts his fly across the flow and leaves it to fend for itself.

Usually, particularly in faster water, an upstream mend is required to slow down the pace of the fly, but sometimes in very sluggish water a downstream mend is called for. This increases the belly in the line and gives the fly a little more movement and speed to make it attractive.

On very sluggish rivers, such as some stretches of the Thurso, it is common practice to indulge in what is known as 'backing up'. This means starting at the bottom of the pool and taking a pace upstream as the cast swings round, which imparts even more movement to your fly, though it does have the possible disadvantage of showing the line to the fish before it sees the fly. Sometimes, in very dead water, I find that it pays to handline the fly back slowly so that some lifelike movement is imparted to it, but in all these instances of very sluggish water I like to have a good wind ripple on the surface to help camouflage any clumsiness on my part.

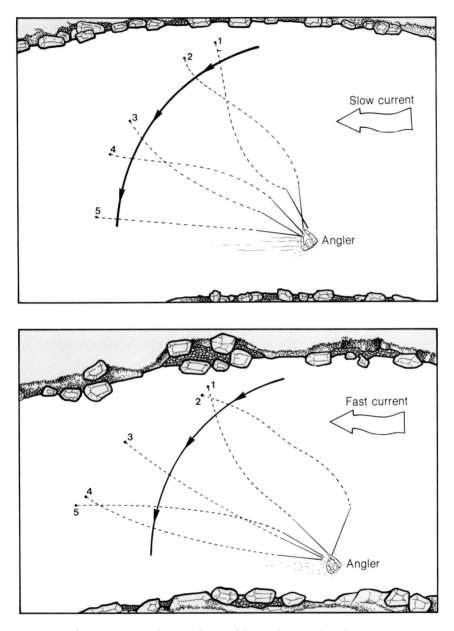

Slow current

Angler

Fast current

Angler

Figs 18 and 19   Various forms of 'mends' may be employed
to suit current conditions. A slight mend may be necessary in
a slow current and a bold mend in a fast current. The
important thing is to have the fly swimming slowly at points
3, 4 and 5.

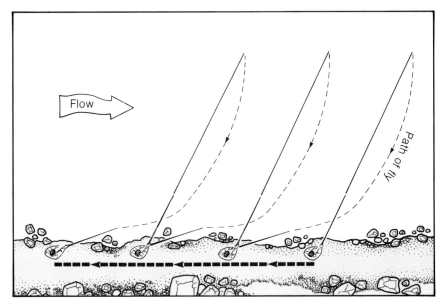

Fig 20   Backing up a pool. In sluggish water it may be
necessary to cast and then walk a pace or two upstream as
the fly swings round.

An understanding of the degree of movement required of your fly
– and thus the speed and angle at which it should be fished – comes
only with experience. A fly which passes over a lie too quickly may
not incite the fish into taking mood, while one that passes too slowly
may be seen for what it really is or fail to initiate the attack reflex
mechanism. Then again, what triggers off a suitable response at one
moment or on one day may not do so on another. There are also the
variables of air and water temperature, water clarity, climate,
barometric pressure, visibility, oxygen content and the general
demeanour of the fish at a specific time of the day or night – all of
which add to the permutations. I know of no formula which can
provide the certain downfall of a fish.

A friend recently said to me that he hoped that this new book of
mine would do something that no other book on salmon and sea-
trout fishing had ever done for him – provide some clue of where
and when to fish, where the fish might lie, and how best to get one
on the end of his line. Of course, the aim of this book is to help you
do all of these things, but I doubt if anyone alive could enlighten us

on anything other than some tactics to experiment with. This is not
an exact science. We are dealing with fish that do not feed in fresh
water and have no need of food at any time during their spawning
migration.

Were you to ask me how to catch trout, I would suggest offering
them something they are seen to eat from time to time, or an
acceptable imitation of that food – a worm perhaps, or a grass-
hopper, or any of a wide range of insects, or even a tadpole. But
when we go after fish with a suppressed appetite, we don't know
what induces salmon or sea trout to take our offerings, so how can
we gain anything but superficial knowledge until we have acquired a
deal of experience of what salmon and sea trout may do at times?

OVERFISHING

Of course, it is one thing to be on a water well stocked with fresh-
run fish straight in from the sea. It is quite another to be casting over
pools which, although full of fish, contain only those which have
been there a long time and which may have seen the offerings of
several other anglers. Hugh Falkus, in his excellent book *Salmon
Fishing*, suggests that it is impossible to overfish a salmon lie. In the
sense in which this comment is made I am sure that he is right; but I
am equally sure that, given the choice, he would be the first to
choose to fish a pool that had not been thrashed too much rather than
the sort of pool, perhaps one adjacent to a car park on association
water, that seems to attract every visitor to have a cast or two, and
also has its share of stone-throwing kids and stick-retrieving dogs.
This is why, as Falkus well knows, access to a private beat is so much
more desirable than being restricted to well fished association
water. It is not that it would ever be *impossible* to catch a fish from an
overfished pool or lie, but the chances of a catch are increased on
those waters that are not over-molested.

I am sure that there are many instances in salmon and sea-trout
fishing where it is possible for familiarity to breed contempt. Also,
you have to ask yourself what advantage is to be gained by the
continual flogging of a piece of water when there is a total lack of
response. Would it not make sense not only to rest yourself but to
give the fish some respite as well? The question of resting a piece of
water, of course, poses many imponderables. On many rivers it is

impossible to note exactly what is taking place beneath the surface. Only by having a fish counter at the inlet and outlet to every pool might it be possible to determine just what stock it contains from one minute to the next.

Of course, there will be times when there is a continual migration of fish moving through a pool which already holds a good stock of resident fish. In these circumstances you may never know exactly when the situation may change and a fish take your fly. If, on the other hand, there is no change of stock for several hours or days, then it might pay to assume that, other than at specific times, such as the last hour of daylight, continual flogging of the water will have a slightly adverse effect. Only very rarely are you likely to know what is happening beneath the surface and I cannot think of more than one or two rivers where it is possible to indulge in a meaningful assessment of fish movement merely by observation. Falkus undoubtedly did it on the little River Esk near his home in Cumbria, but this only gave him the very limited experience of one small river – a river, incidentally, much more suited to the study of sea-trout behaviour than that of salmon. The only rivers where I have been able to watch fish I was hoping to catch, other than in very low water, have been the Laerdal in Norway and on Lune and Awe in Britain.

Resting a pool, therefore, will reduce the chance of familiarity breeding contempt and thus enable you to hope that the next time your fly is shown to the fish some new stock will have moved in or one of the residents will have changed its mood.

Another example of undesirable overfishing sometimes occurs when fish in low water are intimidated by bait fishermen. This can certainly cause such a continued disturbance that in some instances the fish will move to a fresh pool. In very low water, of course, they may be confined to the pool in which they are resident and the fact that they do not move must not force you to the conclusion that they are not being overintimidated. It may be more difficult for a competent angler to cause a disturbance with a fly on a floating line but, if I have fished through what seems the best time of the day and have found that fish response is totally unrewarding, I would rather sit around or do something else until I sense or suspect there has been some subtle change in conditions to alter my chances.

WATER HEIGHT

That great salmon fisherman, the late J. Arthur Hutton, suggested that the height of the water was the most important factor in successful salmon fishing. Every pool has its ideal height – but only when related to water and air temperature and sundry other factors of which we may not be fully aware. Anglers fortunate enough to have access to the Upper Floors beat of the Tweed are given not only a list of the names of all the pools but notes of the heights at which each pool will fish best. With seventeen named pools there is a lot to learn – more than may be learned in a season or two of casual visits. For many, however, salmon fly fishing tends to become a ritualistic exercise. They achieve modest competence in casting and then rely on tedious flogging of the water to give them the odd fish. Of course, there are many instances when sheer persistence is likely to prove more effective than applied science. I am thinking particularly of those days in March, April and early May when the bulk of the fish migrating in from the sea are still travelling and only resting briefly in temporary lies. In these circumstances it is possible for a pool to be occupied with several fish at, say, 10.30 a.m. and totally vacated by midday. If this is when an angler comes down for a casual cast, no matter how competent, he is not going to fare as well as the plodder who keeps his fly in the water all day. Fishing the Spey in spring I would not rate my chances any higher than a competent novice and, as I lack the enthusiasm I used to have in my fish-hungry days, I do not worry in the slightest when my guests catch more fish than I do – rather the reverse in fact!

In so far as spring fishing is concerned, therefore, it is not easy to predict exactly where salmon are or when they may take. There are several influences which induce fish to run and which, equally, cause them to rest briefly before continuing their slow migration upstream. Hutton was right, I think, in his belief that water height is of paramount importance; but there are other factors to be fed into our mental computer, as well as a deal of sheer speculation. The result is that it is often little more than a feeling, a sort of sixth sense, that urges us to fish a specific pool in a certain way at a chosen time.

I recall arriving on my Spey beat one morning in early May at about midday. My guests had fished hard all morning for one small fish taken on a spinner. The river was at a superb height, but I was

perturbed by the apparent lack of fish. After lunch my gillie urged me to have a cast or two in the March Pool with my fly rod. Frankly, I gave him a rather old-fashioned look, suspecting that he was merely pulling my leg by inducing me to fish when the rest of my party were heading back to the hotel for an afternoon siesta. But I also had a slight feeling for the water and I did not need much further persuasion to assemble my rod, don my breast waders and take the boat over to the other side of the river, where I could fish the March Pool from the right bank. Whatever induced me to go fishing cannot be fully explained. There was no logical reason, merely a vague sort of feeling or suspicion that I might be lucky. I had no knowledge that a shoal of fish were about to take a rest in that pool nor have I read any book on salmon fishing or yet met the man who could give me a reasoned formula to follow. But by 2.30 p.m. I was wading in at the neck of that pool and by 4.30 p.m. I was back at the hut with four salmon, having lost another two and missed hooking another four pulls – a total potential catch, if all had gone right for me, of ten salmon in two hours!

I had started in at the neck of that pool and had merely extended my line to about twenty-five yards and then made double Spey casts all the way down until I got to our bottom boundary. Any other competent angler could have done exactly the same and it was sheer luck that I made the decision to do it. In these circumstances, how arrogant it would be for me to pontificate or pretend that I had some divine knowledge denied to other mortals! I would do you a great disservice if I suggested that anything more was involved than a combination of sheer good luck, a good knowledge of that water, good casting ability and the information that the river was at a perfect height. If the fish had not chosen that specific two-hour period in which to rest in the March Pool, I would have drawn blank.

Back at the hotel one friend who had taken a siesta was quick to remark, 'You crafty old devil, you knew something we didn't know. What was the reason for your good fortune?' The answer, of course, is that I did not *know* – and nor does anyone else.

That taking times can *never* be predicted is not strictly true. As soon as our spring rivers start to settle down to summer levels there will be a strong inclination for fish to settle in the main pools until a summer spate drives them on upstream towards their goal. Fish which settle in lies for several weeks are known as residents. You

In the low water of summer it is frequently possible to see fish lying in the pools from this right bank of the Lune at Newton, Lancashire.

may even begin to recognise some of them, from the positions in which they show, their leaping style, their size and colouring. For me, this is when salmon fishing is at its most interesting, and it may even be possible to indulge in a little mild speculation on the best possible taking time. Even then I must caution you never to utter dogmatic statements about salmon behaviour.

Many years ago I recall standing on a bridge and watching three salmon lying behind a rock. The fish on the outside was having to fan its fins a little more quickly than the other two in order to keep station in the current. I even tried a cast to these fish, but my flies and spinners were totally ignored and I went back on the bridge merely to watch. Eventually, after about half an hour, the fish which had been swimming a little harder than its companions took off on an upstream jaunt and then jumped out of the water before circling round to come back to the rock. Once there, it pushed its way in between the other two fish, causing one of them to take up its old position. This fish then demonstrated that it too had to work a little harder to keep station and when another half hour had elapsed it took off on a similar upstream sortie, did a lazy jump and came back to push its way into the middle again.

Frankly, I did not wait any longer to make further study of what might happen. But, had I not been watching and noting exactly what

the realities were I might well have come to some very erroneous conclusions. I might, for instance, have deduced that the first leaping fish was the same as the one that showed on the second occasion and I could well have concluded that they were not in fact lying where I had noted them underwater, but merely where I had seen them jump.

On the vexed question of taking times and overfishing a lie, I have on numerous occasions seen all the long-held doctrines firmly reversed. On one memorable occasion my wife and I were together on the Lune. There had been a little summer spate and we had gone over one evening with the intention of staying as long as the sport lasted. I caught a fish the first evening on a small fly, but on the following morning the sun shone out of a cloudless sky and the mercury moved up into the eighties. By lunch time I was ready to throw in the towel and concede defeat. My wife, however, had yet to catch a fish on a fly so, stripped down to her bathing suit, she was prepared to cast merely for practice. I was virtually asleep on the bank when I heard the cry of 'Help!' Thinking it would be a small trout or parr, I did not hurry to her side, but when I heard the reel snarl into a fine pitch like an aeroplane propeller I was quickly offering advice. Eventually she safely beached a nice little 8-pounder, and then went on to compound my confusion by taking a playful fish of 10lb from the same lie about thirty minutes later – both fish hooked firmly in the back of the mouth.

It was assumed that those two fish had been resident in that pool all the time, but I am forced to wonder if they were not two fish which had just recently moved in to take up residence and then showed their resentment at the intrusion of that small fly. One thing is certain: we shall never know the answer.

To add to the confusion I recall an early June week spent with friends on the Spey. A ridge of high pressure dominated the weather in Strathspey, giving low cloud and cool conditions until midday, when the cloud swept aside and a torrid sun took command. Most of us concluded that the best of the fishing would be over by lunch time and I have to confess that I shared this opinion. On most mornings, therefore, I was on the water for a prompt 9 a.m. start and ready to pack up just as soon as the sun appeared about midday. Despite there being plenty of fish in the beat I never did get an offer until the cloud was swept away and the hot sun bore down on the water. Most of my fish that week were caught while my friends were

having lunch, but there were also a few taken during the last hour of daylight.

If there is a predictable taking time, therefore, I suspect that it has to be the last hour of daylight. It does not seem to matter if it is winter or summer, spring or autumn. Providing that the air is warmer than the water and that cooling winds do not chill the water surface, I lean to the view that salmon may be likened to the proverbial commercial traveller – they go about their business for most of the day and then, as night falls, they seek some resting-place or hostelry where they are likely to succumb to temptation. In suitable conditions, fish might well be in the same resting lies and frame of mind to take an angler's lure as the first glimmer of daylight kindles into flame on the eastern horizon. But these are only suggestions, not predictions.

LINE COLOUR

Throughout this book I want to try and avoid dogma. Line colour is one subject upon which I have tried to retain an open mind. Arguably, since the underbelly of a fish is white, white lines will be less easily seen than those of any other colour. Always bear in mind, however, that lines of any colour will cast similar shadows. Usually, the leader will eliminate the chance of fish getting a sight of line shadow, but the colour of line can have an effect if any part of it is below the surface. My preferred colour for sinking lines is either green or brown. Most fish are accustomed to strands of grass or brown weed waving in the current, so what would be so disturbing about a green or brown line? For a floating line, on the other hand, I think that it is important to consider the type of water to be fished and the condition of the line in use. Flat, gliding water and a well worn white line may cause the front section to submerge slightly and thus be seen by the fish. Here my experience tells me that a brown or green floating line is the more effective. But for all practical purposes a good-quality white floating line in an average stream offers so many more advantages than lines of other colours. You can see it plainly and you know at all times the precise placing of your fly. You can mend the unwanted belly formation and rest assured that its shadow will be no more dense than that from any other line.

For most of my sunk-line fishing, therefore, I use a green line and a short leader, while for the floater I prefer a white line and a leader as long as I can comfortably handle and probably nigh on twelve feet. The long leader helps prevent any chance of the fish seeing line shadow and it also enables the fly to fish or swim round without skimming on or near the surface. Sometimes a tendency for the fly to skate may be eliminated by rubbing the leader with a paste made from a mixture of fuller's earth and glycerine. Alternatively, any concentrated detergent will have the same effect, as will good, clean mud or clay from the river bank. The longer the rod the easier it is to fish with the longer leader, but problems can arise if the knot joining leader and line comes through the rod tip while a fish is being beached or tailed by hand. If the fish makes a last-minute dash for freedom, the knot can momentarily catch in a rod ring – with dire results. However, I believe that the benefits of a long leader outweigh its disadvantages, and knots can be tied carefully so that they slide easily through the rings.

EFFECT OF DISSOLVED OXYGEN

Some writers advance the theory that the amount of dissolved oxygen in the water has a direct and dramatic influence on the behaviour of salmon and sea trout. The basic theory suggests that during high levels of sunshine or high pressure the increased evaporation removes a lot of oxygen. Cloud and low pressure, on the other hand, with the possible addition of modest amounts of rain to aerate the water, increase the oxygen content of the water and thus make it more agreeable to the fish. Somewhere between these two states there are predictions as to the best taking times based on an assessment of oxygen availability.

Frankly, science does not support this theory. I do not know if the oxygen content of water varies much on the average salmon river or if it has any measurable effect. I do know from long experience those weather and river conditions which persuade me to fish hard and those which induce me merely to sit and watch, take photographs or go home. Even then, as I have tried to demonstrate, the salmon and sea trout are not always as aware of these factors as I may be. They have not read my books and seem reluctant to conform to any formula I might insist they follow. There can be

little doubt that wind, weather, relative water and air temperatures, barometric pressure, humidity and a host of other factors all influence fish behaviour somehow, just as they influence hatches of the insects on which some fish feed. In all my many years spent in a casual study of hatching insects, particularly on the Spey when I am on the river every day for nigh on two months, I have never found a formula to enable me to predict when or if a hatch of fly would appear at a specific time on a given day. In this instance I was merely attempting to predict the taking time for trout – fish that feed in fresh water. How difficult it must be, therefore, to suggest a taking time for a fish that does not feed in fresh water.

RISING AND FALLING WATER

An awareness of variations in the height of the water and how they influence the chances of a catch is invaluable. Classic spring rivers rely on a combination of snow and rainfall to sustain them. During the early season extra rain or melting snow causes the river to rise, and, depending on its temperature relative to the sea, might well induce the first fish of the season to come in. Again, depending on many factors – which might involve relative water and air temperatures, suspended matter linked with water clarity, excess acidity or the time of the year – the fish may run slowly or quickly.

As a general rule, a rising river – particularly if it is a big rise which is accompanied by much suspended matter and debris after a long period of drought – does not bode well for running fish. They prefer to wait until the maelstrom has passed and the river is clearing and falling. This is a good time to start fishing. If there are weirs, the fish may await water of a specific temperature, as well as an adequate flow level, when they can negotiate them comfortably. Too much water may cause the current to be too strong, while in too little the fish may be unable to swim or leap through.

Normally I watch carefully for any rise of water to reach its peak and then start falling slowly. Initially I am content to start with a large fly on a sinking line, but I am ever watchful for the moment to revert to a floating line and smaller flies as the river falls and clears. Sometimes this moment may be determined by the amount of acid still remaining in the water. A deal of foam on the surface may indicate a high acid level, and frequently follows a late spring or

summer flood. A lack of foam, on the other hand, and particularly when water temperatures have reached the high forties, may suggest that it is time to try the floating line.

On certain rivers, notably the Tweed, any substantial rise in the water causes the more experienced anglers to pack their tackle and go home. It is not that it will be impossible to catch fish on a rising water; it is just that the effort involved usually brings paltry reward. Other than during the initial flush of fresh water hitting the river, I refuse to fish when I know the water to be rising. Too often I have experienced total frustration in trying to catch fish at this time. As soon as the river starts to fall, however, it is a different story. Depending on the time of the year, the fish may run fast or slowly. During the spring, as I have noted, the run continues spasmodically until the river falls to near summer level. This is when fish become resident in pools and fishing for them becomes more interesting, as tactical angling skills take over from mere industry and persistence.

In pausing awhile during the writing of this chapter, as if to take a deep breath, I took time out to read through some of the many books on the subject of salmon fishing. So many varied philosophies are put forward that one wonders if it is possible to say anything meaningful about salmon with any certainty. Of the many writers I have read I find I am often in agreement with the late G. P. R. Balfour-Kinnear. In Chapter 8 of his book *Catching Salmon and Sea Trout*, when speaking of sunk-line fishing, he writes: 'A long line not only practically ensures a correct fishing depth, but gives the fisherman infinitely more control over the speed of the fly than could be obtained on a short line.' Then, as though to illustrate what I mean by 'effective water command', he writes:

In order to fish a slow moving fly, in cold water, it is necessary to be reasonably close to where the fish are lying. As an example: I was asked to fish from a boat and to bring a friend who was to use long waders. I caught seven fish and he never had an offer, although he is a first-class fisherman and, notwithstanding the awkward height of the river, was able to cover the fish. The reason was that the river was not high enough to bring the fish near to the edge, but too high for him to wade in as far as was necessary. He had therefore to fish from a point much farther away to reach the lies, which, in spite of his placing of the line or initial mend, made his fly sweep over the

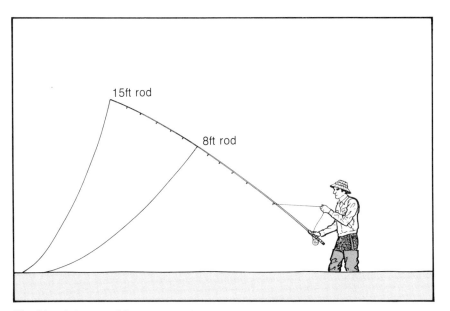

Fig 21   A long rod keeps more line off the surface,
meaning less drag and better control of speed with the fly.

fish faster than it should. Naturally, had our positions been reversed he would have had seven fish and I the blank.

A brief dip into Balfour-Kinnear's book was followed by a perusal of *The Floating Line for Salmon and Sea Trout* by Anthony Crossley. Here in Chapter 6, in a question and answer mode, I read the following:

Q.   Why wade out as far as possible in order to be above your fish in fast water?
A.   Because if you fish fast water across the stream your fly passes over the fish too quickly. A salmon is rather a lazy fish; and likes time to see the fly. Indeed, if you can hold a fly over a fish in water that buffets it about, he will usually take it in the end. You cannot be too slow.
Q.   If you cannot wade out in fast water, is there any way of catching them by fishing across the river?
A.   Yes. Put on a larger fly (often two sizes larger) and mend your

line by keeping an upstream belly to check it.

Q. Why hold your rod point high in the air when fishing fast water?

A. For two reasons. The first, so that there should be a belly of loose line in the air. Then the fish does not rise against a tight line. The second, because if you do you will find your fly will 'dab' round slowly and close to the surface without drag.

Crossley's comments on the size of fly are particularly worthy of note. Sometimes a fly of one size appears to be unacceptable to the fish, while one of a different size may be taken. Most writers suggest going down a size whenever a change of fly size seems desirable but there are several instances when, if I suspect that a fish has shown interest in my fly, or has given it a brief inspection or pull, I would rather show it something larger and perhaps make the fly move a little more quickly. With sea trout, on the other hand, changing up a size is the general rule – but it is a rule that will stand frequent breaches.

My philosophy is closely linked with that of Balfour-Kinnear and Crossley, but practically all our salmon anglers of earlier years and even many today are totally conditioned into the exclusive use of double-handed fly rods for all their fishing with sinking and floating lines. Indeed the long double-handed rods, such as those I have mentioned, make excellent tools in the pursuit of effective water command. In my view they are indispensable so long as water height and temperature make long casting an essential requirement. There comes a time, however, when many salmon rivers fall down to summer level and when deep wading to the hitherto most inaccessible parts of the river is easily accomplished. Now, fishing with a shorter, single-handed rod may not only be more interesting, but it could be more rewarding as well, and this is the subject of the next chapter.

9
Fishing with the Single-handed Fly Rod

Rods over twelve-and-a-half feet are becoming relics now, used for sentiment. In their time there was no other way to cast a fly as far as easily. Modern rod materials and modern line tapers have increased the casting distance of the shorter rods and made the very long rods no longer necessary.
Lee Wulff, in defence of the ultra-short rod, The Atlantic Salmon

The trend to the use of single-handed rods for salmon fishing in Britain represents a big break with a long tradition. We have used them over many years for sea trout but little more than a decade ago it was almost sacrilege – a breach of the lore – to use them for salmon. Much of the rethinking was caused by that wind of change which blew over our stillwater fisheries when, almost overnight, thousands of coarse fishermen took up fly fishing for trout. Having quickly savoured the delights of catching larger-than-average trout in our stillwaters, it was not long before some of them were turning their attention to the many salmon rivers offering ticket or association water. Their single-handed rods and other tackle had been quite capable of commanding superb casting distances and handling big fish on the reservoirs. Why should they not be just as successful on the classic salmon rivers?

In North America, only a few diehard anglers of the old generation cling to their long double-handed rods. Until the discovery of carbon fibre the continued trend there was for rods to become shorter and therefore lighter. As I have noted, the veteran American angler Lee Wulff came up with perhaps the ultimate in Lilliputian tackle when he appeared with a six-foot wand of a rod and proceeded to catch large salmon with it. He was quickly accused of gimmickry at that time and certainly the traditional British anglers and the press gave him a rough time when he first

Arthur beaching a salmon of 16lb, caught using a single-
handed rod, late one evening from the Bolstad fjord, River
Vosso, Norway.

came to Britain during the late 1950s. No American upstart was
going to tell us how to do it! Well the facts are that throughout a
lifetime of salmon fishing Wulff has caught over 5,000 Atlantic
salmon and all on a single-handed rod. That other great American
angler, Al McClane, once declared to me on the banks of the Spey
that he failed entirely to see any necessity for a rod of more than
nine feet.

I think that this preference may be due largely to the fact that a lot
of salmon fishing in North America is done from canoes, where long
casting distances are not required. Transportation into the back-
woods is either primitive or limited to a float-plane with the
consequent meagre baggage allowance. Americans are renowned for
innovation and light travel. Why bother with a cumbersome 14-

footer or a 16-footer inherited from grandfather when the eight or nine-foot wand will do all and more than is required?

As I have tried to demonstrate elsewhere in this book, the length of the rod has little effect on the playing of a fish. In fact, the short, stumpy rod is likely to kill or subdue a fish more quickly than a slender one of greater length. Of course, a lot depends on who is playing the fish, the length of his experience and how he tackles the problem. Where the length of the rod does have influence is in its ability to give us water command.

I am firmly convinced, therefore, that there is a place for both long and short rods – particularly here in Britain where we have an extended season from February through to November and are not merely confined to the months of June, July and August, as they are in so many other countries. If you are prejudiced against short rods then it may be that the Americans are equally prejudiced against long ones. But these prejudices do not seem to be based on logic and I have already tried to demonstrate some of the superb benefits to be derived from fishing with a short rod when conditions are suited to its use.

On such a river as the Spey there is usually a vast difference between the character of the river in March or April and the low water of June or July. A pool that will barely accommodate a deep-wading angler in April may be totally fordable in June. Other than at times of flood, the salmon and sea trout will now have slowed their pace of running and will for the most part be confined to the deep pools and streams. Here, with deep-wading, it may be that a fifteen-yard or twenty-yard cast will do all that is necessary to get effective water command. Usually the water will have gin-like clarity and the angler who can fish with a little bit of delicacy and finesse is the one most likely to catch fish. Why then do so many anglers continue to use the big and now cumbersome rods and tackle that seemed so essential in the spring? No. 11 lines are now totally unnecessary and, in the clear and shallow water, are going to look more like ships' hawsers than useful fishing lines. Far better to put this tackle to one side in readiness for the big rivers of the autumn or the next flood. Now is the time for the light single-handed rods, small flies and slender leaders.

Tactics for fishing with shorter rods, lighter lines and leaders and smaller flies are pretty much the same as those used with larger outfits, and described in the preceding chapter. It is normal

procedure to merely cast across the current, mend the line as required and when the cast comes to the dangle, handline some of the backing in, take a pace or two downstream, and then make the next cast. This is the basic technique for catching fish, be they salmon or sea trout, in almost any situation. It may be unimaginative, but it is a fact of life. As with fishing a double-handed rod, much of what we do is merely because the gillie suggests it or because we are reluctant to try other tactics which have not stood the test of time.

One aspect of fishing with a single-handed rod which appeals to me is that it provides an opportunity to exploit the same dexterity in casting as is required in dry-fly and wet-fly fishing for trout. In my formative years as an angler I was virtually weaned on trout fishing, and the epitome of my sport was the challenge of dry-fly fishing for trout. The single-handed rod gives opportunites for more flexible action than the more cumbersome double-handed rod, and it was for this reason that I came to admire Lee Wulff when he wrote his book and devoted it entirely to catching salmon on a single-handed fly rod.

His philosophy, and one I stoutly defend, is that there is more to salmon fishing than merely casting a fly out across the current and waiting for it to be taken before it comes onto the dangle at the end of its arc of travel. Of course, it has to be realised that Wulff's book is directed principally to North American anglers, who only have that limited season from June through to August. They may occasionally catch fish by tactics and methods which are not frequently used in Britain. North American fish leap more often when hooked and while in play, and there are subtle differences in their behaviour patterns which make us reluctant to experiment with transatlantic tactics. But I do suggest that during the period when our water conditions, weather and season coincide with the main seasons in North America the use of the single-handed fly rod can give us an opportunity of prime sport with salmon and sea trout.

Although salmon seem willing to take a dry fly only occasionally on British rivers, this is a normal method of fishing for them in North America. Only twice have I caught salmon on a floating fly and I reckon they were flukes rather than demonstrations of normal behaviour anyway. I am quite sure, however, that if we were to have runs of salmon in June and July, with fresh fish concentrated in pools to the exclusion of earlier runners, many rivers in Britain

Joan Wulff casting with her 7-foot fly rod on the Spey at
Castle Grant. Note the tight loop and high delivery point. A
superb style in single-handed casting.

would produce a higher incidence of salmon taking a dry fly.

The fact is that very few anglers bother to experiment with a dry
fly even at the more propitious time of the year. I have only tried it
by way of casual experiment and in the same manner as I have tried
the riffling or Newfoundland hitch. This technique involves tying a
half-hitch knot on the fly after it has been tied on in the traditional
way. The extra knot makes the fly hang at right angles from the
leader, and is tied on one side of the fly or the other depending on
which bank you are to fish from. The idea originated on a small
Canadian river at Portland Creek. This area was visited frequently
by British naval officers in the old days, and they were in the habit of
leaving gut-eyed flies as gifts for the local fishermen. Not trusting
the gut eyes, the locals used the riffling or Newfoundland hitch
merely for added security. Only some time later was the fish-

catching ability of this device appreciated.

Nowadays many American anglers swear that when the going gets tough the hitched fly is more successful than the traditional wet-fly presentation. Quite a few highly successful anglers in Britain tell me that they have used the hitch to good effect on such rivers as the Dee and Spey. I have never given the method extensive trial, but I am convinced that at times it would work exceptionally well – particularly when fish have been subjected to continued trial by traditional methods and have become slightly potted. This is also the time to try lots of other tactics – some surprising results may be achieved.

I recall a bright summer day many years ago on the Lune when, in the company of the late Ian Wood, the founding editor of *Trout and Salmon*, I was trying to interest some fish in the neck of a fast stream. Traditional fishing did nothing and I sat idly at the head of the run wondering what to do next. It was while pondering on what to do that I let my fly dangle in the fast current. It hung there for several minutes, with the rod propped casually against a pile of stones. After about ten minutes I saw the line tighten and as I quickly grabbed the rod I realised that a fish had taken my fly. I jumped to my feet and quickly hustled that fish out of the fast water and into deeper water, where I played it out before hand-tailing it ashore. With that one safely knocked on the head I went back to the neck of the pool and let my fly dangle again. Occasionally I would *trot* the fly downstream by paying out extra line from the reel. Then I would wind it back and repeat the process. I spent the best part of the afternoon fishing in this style, but at the end of the day I had five salmon to take home. All had fallen for a little fly fished on a single-handed rod and all had been taken with a technique which, at that time, I had never tried before.

Another method of catching the occasional fish is to cast a fly upstream over known lies and then handline it back as quickly as possible. Here it is important to know where the fish are lying, and it helps if they are fairly fresh-run. Stale fish too will occasionally respond to this tactic, particularly if they have refused flies fished in the traditional manner and the upstream technique has not been overdone. This tactic is also highly successful with a spinning bait. But then there is a grave chance that fish will be over-intimidated or even foul-hooked. The fly cast upstream will sometimes work when

other methods fail, but I am not suggesting that it is worth more than occasional trial.

In water of average to strong current – and also on stillwaters, lochs, etc. (of which more later) – most salmon are caught on slow-moving flies and it is the sea trout that seem keener to take the fast-moving lures. Even in these conditions salmon may sometimes be induced into frenzied action and perhaps never more so than when they are being continually intimidated with something like one of Lee Wulff's skater flies. The technique involves the use of a very bushy fly, one so anointed with floatant that it simply refuses to sink under the surface. Normally it is cast across and downstream in the traditional way on a light leader and then caused to skate about in the immediate vicinity of a known lie.

Watching Lee employ this technique on a bright August day on the Spey in 1984, I was amazed at his persistence under apparently hopeless conditions. The fly, which resembled a large daddy-long-legs, was caused to skate on the water in wild gyrations. It was cast again and again, as if to remind me that it is impossible to overfish a lie, but there was no apparent response. I watched spellbound as Lee continued his bombardment and was utterly amazed when a salmon came up from the depths and grabbed the fly as though it repre-sented the last meal of its life. Sadly, the hold of the small hook was not sufficiently secure and the fish got free. But Lee had made his point and helped confirm the Falkus tenet that it is indeed impossible to overfish a lie.

An enjoyable way of catching salmon and sea trout in midsummer and during the daylight is to select pieces of water which are not normally fished – little streams with deep pot-holes and with barely sufficient room to hold more than the odd fish. Such places are not easily found in one or two casual visits to a water. They are discovered only through continued experience of the same piece of water and seeing it under the low water of a summer drought. At normal river height, of course, these places may be far too fast to hold fish, but when the level is down, and providing that effective water command can be achieved, they may well offer up the occasional fish. There is one such place on the Spey at Castle Grant. It does not have a name, but it is a small place where by wading out under bushes and into shallow but exceptionally fast water you may hang your fly over a pocket and expect to have it taken by a fish. Of course, you must not fish these places too frequently or expect them

David Hield hand-tails a salmon from a short and little
known piece of water on the Spey at Castle Grant.

continually to yield the quantities of fish which you might sometimes get in the main lies. But they are good places for the occasional
try when conditions get tough.

Frequently it will take some time just to get the feel of the
current and of the amount of fly movement required to interest the
fish. Usually, if the first time down does not produce an offer, it
will pay to alter tactics slightly and go down again on a different
tack. In very fast water I frequently fish the first time down without
wading too deeply. If this does not produce an offer I then go back
to the top of the pool and wade out as far as comfort and tactical
necessity allow. The hanging fly, in fast water, as I demonstrated
that memorable day on the Lune, will often prove more effective
than the fly fished more quickly.

There are some anglers who incline to the belief that once the
best of the spring run is into the river and getting slightly potted the
only successful way of coming to terms with the fish is by some form
of natural bait fishing. In Britain and on certain rivers in Ireland and
Norway it is frequent practice to resort to worm or prawn fishing at
this time. Indeed, it cannot be denied that skilful use of a worm or
prawn will often get fish which seem uncatchable by any other
methods – particularly the artificial fly. But these methods are
banned on all North American rivers and we may be coming to a
time when there will be a necessity for restrictions on angling
methods in Britain. It is not that careful and occasional use of the
worm or prawn is so disastrous in its effect; it is just that these
methods offer the unscrupulous the opportunity to indulge in many
types of skulduggery, such as deliberate foul-hooking and general
intimidation of the fish. My view is that a well managed fishery,
unless it be a little spate river, will continue to provide sport with
the fly provided fishing pressure is not too high and the anglers
participating do not over-flog the water. Late evenings and early
mornings often offer the best chance, though when water temperatures get much over the 70° mark there is a marked reluctance on
the part of the fish to do anything but sulk.

In my experience August is a notably bad month unless there is
heavy rainfall and the weather is much cooler than that prescribed
by the holiday brochures. A summer such as we had in 1985 proved
to be ideal for many rivers. Indeed, there was sometimes so much
extra water that the problem was not in finding stocks of fish but
merely in finding a piece of water with a sufficiently modest flow to

Noted American angler, Al McClane, playing a salmon on a
single-handed 9-foot fly rod.

get a fly to move properly. In a normal year, however, the end of
August usually sees an end of the dog days and this may be a time
when some rivers will give of their best. Unless stocks are revived by
fresh runs, however, there is a tendency on such rivers as the Spey
and Dee for the fish to be soon past their best and I can share some
sympathy with that school of anglers who think that the best salmon
fishing is over by the end of August. I do not really condone the
killing of red, stale salmon and black sea trout and September does
seem to be a time on many rivers when the red fish would be better
spared. Of course, there are other notable rivers and many on the
west coast of Scotland where the runs of fresh fish are just reaching
their peak. Here it may still be permissible to catch fish and the use
of a single-handed rod can offer superb sport. Even then it must not
be assumed that fishing with a single-handed rod will be confined
merely to the low water of summer. In any situation where boat
fishing is undertaken there will be many occasions when you may
use a single-handed rod as successfully as the double-hander.

It would be a pity, however, if those who have recently come to
salmon fishing with their single-handed reservoir rods took the view
that such rods are adequate for every fishing situation in Britain
throughout our longer season. Equally, it is a great mistake for those

who cling to the tradition of the double-handed rod to assume that it is the only rod to use throughout a season. Until the advent of carbon fibre there was an undoubted trend towards lighter and therefore shorter rods. Carbon fibre has altered all this and I suspect that the trend to ultra-short rods has been firmly reversed.

DROPPERS

Usually, when I am fishing with a single-handed rod, whether on rivers or lochs, I do so with an additional fly on the dropper. Just occasionally I will use two droppers, but they may present problems, particularly with big fish and especially when one takes the top dropper, leaving the other two flies dangling beneath the fish all the time it is in play. In one such incident my tail fly fouled some obstruction and broke off, and I was extremely lucky that the fly on which the fish was hooked miraculously remained attached to the leader. It could all have ended very differently.

On one memorable occasion I was fishing for trout in the famous Pollowick Pool of the Spey at Castle Grant with my 10-foot trout rod, a no. 6 floating line and a team of Yorkshire trout flies, the Waterhen Bloa, the Partridge & Orange and the Snipe & Purple on a 3lb test leader. I had caught a few nice trout when a particularly heavy pull caused me to think that I must have hooked one of the occasional Spey specimen trout. The fish backed away in the heavy water and it took me a little time to realise that it was no trout that had taken me, but an active fresh-run salmon. Fortunately, I had a companion fishing close by and he was soon at my side offering help. The fish had taken the top dropper and I asked my friend to lift it out and knock it on the head – a lovely salmon of 7½ lb.

When I am after salmon with the single-handed rod, therefore, I tend to concentrate on just one dropper and do not much care whether I catch salmon or sea trout. Fresh-run sea trout in the spring are not nearly so timid as those that have been in the river for some time or fish in low water. On many occasions they will take quite well in daylight. Usually these fresh-run sea trout seem totally unconcerned whether your fly is a salmon pattern or an accepted sea-trout pattern; nor do they care whether you are using a single-handed or a double-handed rod. So it does not seem to matter if you overlook the rules at this stage, though after a fairly short time

in fresh water the fish will develop their traditional shyness.

Pay particular attention to the length of your droppers and to the best knots used to make them. Most droppers are too long, which tends to cause the dropper fly to entwine itself around the leader, in which case the fish will find it wellnigh impossible to take properly. We can all recall instances when we have felt a vague pull or seen a splash in the vicinity of our flies but no fish has been hooked. This is the time to examine the dropper to see if it is wrapped round the leader.

Using the correct dropper length for the breaking strain of the nylon will help to eliminate this problem. With light monofilament the dropper should be quite short and is best tied with either a blood knot or a water knot. With stronger monofilament a little more length might not matter too much, but in no circumstances should the dropper be more than 4 inches from the knot on the main leader to the fly and it may well be better at nearer $2\frac{1}{2}$ inches. There is nothing to prevent you using a dropper with your double-handed rod and many anglers employ this technique to good effect throughout the season. But I prefer to use it only with a single-handed rod in the late spring and summer, when fish seem more inclined to come to the dropper.

A nice sea trout taken in May from the Spey at Castle Grant.

10
Wading, Boating
and
Gillies

Avoid standing upon rocking stones, for obvious reasons: and never go into the water deeper than the fifth button of your waistcoat: even this does not always agree with tender constitutions in frosty weather. As you are likely not to take a just estimate of the cold in the excitement of the sport, should you be of delicate temperament, and be wading in the month of February, when it may chance to freeze very hard, pull down your stockings and examine your legs. Should they be black, or even purple, it might perhaps, be as well to get on dry land; but if they be only rubicund, you may continue to enjoy the water, if it so pleases you.
William Scrope, Days and Nights of Salmon Fishing in the Tweed

In order to achieve effective water command it is essential for the angler to take up a position in which he can cover fish in such a manner that they might be interested in taking the fly or lure. In certain circumstances, particularly in high water, it may be perfectly feasible to cast from the bank and have your fly come into a position where a fish might be interested in it. Indeed, it is frequently possible to do this with spinning tackle; but opportunities are not always so plentiful with a fly and you may well have to resort to the use of a boat merely to act as a platform or employ what for me is the most desirable form of fishing, fly-casting in breast waders.

On the lower beats of the classic big salmon rivers, however, and particularly in the early spring or late autumn, it is quite likely that you will have to use a boat and boatman. It is the boatman's prime task to put you in a position to cover the fish and it will usually be left to him how he then manoeuvres the boat in order to make the fly travel in the right arc to cover the lies at the right speed and depth. In such instances a good boatman can quickly convert a modest fisherman into a highly successful one, but such boatmen

A good boatman will manoeuvre the boat to make the fly travel in the right area to cover the lies at the right speed and depth.

tend to be hard to find. As noted earlier, other ways of manipulating the boat may involve the boatman standing on the bank and holding the boat on a rope, with one oar placed to act as a paravane or rudder so that he can manoeuvre it where he wishes. Even bad casts may be transformed into effective ones by a good boatman who knows his water intimately.

Failing the assistance of a boatman, it may be possible to position yourself single-handed by the use of an anchor and a rope. Care will be needed to get a good original anchoring position and then you must be able to keep paying out a short amount of rope after each cast so that you can let yourself downstream slowly and cover the pool properly. It is fairly plain sailing until a fish is hooked, and then you need all your wits about you plus a slice of good luck to be able to up-anchor, make for the shore, and then play and land your fish. In my younger and more agile days I have done it many times, but the outcome was never predictable, particularly if the fish got playful near the anchor rope before I had got it aboard.

Much of my fishing these days, be it for salmon or sea trout, with single- or double-handed rod, is done by deep wading. I am now

fortunate in that, on most of the rivers where I fish, I know the water intimately and no longer have to spend several seasons learning where I can wade safely and at the same time fish my fly over the best lies. Initial attempts on a strange water are best done with the assistance of a wading stick. Ideally this should be weighted in the base so that, with its base already firmly on the bottom of the river, it comes easily to hand. Wooden sticks which float when released are an abomination. Not only are they useless when left free; their very presence in the water while tethered ensures that they usually cause any shooting line to foul up on them. Great care should be taken to ensure that you are not overencumbered when wading. All encumbrances present an additional hazard and although I am now on the wrong side of sixty I have yet to resort to the use of a wading stick in those rivers and pools where I have a long experience. All I carry into the water is a small box of flies and a small spool of leader nylon. Anything else I regard as an added and totally unnecessary burden.

Of course, I have an occasional ducking and it must be admitted that no form of deep wading is without moments of tension or danger. But it is panic that drowns unless, of course, the encumbrances you deem it necessary to have with you ensnare you by fouling up on some obstruction and dragging you under. For me wading represents the most challenging way of fishing. There is the sensation that I am sharing the element with my quarry. I get a feel for the current and where a fish might choose to lie. Many anglers miss this experience because they are afraid to wade. They believe the fiction that air trapped in their waders will cause them to bob up feet first, with their head down and possibly submerged. Others are frightened for the reverse reason – that their waders might fill with water and weigh them down like an anchor.

These fears are contrary to logic. If you are standing in water the pressure on your legs will not permit much air to remain and that already trapped in your clothing is sufficient, in the event of a tumble, to give the right amount of buoyancy. Should water get into your waders it cannot weigh any more than it does when outside. Its weight is neutral until you try to walk out on to dry land. So, in many instances, other than feeling slightly damp, you may be totally unaware that your waders contain any water until you reach the bank and start to walk normally.

One occasion which comes to mind was when I was wading the

Into the drink! No form of wading is without its occasional moment of tension or danger. If you do stumble or fall, get onto your back in a position with your feet going downstream. Then, slow arm movements should bring you safely to the bank. (Photographs by Sandy Leventon)

Wintercast Pool on the Upper Hendersyde beat of the Tweed one February. It was a bitter cold day with ice floes occasionally passing by. Around mid-morning my legs began to feel as though they had both been amputated. They went totally numb and felt much colder than they should have done normally. What I did not realise until I waded ashore was that my waders had sprung a leak and both legs were full of ice-cold water. So much for the weight of water weighing me down!

Should you get into water which is too fast and deep and are then swept off your feet, it is important to get onto your back and into a position with feet first going downstream. Slow arm movements should bring you nearer the bank, but make no attempt to swim back against the current or to raise your hands in despair. As Hugh Falkus very ably pointed out in his excellent film *Salmo The Leaper*, 'Arms up and the body sinks. Mouth open, with a cry for help, and water rushes in.'

It is important to be fully aware of the varying effects that even minute changes in height can produce on a piece of water. For this reason the desirability of intimate knowledge of the water to be fished cannot be emphasised too strongly. There is no book printed that will teach you how different water heights and temperatures can affect a piece of water. I might produce diagrams of a typical run or pool, but let me remind you that salmon pools are like fingerprints – no two are identical.

On the question of waders, there are too many which are not suited to their task. Most classic salmon rivers require breast or chest waders. They are available either as one-piece garments or with stocking-shaped feet over which separate brogues or outer boots of sturdy proportions are worn. My preference is for the one-piece arrangement, but I do take care to ensure that they have non-slip felt soles and that they are not too heavy. Early spring and late autumn may call for something which will retain some body heat, but the same waders in summer may make you too hot for comfort.

In most wading situations on big rivers, thigh waders are virtually useless. They may be used on small spate rivers, but the serious fly fisherman would be wise to think only in terms of breast waders and to buy the best. Some experience of deep wading must be achieved before you will be truly relaxed doing it. In this connection I emphasise again that there is no substitute for an intimate knowledge of a piece of water and that this knowledge is not gained by

A friend often makes a good
gillie. Here Grace Oglesby stands
by to assist Sarah Myddelton land
an 11lb spring salmon.

making occasional visits to a beat.

Only a week before writing this chapter I was wading a pool on the Tweed at Upper Floors known as the Bushes. It was November and the water just about made it to a chilling 38°F. A casual move suddenly found me base-over-apex in the swirling water. It was a thoroughly miserable experience which sent me scurrying back to my hotel and a hot bath and inspired total reluctance to fish again that day. No matter how well you know a piece of water, therefore, there will be the odd occasion when you have an immersion and when you must seek to get out as quickly and as safely as you can. The danger of drowning is one thing but there is always the additional hazard of hypothermia – particularly when youth is no longer on your side!

An opinion which I make no apologies for continuing to plug, assuming that your fishing trips are restricted to one week a year, is that it will take at least ten years before you are on the sort of intimate terms with a piece of water to get the best from it. I have now been fishing two of the Spey beats at Castle Grant for nigh on twenty years and there are still places on those beats which I have not yet thoroughly learned. On the pools I know intimately, of course, I could almost wade blindfold; but the precise height of the water will alter conditions from day to day. The height as well as temperature of the water will also influence the precise locations of the best fish lies. It is not an exact science and only continued experience will enable you to wade down the correct line (for a given river height) and thus cover the lies to best effect.

Some anglers think it impressive to show their prowess as competent waders. Although it is highly desirable to wade confidently it can be a grave mistake to over-wade the lies. This may just scare the fish and send them on up to a beat above, although in my considered opinion deep wading is less disturbing to a piece of water than many might suppose. It is the activity above the water level which the fish often find more frightening than what takes place below. Most fish seem to get accustomed to odd bits of flotsam and old junk floating down. Old plastic bags are often seen, semi-submerged, tumbling their ponderous way downstream. Are a pair of slow-moving legs and feet any more likely to cause fright than a brightly coloured plastic sack? No, it is the effect of those movements you make above the water line that will have the most effect on the fish.

Where effective water command is impossible, good fishing positions can sometimes be achieved by other means. Certain Norwegian rivers have special casting platforms in the best spots, and on some of our rivers groynes sometimes provide good access to known taking places.

Most gillies or boatmen are employed for the prime reason that they know their piece of water quite intimately. Few anglers visiting their beat for one week a year could ever acquire similar knowledge. This ability to place a boat or a wading angler in a prime position is also determined by casting ability, which is not constant but varies with all of us. This is where a good assistant may be of tremendous help. Gillies come in all shapes and sizes and with varying degrees of ability and enthusiasm. Some are little more than purveyors and consumers of strong drink, while others take a professional delight in seeing that you get the best chances.

In order to bring out the best from a gillie or boatman, you must remember that most are exceptionally good anglers – particularly on their own water. Most respond well to being treated as fellow sportsmen and not merely as serfs out of the Middle Ages. Many of the gillies with whom I am associated are firm and lasting friends and I would not have it otherwise. Any attempt by you to treat your gillie too haughtily may be quietly remedied by him. To my certain knowledge there are many pompous anglers who have spent at least one day fishing a totally useless piece of water – on their gillie's advice!

A good gillie has to be a great student of human nature as well as knowing his water. He must maintain your enthusiasm and do all he can to keep you fishing over the best places. Many years ago, when I could not afford good salmon fishing, I had the fortune to be invited to a classic beat of the Tweed. The only slight snag was that it was during the month of May – not at a prime time for that beat. On arrival I naively asked my boatman about our chances. His prompt reply that there were 'nae fush in the beat' did not exactly help to kindle my enthusiasm; but, sad to relate, at the end of a fruitless week I had at least to concede that he had spoken the truth.

On the other hand, I know at least one Spey gillie who, whatever the situation, always maintains that his beat is full of fish. 'Och, they're there, ye ken, even though they're nae showin'' is his frequent response to my suggestion that we are short of stock. If my

The gillie wades out to net a salmon which is snagged round a rock. The angler is John Lee, M.P.

experience is worth anything on this score, I have to state that the presence of a lot of fish in a beat is usually demonstrated by a lot of fish showing. A low stock, on the other hand, may mean few, if any, seen at all. Of course, fish do tend to show more frequently when they are settled in the pools or when water temperatures have warmed into the fifties. But many anglers of long experience of the more prolific years talk of the vast numbers they saw jumping in February or November when certain pools on the Tweed were known to contain an abundance of fish.

The fact that you see a lot of fish does not necessarily mean that you will catch a lot. The two factors are not directly related. Indeed, it may be that catches will be more plentiful when fewer fish are seen and when they only tarry briefly in a known lie or resting place. That is a separate thing entirely from my opinion that a good stock

Gillie John Thompson and angler Jane Blakeney with a fish of
30lb from the Garrapool of the Spey at Castle Grant.

of fish is usually demonstrated by increased surface activity and a
poor stock by little noticeable activity of any kind.

Unless you are to use a boat with your own boatman it is now
more common to find one gillie being shared by more than one rod.
In those rivers where I am to wade and which I now know fairly
intimately, I prefer it this way – although there may come a time
when advancing senility will cause me to seek the assistance of a

full-time gillie.

For the beginner, on the other hand, the services of a gillie or boatman can be of inestimable value. Whether he is an enthusiast or a pessimist it makes sense to make friends and there are few who do not have a taste for Scotch. Dispensed in modest amounts, this may be a key to the treasure chest, the fountain of all knowledge. George Smith, our jocular gillie on the No. 3 Castle Grant beat of the Spey, is also known to take the occasional dram of Scotch, as well as taking a morbid delight in ensuring that my wife catches more fish than I do. Some years ago, while we were fishing the beat in July, he was busy chatting with my wife as I waded out to make a cast in Pollowick. Chuckling quietly, he quickly suggested to my wife that I had started fishing too far down the pool and that the best lie at that height of water was slightly upstream of where I was wading. Urging her to come in and fish it all down behind me, he was in sheer ecstacy when she eventually hooked and landed a fish while I eventually came out of the pool having drawn blank.

11
Reading Rivers

But alas and alack, the span of human life is too short to enable one to gain even the rudimentary knowledge necessary for the successful catching of salmon. Even on the river that one knows well, each pool has to be treated separately, and all one can do is keep an open mind and learn what is possible from the specialists, always remembering that the more one is willing to learn the better chance one has of becoming one of the few who can hold their own on any and all rivers.

J. Hughes-Parry, Fishing Fantasy

One of the greatest problems confronting the newcomer to a piece of salmon and sea-trout water is that of reading it, together with the conditions, and quickly establishing which bits are worth fishing and which may be virtually unoccupied by fish and not worth the effort. It is for this reason that many of our classic salmon beats have a resident guide or gillie to give advice on the best places to fish. In many instances this gillie has spent a virtual lifetime on or near the water and he should know it like the back of his hand. He sees it in the drought of summer and the flood of winter. He becomes aware of its moods and of precise locations where fish are regularly taken, as well as the places where even the sight of a fish is rare. Usually it will have taken him several years to acquire this experience and such knowledge cannot be acquired from books or from a casual acquaintance with a piece of water. It is for this reason that I am continually urging you to get to know one piece of water as closely as possible. It may be great fun to try a new venue every year, but unless you can have continual help from a gillie this is not going to put you in the best position to ever get the ultimate from the water. Even with the most capable gillie there will be subtle tactics required on one piece of water which are best learned from experience.

In learning a piece of salmon and sea-trout water the ideal is to see it at a time when it is showing some of its bare bones in very low water. In these conditions the main channel over the river bed is

easily seen and parts usually covered with water are exposed. It is in or near this channel that the fish generally run and lie, and the exposed gravel near the shallow stream may contain pots or dents where the fish may lie – and can profitably be covered with the fly – in much higher water. In very high water, of course, the fish may well be compelled to seek temporary shelter immediately under the bank and literally under the angler's feet.

Places where the water is deep and slow tend to be occupied only in the very cold weather when the more sluggish water attracts the slow-moving fish. Usually they will be worth fishing only when it is very cold and when the river is slightly higher than normal. The fish are likely to lie in any small indentation in the river bed and, in general terms, the angler who can comb the water with his fly will score over the casual caster. While effective water command will always be important, precise casting distances will not matter much. The fish will rarely have specific lies and may well be congregating in small shoals during the very cold weather.

As soon as the water warms up to a good running temperature, say in excess of about 45°F, it is quite likely that the deeper dubs will be quickly vacated and not much occupied again until the very low water of summer forces the fish to take cover wherever it is available. Deep pots at the edge of a fast run will also hold fish in a very low water, but there may be times, such as the onset of dusk, when the fish will either move into the shallow streams, presumably for better comfort in the more highly oxygenated water, or into the shallow tails. Sea trout particularly like to move into the tails of pools at the onset of dusk and seem quite likely to stay there until the first glimmer of daylight. This is why a daylight reconnaissance to find sea trout is not always quite so informative as we might wish. In low water all fish will be inclined to move at night; if the summer gets well advanced without much sign of extra water, practically all upstream migration is done under the cover of darkness.

Late on in the season if there is insufficient water for fish to run you may see them squirming their way through shallow pools, just on dusk, with their backs half out of the water. I well recall an October day during the late fifties when the little Yorkshire Esk near my home was at drought level. An average-size drain pipe could have carried the total flow over the weir at Ruswarp, but there were fish below the weir which seemed so frustrated that they continually leapt onto the dry sill of the weir in their attempts to get upstream.

Late summer on the Yorkshire Esk at Ruswarp weir. Fish are being lifted over the weir and released upstream. An extreme example, perhaps, but to understand the contours and learn where to find the holding pools on any river you need to see it at low water.

The river keeper, David Cook, and myself spent an entire morning just picking the stunned fish off the weir apron and carrying them to the top to be released into the deeper water there.

The spring fisherman, particularly, has to be aware of the more intimate contours of his river before he can expect to get the best from it. Normally in spring he will find his river at a good height and he may expect the running fish to be creeping up the edges rather than through the heavy water in the centre. It is normal to assume that these fish will take frequent rests and they may prolong their residence in one specific place if they find comfort and all the other requirements to maintain a quiet life. On the other hand, if the lies on the lower beats are well tenanted, the later-running fish may well press on into the middle and upper reaches. It may be quite normal for them to take periodic rests and then they may occasionally succumb to temptation if your lure happens to cross their path. There is a theory that classic salmon rivers tend to fill from the

There is no such thing as a typical salmon pool. You will
have to learn the water you intend to fish; only experience
will give you a better catch potential than the casual visitor.

source downwards, but I do not know if it has any basis in truth.
Most certainly there is evidence that in milder years there are times
when the Spey quickly stocks itself in the upper reaches. I recall one
season there when the fish were well up into Loch Insh and the
tributaries Feshie and Truim by mid-May.

There is no such thing as a typical salmon pool. You will have to
learn the piece of water you intend to fish and only long experience
on one piece of water will give you a better catch potential than a
casual visitor. Even a lifetime of experience in salmon fishing, in a
great variety of waters, will not qualify you to go to a strange piece
of water and make profound comment on the best taking places –
some mild speculation, perhaps, but no more.

Nevertheless, every salmon angler of long experience gets a

feeling for the best taking places. The fact that he is often totally wrong does not alter the fact that there are other times when he gets it right. But it does not do to be influenced much by the fish leaping and cavorting on the surface. There are, to my certain knowledge, places which merely hold fish and others where they are more likely to take.

In my experience some minor inferences *can* be drawn from leaping patterns – signs which may give a clue to the likely status of the fish we are seeking to catch. The most popular image of a salmon is a fish making a forward plunge with its back arched in purposeful intent. Indeed, many of the fish seen behaving thus may be assumed to be running fish moving upstream as conditions dictate. Such fish are likely to be seen at the head or tail of a pool when the river and weather conditions are suitable for fish to run. But the forward plunge may also indicate fresh-run fish which are temporarily **resting** in some pool or lie. In much the same manner a fish will

A red salmon jumps tantalisingly in front of American visitor, Phil Burnham, on the Manse Pool of the Spey at Castle Grant.

occasionally do a porpoise-like head-and-tail roll when running or taking a brief rest. A persistent head-and-tailer in one location may induce you to fish hard for that fish in the hope of a take, but beware that it is not a fish which you have disturbed by deep wading over the lies. Quite frequently I have had the impression that a fish so disturbed will do a head-and-tail roll in a position in which it would not normally lie.

Fish which skitter on the surface and do an awkward vertical jump, frequently falling back on their tails or on their backs, are often residents in a pool. Kelts making their tedious way downstream also have a habit of indulging in similar behaviour. Once the pools are full of resident fish it will frequently be possible to identify specific fish by their size, colouring and leaping patterns alone. The sight of fish will also give you a good clue to where they are lying, but do remember the incident described in Chapter 8, where the fish which I saw leaping were actually resting in an entirely different part of the pool.

One of the many questions with which I am confronted by guests who join me on my fishing courses at Grantown-on-Spey is 'What is a pool?' Of course, they know the grammatical meaning, but not all are aware of the terminology when applied to the average rock-girt, rain-fed salmon and sea-trout river. Usually it is necessary to see a river at a fairly low level in order to identify those areas where the water rushes down from one cataract, smooths out into a semi-placid and deeper section, and then increases in tempo in readiness for the next tumble into the pool below. Our *pool*, therefore, may be anything from a few yards in length on a small spate river to several hundred yards on a very big river. It will start at the *neck* as the water cascades down over a firm river bed. The top part of this neck is known as the *stream* or *run*, while the portion which trails away is the *glide*. The very bottom of the pool, before the river rushes away to become the neck of the next pool, is the *tail*.

The height and temperature of the water always influences the position of resident fish. Some pools offer better holding water than others. Some are worth fishing at a specific height and not worth any effort if they are higher or lower. And there is no blueprint for one pool which will apply to another. Some fish will choose to lie in one place and not take the slightest interest in your fly while others may take in places where you might not expect to catch them. There will be *taking* lies and holding lies and there may be lies which are

A small fresh salmon leaves a Hebridean sea pool on its upstream migration.

Early spring may find the river
still in winter's grip. The Spey
at Grantown.

Late spring on the Lune.

High summer on the
Cumbrian Esk, following a
spate.

Autumn on the Stinchar.

Left: Fresh-run fish may be taken from very small Hebridean streams, if the pools are approached with all the stealth of the hunter.

Centre: Loch Voshimid, North Harris.

Below: Grace Oglesby playing a spirited Hebridean sea trout.

Flies used by Arthur Oglesby for sea trout. Top: Muddler
Minnow and Black Chenille. Middle: Oglebug and Falkus
Secret Weapon. Claret and Mallard in solo space with two
special variants at bottom.

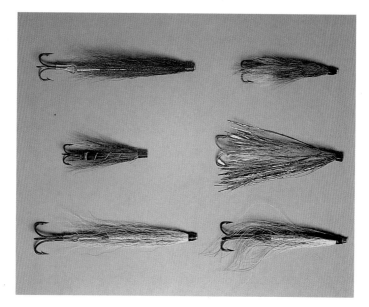

Salmon tube flies as used by Arthur Oglesby for fishing early spring and late autumn. The Lureflash (middle right) is very useful in turbid water.

Treble-hooked flies for early season fishing with the floating line. The Lureflash (low right) is useful in cold and coloured water conditions, while the Oglebug is useful in high, clear and cold water (46-50°F).

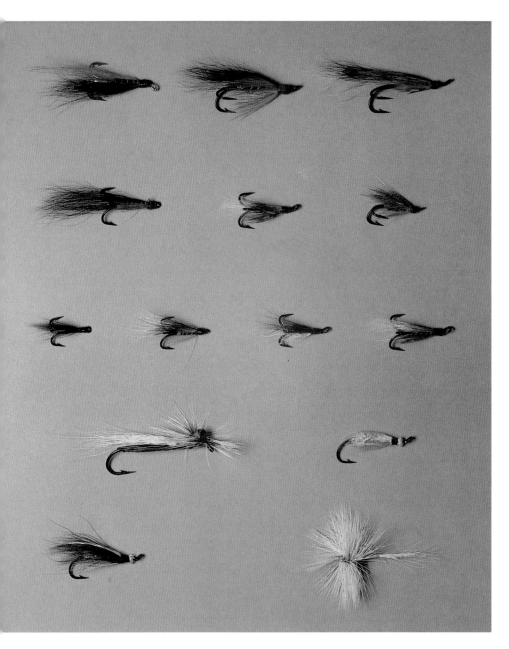

Assorted flies for use on the classical rivers in May and June.
Popular with Arthur Oglesby are the Munroe Killer variations
on the top row and the smaller trebles. The four flies at the
bottom are Lee Wulff patterns (top left – Surface Stone Fly;
the two with collars for a Riffling Hitch; and his special
Skater Fly, bottom right).

Flies and lures principally for sea trout. Fly at top left, the Goat's Toe, is an excellent Hebridean pattern for both salmon and sea trout. Alongside are dapping flies. Underneath are a set of tandem lures for sunk line night fishing for sea trout. The Falkus Lure is at bottom right.

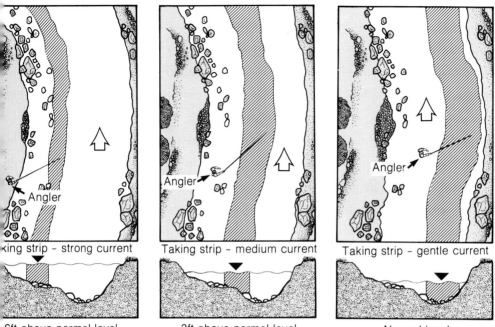

Taking strip - strong current | Taking strip - medium current | Taking strip - gentle current

6ft above normal level | 3ft above normal level | Normal level

Fig 22   Effective water command. In a high water (left) the fish may be close into the bank and the angler will achieve EWC from the bank. In a normal water (centre) some wading may be necessary. In a very low water fish will be confined to the main channel and deep wading may also be necessary.

both – but not always.

Mere knowledge of where fish may be lying, therefore, may not be enough to provide the best clues as to where they might take a fly. I can think of one specific pool on the Spey, Pollowick Pool on the lower Castle Grant water – possibly one of the finest holding pools on the entire river. It consists of a fast run-in from a small sluggan, or long piece of rapid water (which also holds fish when the water is very low), followed by a slow left-hand swing of the river into a deep dub under a high bank which once supported a railway. This in turn shallows off into thinner water at the tail of the bottom portion of Pollowick known separately as Green Bank. During the early spring and before the water has warmed above the 50°F mark it is rare for running fish to reside in Pollowick for very long. The occasional fish may be caught as it pauses temporarily on its way upstream. Those caught there are frequently taken during the late afternoon or early evening, but there is no great resident stock of fish until the water tops 50°F.

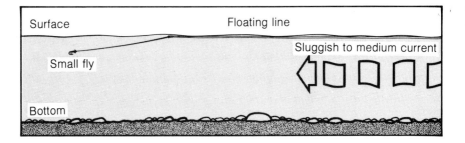

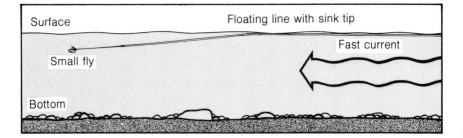

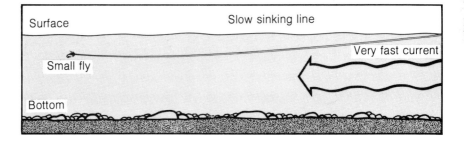

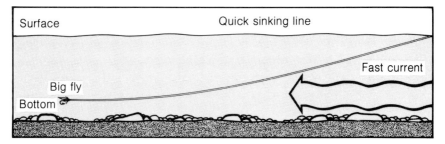

Fig 23 The effect of different line densities and current strengths must be known before the fly can be presented at a depth suitable to the water temperature.

A pool on the Spey where water height is critical for success.

Over many seasons the first fish caught in this area of the river has come from a small portion of the bottom of the pool in Green Bank. This has to be just at a critical height to get the best from it. With too much water it is impossible to wade it properly to cover the lies and with too little insufficient swing, draw or movement is imparted to the fly. The pool will occasionally fish in a low water providing there is some wind ripple to break the smooth surface.

As soon as the water warms in early May more fish, both salmon and sea trout, show in the deep dub of Pollowick. There will be a great temptation to fish for them there, but in all my experience of fishing this pool I have yet to take more than the very occasional fish from this deep middle section. Usually you have to wait until the fish are occupying the main stream in Pollowick and then sport may sometimes reach hectic proportions. In most instances this pool fishes much better from the left bank than it does from the right, but

here again there is a specific height when superb sport may be expected from the right bank and also on that same side in the sluggan above it. Although the deep dub may still hold the bulk of the stock of fish there is never a time when it is really worth fishing or when it produces more than a few oddments. Most times it seems that this dub merely contains a stock of fish which will move up into the Pollowick stream before they become inclined to take.

As the season advances the pool fills with both salmon and sea trout. On an average June evening it is difficult to decide whether you have hooked a salmon or a sea trout until it is firmly in play or even on the bank. Over so many June and July nights I have gone down there to fish at about 10.30 p.m. and have come away at midnight with a mixed bag of both salmon and sea trout. On one occasion I hooked a salmon on my top dropper only to have a sea trout snatch the tail fly. Sad to relate, it was the salmon that broke free, leaving me with a diminutive sea trout of less than two pounds. On another occasion I hooked a sea trout on the tail fly only to have a bat take the dropper during play. The sea trout was a beauty of about four pounds, but the bat was highly resentful and aggressive following its several baptisms. It bit me!

By the time we get the low water of mid-summer it is normal for Pollowick and its deep dub to be literally heaving with fish. Careful fishing of the streams during the early mornings and late evenings will produce a few fish, but there is never a moment when the deep dub is worth more than an exploratory cast.

Such is the taking style in one small location on just one salmon river.

I fish or observe the River Spey at Pollowick for at least a month of the season and a few years ago I used to fish it for at least six weeks. Multiply these figures by the twenty years I have known the water and you may begin to glean just how long it might take to acquire the intimate knowledge of a piece of water to get the best from it. I could not begin to tell you how to *read* that 150 yards of water from the Sluggan of Pollowick down to Green Bank in a short chapter. Nor could I explain what any subtle differences in height would do to fish movement and reaction. It is one thing reading a piece of river geographically and geometrically, therefore, and quite another learning the effects of different water levels, temperatures and conditions.

Another aspect of water that might materially affect the chances

At certain heights it is possible to fish the neck of Pollowick
from either side. When this photograph was taken, the angler
nearest the camera had just landed a fish.

of a catch, often associated directly with water height, is its
chemical quality. Excess acidity may sometimes be detected as
flecks of foam. Sometimes this may collect in odd corners and,
depending on the time of the year or the duration of high water
levels, it may take some days for it to be dispersed. Excess acidity
may also cause the water to change colour and you must try to
become aware of the influences all this will have on the fish. As
suggested elsewhere, it may prompt you to change from a small fly
on a floating line to a big fly on a sinking line.

   As I am constantly citing water height as a paramount factor in
successful salmon fishing it is important to realise that it is the slow
erosion of flood waters over the centuries that has formed the river
bed and adjusted the course of flow. Floods have slowly gouged
their way through most rock-girt waters. Many of our classic rivers

The River Lune is based on gravel and is subject to flood. At least one beat which I fished during the 1950s bears little resemblance to the one today. On rivers such as this it is often necessary to completely relearn the river contours each year.

on a rock base retain the same basic contours from year to year, but other rivers, mainly those based on gravel, are subjected to the most violent changes following each major flood. Such a river is the Lune in Lancashire. A stretch which I used to fish regularly had almost to be re-learned at the start of every new season. This beat I once fished now bears little resemblance to what it was when I first saw it in the fifties. Man-made groynes had to be used to arrest bank erosion and the water authority has waged constant battle to maintain the river within its banks. Even so there has been some dramatic gravel movement over many years – to such an extent that when the river changed course slightly the ownership of part of it also changed.

Other rivers are also influenced by flash floods and over the years there is no way of predicting just what might happen to traditional fish-holding lies. One year a pool might hold a fantastic number of fish while the following year it might be a complete waste of time

A hand-tailed fish from the Lune at Newton, where man-made groynes are maintained annually to prevent erosion.

even to cast over it. But not all is sacred on the rock-girt rivers. The interference of man has frequently had the opposite effect to that desired. Man-made concrete groynes are all too often badly sited and it is a bold and perhaps a stupid man who would say with certainty just where a groyne should be placed to best effect. Nine times out of ten we get it wrong and not only ruin the pool we hoped to improve but also cause some drastic change in a pool or pools further downstream. We should meddle with nature only when any harm done is liable to be totally unimportant to the overall effect.

The flows and depths of a river vary as it progresses on its seaward course. Water seeks to flow in a straight line and, impelled by gravity, the greater the volume to be moved and the greater the depth of fall, the stronger will be its influence on obstacles that lie in its path. For this reason at any point where a river bends we can assume that the ground is more solid at its point of deviation than it is on the opposite bank. Thus you will note that the main stream tends to be forced down the outside of a bend while the inside curve contains the calmer water.

Invariably at any point where the river turns sharply the continuous floods scour out a deep depression towards the inside bank and this spot may well harbour good stocks of migratory fish. It follows that it is a sound basic rule (although there are some notable exceptions) that many rivers fish better from the inside curve of a bend than they do from the outside curve. You will be able to make your casts into the fast water in the certain knowledge that your fly will then swing into the calmer water where the fish will tend to lie. With experience of the water you will learn the precise places where fish lie at a given height. In many instances knowledge of the best height for a specific pool is enough to be able to predict the chances of success. In times of flood, of course, fish tend to be under the very bank which is dry land – or at least where you might be wading in shallower water – when the river is at normal height. Knowledge of the ideal height for a specific pool is of the utmost importance in achieving the best fish-catching potential on any water.

If the bends and curves in a river do something to assist in reading the water there is still a lot to learn about that portion of the river we cannot usually see, that important third dimension – depth. Most rain-fed rivers vary tremendously in depth and are also influenced by the type of bed over which they flow. Solid rock may take thousands

The River Stinchar in Ayrshire, a rock-girt but small spate
river.

Despite its right-hand sweep, Polchraine may fish well from
either side. The main current goes down this left bank where
Grace Oglesby is fishing for sea trout.

of years to erode, while gravel, as I have shown, may be shifted from one flood to the next. The only way to learn the geography of a river, or that portion of it that you wish to fish regularly, is to get into a wet suit and submerge yourself in it for a lengthy exploration at different heights. The next best way, as already mentioned, is to study its basic contours at a time of very low water. Even then, unless you can move or think like a fish you are not likely to sense how subtle changes in the flow and movement of the water will affect precisely where fish will lie at differing heights. Such knowledge, while it might not seem to alter your catch too dramatically, can only help you in the presentation of your fly.

Enjoying a better-than-average day involves so many other factors than merely reading the water. A perfectly formed natural salmon pool at perfect height and temperature is one thing; such a pool stocked with fish in a mood to take our offerings is quite another. How, for instance, are we to know if the fish are fresh-run or stale? How do we tell which part of the pool, if any, holds fish which are totally resident, and which holds those just passing through and only temporarily residing there until the onset of darkness or a slight rise in the water? The colouring of any fish seen may betray its length of stay in fresh water, but is this necessarily a good guide to our chances of a catch?

In reading a river we must not only be aware of the geographical and geological influences on a pool or piece of water; we must also take into account the direction of the prevailing wind and other, less desirable, winds which may have an influence. We must also consider the direction in which the river, or our portion of it, travels to the sea and the effect of sunshine, or lack of it, at different times of the year. An apparently perfect pool which is continually exposed to chilling winds and in total shelter from a warming westerly wind or sunshine, no matter how good it is technically, will not make the best of taking places.

The effects of sunshine can be dramatic. The lore holds – and it is a widely accepted belief – that bright sunlight shining straight down a pool and into the eyes of the fish is bad for fishing. This suggests that an eastward flowing river – with the fish travelling in a westerly direction – would give the best sport in the mornings and not be overinfluenced by sunshine until late afternoon or evening. A southward-flowing river, on the other hand, should suffer little adverse effect from sunshine at all, while one that flows north may

be adversely influenced by the sun for the bulk of a day. Even then it might be wrong to assume that all sunshine is bad for fishing. I can recall many instances when a dull, chilly day has suddenly been transformed by a burst of spring sunshine, and my conviction that such a change can induce fish to take has been rewarded too often for me not to respond to it with renewed keenness.

The different values of light between early spring, midsummer and late autumn, and the effects of light and shade all play their part. A grey February day offers an entirely different set of circumstances from one in June. The length of the daylight period, the actinic quality and angle of the light and its possible effect on the fish should all be noted in the mental computer when the best tactics for any given set of circumstances are assessed. Only if you are aware of the many influences which may affect your sport are you likely to become that better-than-average fisherman you would like to be.

This is borne out by an experience on the Lune in the summer of 1966. By that time I had acquired a fairly intimate knowledge of one small piece of water. I fished it regularly almost every weekend and

Arthur Oglesby fishing for salmon in the River Sella in Asturias, northern Spain. Even though it was his first visit he knew to fish the inside bend of a pool.

The Tweed at Innerleithen where the tributary Leithen joins
the main river. Anglers fish the left bank where there is a
main holding lie.

over other days during the week when it was in good ply. Although
subject to sudden changes from floods, it was a water on which I
maintained a constant reconnaissance and I was well aware of the
precise height at which it would fish best.

It was towards the end of July that I went over in the company of a
friend to live rough in our fishing hut for a few nights before moving
on to see other friends in Cumbria. The visit had been planned to
coincide with the run-off from a recent rise and I knew that the river
had vast stocks of fish available anyway. Our arrival on the Thursday
evening was heralded by the sight of more water than I had
anticipated. There had evidently been a storm up the valley and
the river was carrying at least two feet of extra and unwanted
water. I used a tree stump in the water as a gauge of the river height
and thus the catch potential and as I made ready our sleeping bags in
the fishing hut my friend was busily tackling up with his spinning
rod and hustling into his waders. Urging him not to be in too much
of a hurry, I explained that the river was just a little too high and that
he would do better to wait until the morning at least. 'Good God!'
he retorted. 'I saw several fish jumping down there and the river

looks perfect. I'm off to give them a cast.'

I watched him go happily on his way and busied myself tidying the hut, preparing supper over our gas stove and sipping a drop of a very relaxing amber-coloured liquid as the sun slowly dimmed in the west. It was midnight before my friend lurched back to the hut with the news that he had seen several fish but that not one had given his lure so much as a tweak.

The following morning he was up bright and early, clambering into his waders and making for the river. Already, with one cheek still on my pillow, I had noted that the river was still too high for perfection, but I bade my friend good luck with a promise that I would have breakfast ready for 8 a.m. Back at 8 he was too, fishless but hungry and keen to get at the plateful of bacon and eggs I had prepared. Several more fish had been seen, but none had condescended to take his lures. After breakfast he spent the rest of the day and evening fishing just as hard as he could, but by nightfall he was

Midnight on the River Tana in northern Norway. The Fosse Pool where, without vast experience, you would not begin to know where to fish. Finland is on the opposite bank.

again fishless and he came back to the hut more than disgruntled
with his luck.

By 6 a.m. on the following morning, however, it was I that was up
bright and early, climbing into my waders and generally disturbing
his peace. Having noted that the river had fallen to its almost perfect
height I felt some conviction that there were now fish to be caught.
My friend, on the other hand, was now content to have a lie-in and
prepare a leisurely breakfast. By 8 a.m. I was back with three salmon
and I went on later that morning to add another two to the bag. We
departed for Cumbria that lunch time with mixed feelings – I with
some conviction that had I been able to stay all day I might well have
broken the individual record catch for the beat. It is not recorded
exactly what my friend felt, but at least he did catch one fish that
morning as some reward for his stout effort.

Intimate knowledge of a piece of water will always give you a
head start over another angler, no matter what his age or general
experience, who does not know the water as well as you do. I would
not back myself against a veritable novice on his own water, nor
would I expect to catch any more fish than the dedicated enthusiast
who, in springtime, when fish are running and only resting briefly, is
prepared to fish endlessly from dawn until dusk.

In the days when I used to fish the little Yorkshire Esk with
almost monotonous regularity, I got to know some of the precise
taking places very well. Sometimes marching down the river for a
few miles just taking the odd cast in the best lies seemed to work and
a few fish were caught. But once a good run of fish was known to be
in the river it paid best to fish down the pools carefully in the
assumption that every cast might hook a fish.

I recall one occasion on this same river when I went to a pool in
the almost certain knowledge that fresh fish had recently moved
into it. I fished it down meticulously without any success. I then
fished it down a second time with the same result. I was about to
move to the pool below when another angler promptly marched into
it. I tarried briefly over a cigarette and a sandwich and then went
down my pool for a third time, and hooked and landed two nice fish.
Of course, it *may* be that the fish had just come in and had not been
there during my first two forays. I wonder.

There are times, particularly on some spate rivers, when you may
be fishing at the precise moment of the run coming in. If this
happens it is possible to stand in one place all day and continually

Local anglers flock to a known hot spot when the Dovey floods.

catch fish as they swim up to the lie and rest briefly before moving on. Although it has never happened to me I recall one day on the Esk when it was fining down from its first main flood of the season and when fish were pouring in. I watched a fellow fisherman stand at the head of a small stream and cast continuously over the same piece of water. By the end of that day, and almost without shuffling his feet, he caught and landed six prime fish.

The successful reading of a river and its condition is a complex business. Only slowly will you mentally record those places where you hook or see fish. You may have vague memories about the height of the water and the time of year you fished it. You may even recall the type of weather, and water and air temperatures. The keeping of a comprehensive fishing diary will help tremendously in recalling past successes and failures. By the time you have been visiting a piece of water for ten years you may find that you are beginning to catch fish more frequently and predictably. You may also note, perhaps with some dismay, that over the ten-year period only one year has provided you with a mild bonanza. You will also consider yourself lucky if you draw a blank in fewer than, say, three years out of the ten. This is the lottery aspect of salmon and sea-trout fishing, and must be accepted by the sporting angler.

12
Hooking, Playing
and
Landing Salmon

No creature on earth treats the dogmatist more sternly than Salmo salar *the Atlantic salmon. Anyone writing about this extraordinary fish enters a literary minefield – each considered sentence threatening to blow up in his face.*

Hugh Falkus, Salmon Fishing – A Practical Guide

HOOKING

What is the best course of action to take at that magic moment when a fish apparently has your fly firmly in its mouth? Many of the old books suggest that the instant a fish is felt pulling the fly it should be given some slack line. Many contemporary writers agree and offer apparently sound reasoning why this drill must be adhered to if successful hooking of salmon is to be achieved. Their answers bear some examination and, for all that I shall attempt to suggest otherwise, their way is occasionally effective.

In seeking to understand even vaguely this slack-line philosophy we must bear in mind that salmon in cold water take very slowly and deliberately. In many instances I am quite convinced that in a normal current of water it would not matter too much what we did, provided it was nothing too dramatic – the fish would be more than likely to get hooked anyway. On the other hand I find it difficult to understand why I should give line to a fish that I can already feel pulling on my line, a fish that has obviously already got a firm hold of my fly. If I really want to hook it should I not let it continue to pull against a tight line until the barb is in? It just does not seem logical to feed more line and risk the fish expelling the fly from its mouth. The theory that the current will cause the slack line to pull the fly into

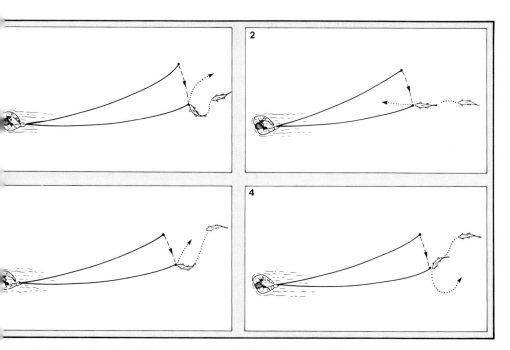

Fig 24   The take. Various ways in which a salmon might
take your fly, but in most instances the angler knows nothing
until the pull is felt.

the scissors of the fish's jaw sounds very plausible, but somewhow
does not seem sensible when elementary logic is applied.

An opportunity to put this matter to the test came when I was
fishing for trout on a well stocked section of the Driffield Trout
Stream in East Yorkshire. A chalk stream, with similar character-
istics to the famous River Test, it had recently suffered an escape of
small rainbow trout from a nearby hatchery. On reaching one
particular pool I was attempting to interest a good-size brownie
when my fly was seized by one of the diminutive rainbows. I quickly
horsed it in and tossed it back only to have my fly continually
bombarded thereafter by more voracious rainbows. By the time I
had returned number six I was seeking any way I could to move my
fly *without* hooking a fish. In the end the only way this could be
accomplished was by feeding slack line to the fish at the moment of
the take. The moral was, therefore, that if I didn't want to hook a
fish I should feed it slack line the instant I saw or felt it touch my fly.
Of course, you may suggest that a hungry rainbow trout is a
different kettle of fish to a salmon. Indeed, there are, as I have

Gerald Panchaud playing a small salmon on the outflow
stream to the sea at Amhuinnsuidhe, Harris, Hebrides.

demonstrated, vast differences between a fish which does not feed
in fresh water and one that does so voraciously. But are those
differences so marked as to make all that difference in hooking
techniques? Both fish are attacking my fly!

When faced with a dilemma such as this I often turn to other
authorities. The first writer I sought on this subject was that sage of
salmon fishing, Lee Wulff. Although not so well known to British
anglers, Wulff is regarded as a Messiah by most North American
salmon anglers. Although born in Alaska, the great domain of
Pacific salmon, he is specifically interested in the Atlantic species –
the same as our own. In the rivers of Quebec, Labrador and Nova
Scotia he has caught over five thousand on the fly. In Chapter 9 of
his excellent book *The Atlantic Salmon*, Wulff writes:

How important the hooking of fish may be was illustrated by an
event at the Portland Creek camps. When I started them, the river
was barely fished. The proportion of fish hooked was about half of
the rises, a good average. As the fishing became more intensive, the

Lee Wulff about to grip a fish by the gills on the River of
Ponds, N.E. Canada

proportion grew lower. During the second year of operation, we hit
an August slump, when, for a two week period during which we had
rains and high water, only a few fish came into the camp. In talking
things over with the guides in search of a solution, their consensus
was that the fish were rising but the fishermen were not striking
them properly. The guides, all able anglers, were certain that if they
themselves had been handling the rods the catch would have been
nearly normal.

As it happened all the anglers in camp ended their trips on a
Saturday, and new anglers were not to arrive until Monday. It gave
me a chance to let the guides have a day off. Since all the guides liked
to fish and were often uncertain as to whether to have a job and not
be able to fish for salmon, or fish for them and not have a job, I saw a
chance to help along their education (and mine). In announcing the
day off, I also suggested they fish the river for the day, and put up a
bottle of rum as a prize for the guide who would bring in the biggest
salmon. Six of the guides went fishing ... and the bottle of rum
went to the guide who caught a six pounder, the only fish taken by
the entire crew. It was the first time some of the guides had fished

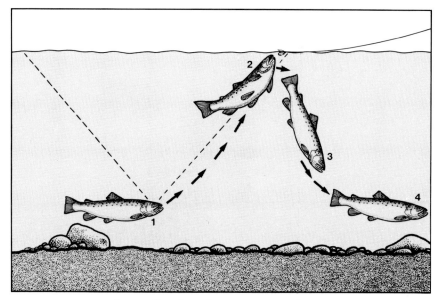

Fig 25 A trout taking a fly often does so with more
determination than a salmon because it is actually feeding.

under conditions where salmon make false rises or come short, a
situation that usually develops where fishing is intense and when
fish have been long in the stream. It gave the guides a new
appreciation of the problem their sportsmen faced. Those guides
were unanimous about one thing though. They believed a fisherman
should strike when the fish takes his fly.

Turning to Balfour-Kinnear and Chapter 3 of his book *Catching
Salmon and Sea Trout*, we read:

If you cast your fly on to an obstacle, you try to get it clear by pulling
it very gently, as you know that it is less likely to hook if you do this.
The dry-fly man wiggles his rod very gently in the hope of
disengaging his fly from the leaves or grass into which he, or the
wind, has thrown it. Why should it be any different when a salmon's
mouth is concerned? If you *do not* want to hook the fish, then be as
gentle as you can – even to the extent of throwing loose line at it.

Another highly experienced angler and writer on salmon fishing,
Neil Graesser, in *Fly Fishing for Salmon* and on the subject of 'To
Strike or not to Strike', writes:

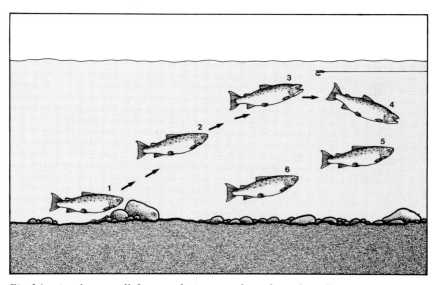

Fig 26   A salmon will frequently inspect the sub-surface fly
at a more leisurely pace, before deciding whether to intercept
or refuse it.

There are three schools of thought. The first school of thought, of
which I am a firm adherent, says that you must raise your rod point
firmly and instantaneously, in other words, strike immediately you
feel the fish . . . The purpose of striking when a salmon takes you is
to drive the hook into its mouth over the barb, the force necessary
to do this will vary with the length of line you are casting, the type of
rod you are using, if it is stiff or supple, and the size of fly. Timing,
confidence and technique are all important but if you wish to test
the necessity and it is a very simple way to experiment, go out with a
friend with a salmon rod and hold the fly in your hand. If your friend
quietly tightens the line by raising the rod gently you will find that
you can open your hand and let the fly go or, at the very worst, the
point will just penetrate the skin. I know for I have done it.
However, a quick pull will produce quite a different story and a
painful visit to the doctor. On this I rest my case.

Another great caster and angler who has caught over two thousand
salmon, Charles McLaren, in his book *Fishing for Salmon*, writes:

To strike or not to strike? YOU MUST STRIKE. A firm raising of

the rod point, and a properly timed tightening of the line, must be made so that after the fish has turned away with the fly, the hook is secured in the fish's mouth over the barb.

Other opinions which I value highly come from those anglers I know who have never committed a word to print, but who, throughout a season, probably catch as many fish to their own rods as would be caught by some of our 'experts' when banded together. One particular angler, Monsieur Maurice Kruch of Belgium, fishes only the best Scottish, Norwegian and Icelandic rivers. Most seasons he catches in excess of a hundred salmon to his own rod and frequently twice that number. He is primarily a fly fisherman and at no time throughout a season of fishing does he feed slack line to a taking fish. In a recent conversation with the Duke of Roxburghe – who despite his youth, has already caught more salmon than many of us will catch in a lifetime – there was little doubt in his mind that any fish felt should be promptly engaged without any yielding of slack line. Yet another angler who comes to mind, Odd Haraldsen of Norway, probably catches more big Atlantic salmon than anyone else in the world. He would not understand what I was talking about if I were to make the suggestion of giving slack line to one of his monsters at the moment of the take. It would seem that some of the greatest critics of the lore, statements which have been handed down parrot-fashion from generation to generation, are sometimes the greatest conformists to the very lore they condemn.

On the other hand, contrary opinions are to be found in several books and one is forced to wonder if it really matters all that much after all. I am inclined to think that it matters very much and it is for this reason that I am taking so much space to debate this point. One of our more modern writers on salmon fishing, Philip Green, in his stimulating book *New Angles on Salmon Fishing*, devotes much space to debunking what he calls the lore and those doctrinaire views which are accepted blindly with little thought for their accuracy or value. Green devotes an entire chapter to hooking and starts by a consideration of that most logical and obvious factor – the sizes and types of hook being used.

I am not going to quote from Green's book here, but it is well worth study and calls upon us to consider the different aspects of singles, doubles and trebles; the time of year we might fish with them; the sizes of hook; and the style (sinking or floating line) in

Odd Haraldsen of Oslo with a fish of 55lb taken from the
Vosso at Bolstadoyri, Norway, in June 1981.

which they are used. Most of the lore to which Green refers in this respect seems to be based on the premise that all will be using single-hooked flies. These are the flies of our forefathers and I have long thought that they could not possibly be ideal instruments for guaranteeing a secure hook-hold. To test my contention you need only take an old single-hook fly in your hand, clasp it between your forefinger and thumb and then pull it away from your hand. Nine times out of ten the hook will slide away without the point coming into contact with you. Try this technique with a hook with outpoints or a sneck bend or one with two or three points and the story is entirely different.

Another friend of mine and an exceptionally competent salmon fisherman admits that he feeds slack line to all the fish he catches on the floating line, but that in all other instances and styles of fishing, from sunk-line fly to spinning, he strikes the instant he feels the pull. He admits that his methods lack any logic and that he was merely indoctrinated into feeding slack line from the first days he started fishing for salmon with a fly. Many of the writers who insist that we feed slack line to a fish when we are fly fishing seem to share this view and are equally adamant that we hit them hard when we are fishing in other styles. I wonder why? Surely a fish that takes a spinner is doing much the same thing when it takes a fly. Why should you strike in one instance but feed line to the fish in the other? You may argue, of course, that the fish on the spinner has usually accepted a multi-hook lure whereas the fly might be dressed on a single hook. Even then I fail to see why a fish should be better hooked with one technique than the other. Most of us know instances when a spinner is taken but secure hooking fails. This is one of the many facets of any form of fishing and it frequently happens in any angling activity, whether for trout, roach, mackerel, marlin or sea trout.

Certainly, many salmon fly fishermen fish with a yard of slack line in their hands. When asked if they are in the habit of fishing this way, they seem totally unaware of what I mean and tell me that they do not consciously give slack line at the moment of the take. It took some time for me to deduce what might be happening, but in reality the answer is very simple. Many people fish with a loop of line simply because they have made a bad cast and have not been able to shoot all of the line that was handlined in from the previous cast. Perhaps there are some loose-liners who merely need an excuse for

being left with a loop!

On the question of hooks, I am of the firm opinion that the treble hook is superior in hooking power to either the double or the single. There may be tactical reasons, as outlined in my book *Salmon*, why a specific type of hook should do better than another in a situation where the drag effect or weight of the fly has to be equated with current strength and clarity or depth. Only rarely do I use single-hook flies these days and then usually in the very small sizes. If I must use single hooks then I feel some conviction that a sneck bend or an outpointed hook is preferable to a straight bend.

One writer, in defence of the single hook, uses the analogy of pulling various types of hook into a flat piece of plastic foam. The single hook does indeed penetrate foam better than the treble hook, and the analogy might be apt if we were fishing for flat pieces of plastic foam! But we are fishing for a fish which usually totally encloses the fly with its mouth when it takes and which, as a result, may be hooked anywhere in its mouth. Within reasonable limits, the more hooks likely to make contact, the better the chances of a successful outcome.

To return to the question of whether to feed slack line or to strike, while I am certainly not a devotee of the slack-line theory at any time I am not fully convinced that a firm strike is always necessary. In this respect I think that it is interesting to note that the authors I have quoted may have had the bulk of their experience on particular rivers or at certain times of the season. For instance, Lee Wulff is generally confined to the three-month Canadian season of June, July and August. Here the fish are usually sought in water temperatures of over 50°F. Their rate of metabolism and reaction is likely to be much higher and quicker than the fish sought in the early months of a Scottish winter, when the water has to struggle to get into the mid-thirties. In such conditions the fish have a low metabolic rate and consequent sluggish reaction times. Any lure they are prepared to take might be taken so ponderously that you may be able to pause before tightening your line and still find the fish firmly hooked. In this instance the necessity for striking is probably diminished.

Much depends not only on the time of year and the consequent range of water temperatures and fish metabolism, but also on the strength and depth of the current, the freshness or otherwise of the fish, and whether they have been fished for hard, and perhaps over-

intimidated, or are occupying comparatively untouched water. Other aspects of salmon behaviour must also be considered but I will not pretend that any formula will provide a sound rule for all conditions.

My method – and, with the exception of worm fishing, one which I follow with all styles of fishing for salmon and sea trout – is to respond with equal and opposite pressure the instant I feel pressure from a fish. In a slow current, or in the very cold months, salmon response may be sluggish and I respond with an equally sluggish but hard hold, so that the fish hooks itself. In the balmy days of midsummer, when both salmon and sea trout respond much more quickly, I think that any sharp pull felt should be followed by a quick strike. Grilse, particularly, seem to have a facility for snatching your fly and departing entirely unscathed. Salmon encountered when I am fishing for sea trout also seem to be able to snatch the fly just as quickly as the most mercurial sea trout. Indeed, there have been many June evenings on the Spey when I have not known which species I have hooked until the playing of the fish was well under way or even until it was safely on the bank.

The only exception I have made to this practice was in my fish-hungry days when I used occasionally to catch salmon on a worm. Here it is important to delay the strike until the fish has the worms firmly pouched in its mouth or gut and is moving away with them back to its lie.

There is one more aspect to consider before we finally abandon this topic. Several apparently competent writers, particularly those who follow the slack-line philosophy, suggest that at all times when the fly is swinging round in the current the rod should be held at a low angle to facilitate the shooting of slack line at the moment of the take. The late Dick Walker used to refer to this technique as the *despondent droop*, and it was only after careful thought that I came up with the notion that the antithesis of this had to be the *expectant erection*. Quite apart from any other consideration, the high-held rod keeps a minimum of line on or in the water so that downstream belly formations of line, and the consequent necessity for mending, do not occur so frequently. This assists in the proper presentation of your fly and is one of the reasons why I often seek a longer rod for essential water command.

I recall an incident one August when I was standing on a high bank on the River Awe in Argyllshire. A salmon could be plainly seen

Dr David Goldsborough fishes on the Shott Pool of the
Tweed at Upper Floors.

waving its fins lightly in the stream below. It would not have been
an easy cast for me, so, calling to a fellow angler who could easily
wade down the opposite bank, I directed his casts so that his fly
would cover the fish. I saw the fish take his fly a fraction of a second
before he felt the pull. In the event the fish was lost after about five
minutes of play, but I would guess that if the angler's response to
that fish could have been quicker the story might have ended on a
more successful note.

The shorter the rod the less the effect the high-held position will
afford, but then you will probably only use the short rod at times of
low water or when salmon reaction is quickened by increased water
temperatures in the late spring and summer, and the technique may
then be of less importance. Be that as it may, I like to hold my rod as
high as is reasonably comfortable and well out at an angle to the
stream. Then I feel some conviction that the sag of line between my

rod point and the hook will provide enough of a cushion for me to respond instantly I feel that my fly has been taken. There will be minute delays in reaction times between brain and hand. Sometimes the fish will be hooked and on other occasions it won't – but is that not the case in all types of fishing? My conclusion, for what it is worth, is that in general terms those anglers who hook and catch a lot of fish usually don't bother to feed slack line at the moment of the take. Those who merely talk about it, speculate and pontificate, are the ones who go into raptures about feeding slack line.

PLAYING AND LANDING

Even when you have hooked your fish securely it is still a long way from being safely on the bank and knocked on the head. For the early part of the play the fish will have some ideas of its own and you

A salmon hooked while Arthur Oglesby was fishing single-handed for sea trout. Here the fish had to be held hard to prevent it going downstream to the next pool on a flooded River Lune.

may have to wage a give-and-take battle until the fish tires and you can persuade it to do more of your bidding. Much tactical comment was given in my notes on tackle in Chapter 5, but there are other aspects which should be borne in mind and they relate to the condition factor of the fish you have in play. Let us imagine that your fish is recently run in from the sea, has travelled about fifty miles upstream in little more than two days and had just settled into the tail of a pool before you hooked it. Although this fish is going to make superb eating it may well give a comparatively poor fight and it will not be long before it is subdued and ready for the net or tailer. This fish has become semi-exhausted in its total dedication to its upstream migration. Little wonder that the bulk of the fight has already gone out of it!

Now let us imagine that you are fishing down near the estuary in May or June. There has been a slight flood and fresh fish are coming in on the tide. Within a few hundred yards of the estuary a fish pauses long enough to take your fly. The water erupts and a violent battle ensues before you finally subdue your fish and knock it on the head. Rarely will the playing style of any two fish be entirely similar. Of course, the size of the fish also has some bearing and there is a law, or lore, which suggests that a minute of playing time per pound of fish weight is a rough guide. Use this suggestion merely for thought; in certain circumstances, it may not be far out.

It is important to avoid prolonged playing times. I recall an incident at Grantown-on-Spey when I had the chairman of a large public company as one of my guests. As I walked down the bank to greet him I found him with his rod only slightly bent and with a fish in play. He had a look of great concern on his face as he announced that he had been playing the fish for over thirty minutes and that, as yet, he had not even had a glimpse of it. He was using a fixed-spool reel with a slipping clutch and every time he wound the handle there was a double click to indicate, to me at least, that he was not gaining any line and that the status quo was being maintained as the fish kept station in the water. I suggested that he tighten the clutch on his reel but he was horrified lest the strain be too much and the fish break off. The contest continued for another ten minutes with the same neutral effect. Eventually, I took the bold step of taking his line in my hands and asking him to wind in the slack line as I handlined the fish towards us. It was completely played out and merely gave a couple of weak flicks as I lifted it out by the tail and

Leading a fish up to the bank from behind is often easier
than standing on the bank and dragging it towards you.

knocked it on the head for him. It is neither safe nor sporting to
prolong the fight unnecessarily.

On the other hand it is sometimes an equally grave mistake to be
overexcited with a fish. During the first moments of play it is
important to establish your fighting ground. Ideally this should be
close to a bay or beach where the fish may be easily brought ashore.
There should be some initial attempt made to keep the fish in the
stronger current where it will tire more quickly. If you have to move
with a fish, bear in mind that it is much easier to take it downstream
than against the current. Initially the fish might fight without being
aware of your presence. It will continually seek to stay in the deeper
water and will struggle against all attempts to lead it into shallow
water. The instant it is aware of your presence it is likely to adopt
frenzied measures. Now the dangers it might not have sensed too
acutely in the early stages of play will be real and vital. By this time

Wait until a fish is lying on its side before bringing it into
the bank for tailing. Arthur Oglesby with a salmon on the
Spey at Castle Grant.

the fish might be aware that it is literally fighting for its life. As the
contest continues you must be prepared to have the fish come into
shallow water frequently only to fight its way back again. Take care
to let it run when the tackle is under heavy strain. You may have to
let the fish make frequent runs back into the centre of the river, but
each time you bring it back it will be slowly tiring and getting nearer
the moment when you may either hand-tail it out or use your net or
gaff.

Although the biggest salmon I have ever caught (a fish of 49½ lb)
was caught on a spinner from the wild waters of Norway there was
much excitement in the playing of it. During its initial run it literally
emptied my reel. Fortunately, by this time I was in a boat and well
able to follow it on its mad downstream dash. Eventually, with a
modest amount of line back on my reel, I was able to come to terms
with it – but not before forty-five minutes had elapsed and the fish
had taken me back down to the fjord from whence it had come. A
more detailed description of the battle is to be found in the latest
edition of my book, *Salmon*. It was quite a memorable occasion!

Arthur Oglesby with his biggest ever salmon 49½lb from the
Vosso at Bolstadoyri, Norway.

Combined British and Norwegian experience has taught me that, purely from the aspect of playing, fish fall into about five different types. For instance, you may go to the Tweed or Spey in spring and catch fish between 6 and 10lbs. These will require firm treatment but not substantial tackle and leaders of from 10 to 14lb test will cope. Such fish are good fun and may provide some spirited sport. Fish in the 12 to 20lb bracket test you a little more. You are conscious of the weight of the fish and the need for slightly stronger tackle or more prolonged periods of play. Fish of between 20 and 25lb – rarely encountered in Britain but commonplace in Norway – really show their mettle, and the capture of a 30-pounder, by whatever means, offers a different challenge again. If you have reasonable luck you might encounter a fish in the 40 to 50 pound bracket and at this stage you may well

Landing a fish with a net. A good net should have a wide mouth, long handle and a strong frame like the one illustrated here.

Lee Wulff demonstrates his method of hand-tailing a good salmon from the Moisie river in N.E. Canada.

wonder if you really know anything at all about playing a salmon.

The same playing techniques are involved whether you are to net, gaff or hand-tail your fish. Little is achieved until the fish is fully exhausted and I am of the firm opinion that many anglers try to hustle their fish out before they are fully played out. This is a pity. Perhaps it demonstrates our greed in trying to get a lovely prize out of its natural element as quickly as possible so that we can knock it on the head and take it home. If we had the dedication of the true sportsman we might well not bother if the fish gets off in play – always providing that it did so without breakage to the tackle. North American anglers are now being urged to fish for salmon with barbless hooks and to adopt a catch-and-release policy. My illustration of Lee Wulff hand-tailing a salmon might horrify the average British salmon angler. What angler in his right mind, you might say, would hand-tail a fish so far from the water's edge when it had every chance of slipping from his grip and getting its freedom?

Questions of ethics and principles are considered in more detail in my final chapter, and here I will merely point out that the true sportsman fishes more for sport than for the pot. Even if it is morally

right to hunt and kill, we must get rid of the idea that the rental should be met by the sale of salmon caught. This, in my view, is a highly unsporting and irresponsible attitude to the wondrous resource we have, and I have little time for those anglers who seek to sell all the fish they catch. Only a few years ago I heard one of these 'fishmongers' retort: 'If it had not been for those damned netsmen we would not only have covered the rental cost, but the hotel and bar bill as well.'

Readers will notice the grip Lee Wulff prefers for hand-tailing his fish. Frankly, it is not my preference and I have sound reasons for believing that a grip with the hand the other way round is better. Of course, it is all a little like picking up a pint of beer: the individual must decide for himself which is preferable. My grip, however, is the one most frequently used by the gillies I have seen and indeed by most of those whose work involves the handling of live salmon.

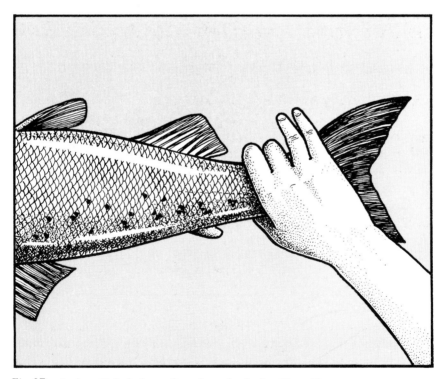

Fig 27   Arthur Oglesby's preferred method of tailing. Note that the main grip has to come on the inside fingers and thumb.

Arthur Oglesby lifts out a hand-tailed Spey fish. With really big salmon, instead of lifting, it is a simple matter to continue leading it up to the bank with the rod point, whilst pushing hard from below.

Most hatchery operatives use the grip as illustrated in my diagram, and it is also the best to use for sliding up the bank a fish that is too heavy to be lifted bodily without fear of it slipping. Large fish may be guided up the bank by the application of pull from the rod point while the hand on the tail merely pushes the fish towards its

intended destination and even fairly steep banks can be negotiated this way.

Some readers may have seen the Benson & Hedges videotape in which I safely beached a fish of 27½ lb in front of the camera. Before starting to fish I had positioned the camera crew where I thought I had the best chance of hand-tailing a fish should I be fortunate enough to hook one. Then, moving some two hundred yards upstream, I started fishing without any thought for the camera crew. Eventually, I felt that electric tug and suspected instantly than I had encountered a larger than normal salmon. Looking round for assistance, I soon realised that I should have to cope on my own and hand-tail the fish as previously planned.

I had been most fortunate in selecting the downstream location for the camera and it was with little difficulty that I soon had the fish floundering about in its immediate vicinity. Had there been a gillie with a gaff or net I could have brought that fish to bank in much less

If you are landing a really big fish – like this 56lb Norwegian monster taken on the Alta – there may be no satisfactory alternative to the gaff.

An angler makes ready with his tailer while playing a fish.

time than it actually took. But, by virtue of the fact that the fish was well hooked and that I was able to take my time I was eventually able to get my hand round its tail and slide it up the bank. It was and still is the largest salmon I have taken in British waters. How fortunate I am to have the entire record of its capture on video!

If you find hand-tailing either too strenuous or too unpredictable in outcome, it is perfectly understandable if you prefer a net or tailer. These seem much more humane than a gaff and I am delighted to note that I rarely see anglers carrying a gaff these days. A mechanical tailer used to be a popular instrument. But, as with the net, it is an added encumbrance I prefer to omit from my list of essentials.

If any of these appliances have to be used then it is important to have the fish virtually played out and lying on its side. On many occasions I have watched anglers stabbing about with a net, tailer or

gaff when the fish was far from ready to be brought ashore, which can so easily result in the fish breaking the short line or leader, leaving you to mourn your loss. Far better, in my view, to be patient and to lead the fish to a convenient landing or beaching place only when it is fully played out. Of course, you will still lose the odd fish, but in that event you will merely raise your hat and bid it Godspeed to the spawning redds.

During the final stages of the fight with a fish – those tense seconds when you are about to tail, net or gaff your fish, it sometimes pays to scratch your feet around so that the water is clouded by the mud of the river bed. Leading a fish into turbid water, where its vision is restricted, will render it less mobile and it may lie impassively on its side while you pick it up by the tail, scoop it into a net (head first if you can) or, if you must, lay the gaff across its back and snatch it out. As noted many times in this book, I do not now carry any of these appliances and rely entirely on my bare hands to get the fish out.

Some writers lay down a rigid rule for hand-tailing fish: that the angler must stand on the bank as he plays the fish and only when it is played out and on its side should he go down and lift it out. This method is fine for many circumstances, and I use it frequently. It makes it possible to apply constant drag effect on the fish. But it also makes the fish totally aware of your presence. It sees you as a monster leering down at it and it reacts continually to your every move. If you remain in the water, on the other hand, you may quietly lead the fish round in front of you and direct it towards the bank with the rod point. This way the fish is not so aware of your presence when you are walking quietly up behind it. Then, as soon as it is on its side, and partially on the beach, you may sneak up behind it and lift it out by the tail. If the fish is too big to lift without risk of it slipping from your grasp, it is then but a simple matter to continue leading it up with the rod point while pushing hard from below.

13

Loch and
Stillwater Fishing

Now I am drifting along the south side of the island, casting the old favourites on the rippling water. Slim chance I have, for the light is brilliant, the whole sky aflame as the sun sets. Yet in the sound of the ripple against the planking of the boat, soft as a mother's lullaby, there is great peace.
                    Terence Horsley, Fishing and Flying

Although I am essentially a lover of the faster-flowing rivers of our upland country, the wild highlands and those rock-girt streams that seem to flourish anywhere in Britain above 500 feet, there is a sense in which advancing old age is giving me opportunities to enjoy some of our more remote stillwaters. I am referring particularly to the lochs of the Outer Hebrides and specifically those of the North Harris Estate in the vicinity of Amhuinnsuidhe Castle. For the past nine or ten years it has been my good fortune, along with my wife, to be invited there every year. Our hosts, Gerald and Hélène Panchaud, not only provide superb hospitality but are among the most sporting and enthusiastic fishermen I have met. Both are highly competent anglers and Hélène has developed a particular flair for extracting salmon, rather than sea trout, out of the several lochs in which we are privileged to fish. Usually I am not greatly concerned whether I catch salmon or sea trout, but there are certain factors, which I will explain in greater detail shortly, which tend to limit my catch of salmon and give me a better chance with the sea trout.

For many years I was inclined to scorn stillwater angling. Reservoir trout fishing was dismissed as a situation where you sit in a boat and cast to the leeward side for as long as it pleases you, stripping the fly back and then casting again. If, suddenly, something stops the line from being retrieved, it probably means that you have a fish on. This, as I saw it at the time, was about all that was involved in stillwater fishing, but the ensuing years have taught me differently. I have learned that there are those who are more

talented at stillwater fishing than others and that you must take many factors into account. Many stillwaters can be likened to a miniature sea: there are variations in the depth of water and the effects of the prevailing wind – not to mention the basic chemistry of the water and, in the case of young offspring of salmon and sea trout, the availability of food. Of course, all lakes and lochs with stocks of migratory fish normally have exits to the sea. Most also have at least a few small feeder streams and it is reasonable to suppose that any loch or lake will only hold stocks until spawning time, when the fish will seek the rapid water of the upland burns in order to complete their spawning activity. The stillwater offers a haven from predators and shelter from hot sunshine during the period from the time the fish enter fresh water to the time they spawn. In many instances fish may occasionally be caught in the rivers which connect the lakes or lochs with the sea, but those in the Hebrides tend to be very short and narrow and only in specific instances do they hold sufficient fish to make fishing in them worth while.

Initially, I shall concentrate my comments on the experience I have had in the lochs and streams of the North Harris Estate, elsewhere in the Hebrides and in Ireland. As a dedicated fast-water man, I had more to learn than I realised and only now, after nigh on ten years of visiting the Hebrides, am I getting some feeling for

A salmon leaping in the sea at Amhuinnsuidhe Castle, Isle of Harris, Hebrides.

Mixed shoals of salmon and sea trout run in and out of this Hebridean bay. Sometimes they will enter the streams, but often they move on along the coast.

where to be and when.

As to just when the fish will run, I have found no logical basis for prediction. Early July seems the best bet for the first batches of fish. These may be a mixed shoal of both salmon and sea trout which come skirmishing into the bay at Amhuinnsuidhe and make the occasional jump in the freshwater outflow nearby. I get the impression that sometimes many of the fish which come into the bay are not actually intending to run the little stream into which they seem to jump with such great glee, but are merely excited at feeling their way, as it were, around the rocky coastline, searching for their ancestral home. This is evidenced by the fact that a large shoal of fish may move into the bay one day only to apparently disappear the next. Careful observation usually proves that they have not run up the little local river. But, of course, there are mixed shoals moving in and out of the bay all the time so it is impossible to

be specific about which are going to run that particular stream and which are merely testing it, as it were, to see if it might represent home. Some days vast shoals of fish, both salmon and sea trout intermingled, appear in the bay like some leviathan submarine and cruise slowly round before disappearing around the next headland. Rarely are any big fish seen and the average Hebridean salmon runs to little more than 6lb. Just occasionally a few big fish in excess of 12lb may come into the bay and on one occasion my wife caught a beauty of 13lb from the castle wall, but such fish are exceptional for that part of the Hebrides and it may be that they are bound for some other destination.

It might be thought that some of these fish could be caught in the sea. Indeed, there are instances where fish can be taken in the salt water and they have been known to follow small spinning baits cast in front of a shoal, but usually they do not want to take the lure properly and shy away at the last minute. Of course they can be foul-hooked, but where is the sportsman who would really enjoy that? No. We owe the fish a bit more respect than to have to resort to those methods. The fact is that the fish will already have lost all appetite. Their vomerine teeth have withered and they seem only interested in their primary task of gaining access to their home waters and eventually spawning. If we could intercept these shoals of fish on the high seas while they were still feeding we would undoubtedly find them much easier to bring to the hook.

While the migrating shoals are fidgeting around the many bays and freshwater outlets there comes a moment, following rain in the hills, when the fish start to run. Much the same will be happening all along the coast and it is particularly noteworthy that each little feeder river or stream will have a precise height in order to facilitate the best running conditions. With too much water the fish get swept back to the sea. With too little there is insufficient flow for them to make it over the barriers. Even then there are some monumental mountaineering tasks for the fish to perform and it only needs a sight of the small stream at Amhuinnsuidhe Castle to marvel at the way they get up there at all.

In most instances it is only a matter of a few hours before the fish have gained access to the lochs. With experience it is possible to pick the right time to observe fish entering the lochs and then fishing the connecting streams may get you the odd fish. But usually you are better advised to wait a day and then try in the lochs. It may,

in fact, take more than one day for the fish to settle into their new home and there seems little doubt that they spend some time exploring their new abode and may not take your fly with great abandon until they have been there for a few days. A lot depends on the overhead conditions.

Angling potential on most stillwaters is heavily influenced by wind and weather. A flat calm under a semitropical July sun (which might just happen in the Hebrides) can make all your efforts a total waste of time. A good southerly or sou'westerly breeze, on the other hand, with odd bursts of sunshine, may transform your day into one of high activity. Shortly after running, fish tend to slash at flies without taking them properly. I recall one day when I counted no less than fifty-five rises to my flies but still went back to base with only three small sea trout. Sometimes the fish merely hang on temporarily and quickly get free. At other times there are big, oily, boils on the water near the flies with not a sign of a pull. Usually I

Two salmon laid side by side (their tails just showing) in the falls at Amhuinnsuidhe, Outer Hebrides.

An almost flat calm on Loch Voshimid renders fishing very difficult.

On the other hand a good southerly or sou'westerly breeze with bursts of sunshine may transform your day into one of high activity.

A Hebridean salmon and two sea trout, Loch Voshimid, Isle of Harris.

fish two flies and I recall one day when a a great slashing commotion near my flies produced not the slightest pull – I did not feel a thing! But when I examined my flies both had disappeared and it was obvious that two fish had come at the same instant and, instead of pulling against me, had pulled against each other and broken free.

Most of the stillwaters of my experience are best fished from a boat. Of course, bank fishing often pays dividends on stillwaters, but a boat gives you greater flexibility and with a competent gillie it may be possible to fish over the best places in a lake or loch without too much energetic exercise. Some of the Hebridean lochs are very similar to those in the west of Ireland and much of what I am going to write about stillwater fishing for migratory fish has been gleaned from experience in these places. In nearly all instances I have elected to fish from a boat and at all times I have fished in the company of my wife and been accompanied by a competent gillie.

TACKLE FOR STILLWATERS

My tackle for stillwater fishing is generally the same. I usually opt for the 10-foot 'Light Line' or the 11¼-foot 'Century', a no. 7 forward-taper line and a level leader, from a spool of monofilament of 6–8 lb test. Fly sizes vary between 10 and 14 and are never very big. I usually fish with just a tail fly and one dropper, but companions sometimes fish successfully with three flies. Usually I put a fly with fairly slender dressing on the tail and one with slightly heavier dressing on the bob. Very often it is the bob (dropper) fly that takes the salmon. Some anglers deliberately put a salmon fly on the point and a sea-trout pattern on the dropper, but the fish don't seem to be as aware of the difference as we are and it is frequently possible to get either fish on either fly.

On our first visit to Amhuinnsuidhe, trying to be the perfect gentleman, I bade my wife get into the stern of the boat while I took the short seat in the bow. The gillie then rowed us slowly and on a slightly crosswind tack over the best water. Just occasionally I would get a fish to make a pass at my flies and then, seconds later, my wife's rod would arch into a bow as a fish took her fly with a

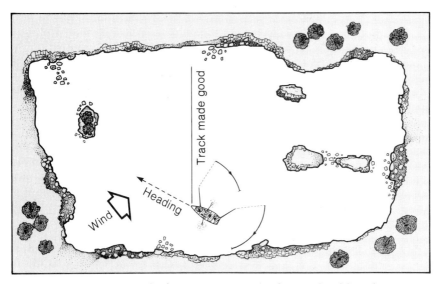

Fig 28   The gillie rows the boat across or into the wind. Although the heading is maintained the track made good is strongly influenced by the wind. Notice how the angler at the rear of the boat has a more commanding position than the angler at bow.

bang. At the end of our first three days her record of fish taken against mine made me look and feel like a veritable novice. My wife is a competent angler, but why the vast difference in the result? Could it, I pondered, be anything to do with the fact that she was in the stern of the boat and that I was always in the bow?

On our fourth day I took particular notice of the action of the flies. The slow passage of the boat was allowing my wife's flies to swing round nicely round the back of the boat, while my flies quickly swung into the vicinity of the gillie's oar. I had to make faster retrieves than my wife and it was often notable that at the moment my wife was hooking fish I was already making a new cast into fresh territory. Of course, I did have the advantage of covering fresh territory before my wife, but it seemed to be the final swing of the flies that gave her the advantage in terms of fish caught – particularly salmon!

Following this, and in attempts to overcome my disadvantage, I began to lengthen my casts to cover more water. This was usually followed by a slightly faster retrieve and it was not long before I started catching more sea trout than my wife while she continued to catch more salmon. Indeed, the very long cast and fast retrieve would often bring some of the bigger sea trout. One of 5 lb was my best, but there were several others in the 3 lb and 4 lb class. Most times it was not worth noting which fly they had taken. Sometimes it would be the dropper and at others the tail fly. In most instances with my wife, however, the salmon took the dropper as it was being lifted from the water and bobbing in the wave.

Of course, there are now plenty of times when things are reversed, but as a general rule, when fishing together on a loch, my wife catches more salmon than I do while I score better with the sea trout. Over the years that followed and in order to put this matter to a test, we have frequently changed places in the boat. But at all times it has been the one in the stern who has scored higher with the salmon than the angler in the bow. One memorable day when our gillie manoeuvred the boat in my favour during the morning I caught five fish to my wife's one. After lunch she got the pole position and promptly caught five to my one. We each came back to the castle with six fish. Had there been just one angler and a gillie in the boat the catch to one person could easily have been doubled.

However, I have to confess that the ladies seem to have a degree

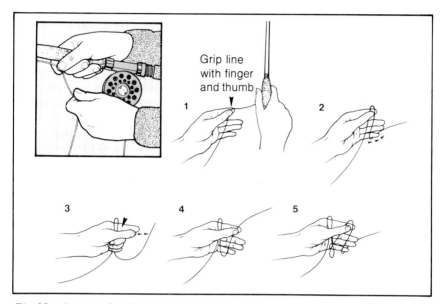

Fig 29   Figure of eight retrieve. Useful in a boat when line coiled in the hand may be re-shot in the next cast.

Fig 30   Salmon frequently take the dropper very close to the boat as the line is being lifted for the next cast.

of persistence with loch salmon that I do not have. Sometimes my wife will literally let her dropper dance on the wave until it is within a few feet of the back of the boat. Quite frequently the fish seem to take just as she is preparing to make the next cast and she admits to being fascinated by the prospect of a gawping mouth coming up from the depths to take her fly. For her that moment when a salmon sticks its head out of the water to take her fly is the most magical in all her fishing. Hélène Panchaud is even more successful and seems to be like a spider weaving a magical web over the fish to induce them into it. I recall one occasion when she came back to the castle with eleven salmon for her day. In her philosophy the sea trout are not even counted and are regarded with slight scorn.

There is little doubt in my mind, therefore, that when fishing the average salmon and sea-trout loch from a boat the angler who makes short casts and slow retrieves from an advantageous position in the boat may expect to catch salmon, while he who casts a long line, followed by a fast retrieve, will get more sea trout. Just occasionally my wife and I hang our rods over the side of the boat as the gillie rows upwind for a new drift. Almost invariably any fish caught are sea trout, but there have been one or two notable exceptions.

Fishing without a gillie on a strange piece of water represents a lot of speculation and a poor chance of making a noteworthy catch. There are some pointers to help you read the water and it may be helpful if the fish can be seen jumping. Most gillies who know their water well have favourite drift lines and it is a strange feature of any sort of stillwater fishing, even in the vast oceans of the world, that any form of cover frequently holds fish underneath it. In the case of sea fish, particularly in tropical waters under a hot sun, the fish will often be found sheltering under old bits of flotsam or floating weed. Indeed, and merely as an aside, I recall many hours spent searching for marlin in the Gulf of Mexico when our skipper spent his entire day looking for floating rubbish. In many instances a slow chug in the vicinity of rubbish, or a piece of wooden debris no bigger than a dustbin lid, would bring us a fish or two. We did not find the marlin, but the dolphin and king mackerel gave superb sport on light tackle.

In the normal course of events, thank heavens, you are unlikely to find floating rubbish on the average Hebridean loch, but there may be lines of scum or foam which seem to run in streets down the wind. These are good places to try for fish and it is remarkable just how much effect this apparently scant shelter has. That aside, of

course, there is no substitute for knowledge of the water and an ability to read the drift lines under prevailing wind conditions. One of the more popular Hebridean lochs which we frequently fish, Loch Voshimid, is studded with small rocky outcrops and islands. These are the places near which most of the fish seem to congregate and it is possible to make casts towards the banks and the overhanging vegetation of these rocks and islands and have your fly taken in a few inches of water.

Frankly, we never do very well in a flat calm and the fish seem not to want to come anywhere near the surface. Doubtless also they may see our flies for what they really are and it may need the ripple on the water to lend some dazzle and deception. On the other hand, there is a lot of evidence to demonstrate that fish are totally unafraid of a boat. When hooked, often very close to the boat, after a short but athletic run or two, the fish will invariably make for the shadow of the boat and may need some extra coaxing to get them from underneath and into the waiting net. I recall an incident when I was shooting some film of my wife playing a salmon. Shortly after being hooked it made for the shadow of the boat and stayed there throughout the entire time she had it in play. I was constantly seeking to get shots of it as it splashed, but it tucked its head down under that boat and did not show again until the final flurry of spray as the net went under it. The edited film shows a bent rod and the final flurry of the fish. Maybe my audience now wrongly assumes that salmon may be extracted in less than one minute of playing time!

NIGHT FISHING

With our Hebridean gillies following a normal daily routine it was not for some years that any of our party tried night fishing for sea trout. This is readily acknowledged as one of the finest ways of coming to terms with shy sea trout, but it was not until 1984 that, on arrival at Amhuinnsuidhe, we were greeted with the news that the party preceding us had spent much time fishing at night and had caught some superb sea trout, with the best one topping the nine-pound mark. Sadly, I am now of an age to be quite content to fish through the day but prefer to savour the delights of civilisation during the evenings. Despite the fact that I know I am probably

missing obvious good chances, I tend to sink back into my chair, drape my fingers around a good glass of malt-stained liquid and chat with my host.

It was not until July 1985 that, on the insistence of my host, there was one day when we altered our routine so that the gillies would be available for a late evening sortie. It was not a night on which I would normally have chosen to go sea-trout fishing, but at least it would eventually get dark and it was this aspect of the test that I was keen to exploit more than any other. There is an old cliché that suggests that a west wind and a wise man go to bed at night. While claiming no great wisdom, I was around sufficiently late that night to realise that the west wind had not got the message either. It blew and it rained and I could barely wait for my host to call a halt and order us all home. By some stroke of fortune I came back with two nice sea trout. The best would make the four-pound mark and there was another of about three pounds. Had the night been different, weather-wise, and had we stayed beyond midnight, I will concede that we might have had a mild bonanza.

In the principal Hebridean lochs where we fish, Lochs Scourst, Voshimid and Ulladale, the water tends to be comparatively shallow. This makes for ideal conditions in salmon and sea-trout lochs, but the influences of wind direction and strength do seem to have great bearing on catch potentials. On top of that, it is a fact that the sea-trout population outnumbers that of salmon by about six to one. What is interesting is that at certain times of the season both fish seem to share a similar behaviour pattern and it would be difficult to draw any conclusions with certainty just how their behaviour differs – other, of course, than the difference between the slow take of a salmon on a short line and the quicker take of a sea trout on a longer line. Both species seem to intermingle with their inward migration and both seem equally at home in each other's company while resting briefly in the short rivers. On those occasions when my wife and I have foraged downstream from the lochs and on towards the estuaries, it has not been possible to find sea trout separated from the salmon to any material extent. Sometimes the fishing in these little streams can be exceptionally easy. I recall one instance when my wife cast her line, with three flies on the leader, into a small but deep bend on the Voshimid stream and had all three flies taken by either salmon or sea trout. Two of the fish broke away in the ensuing affray, but a nice sea trout

of about 2½lb finally made it to the bank.

Fishing down these small outflow streams from the lochs is usually undertaken when a flood bringing fish suddenly stops short, as it were. This invariably means that the late-running fish get caught out with an early lack of water and thus have to hold up in the small rivers until the next flood. More than likely these little rivers would be back to summer level in hours rather than days. You then have to use all your hunting skills to move downstream, carefully reconnoitring each small pool to see if fish are resident. Sometimes the fish will see you before you see them. Even then it is possible to sit down for ten or fifteen minutes before making a cast over the pool from a concealed position. Usually the fish will then come for your flies as though they had never previously been disturbed. Such is the gullibility of some fresh-run fish.

It many instances it is not a long walk from one of the lochs down to the estuary. Here you find lots of fish, both sea trout and salmon, still milling about waiting for access or merely fidgeting around looking for home. Some fishing of these estuary pools may be quite profitable, but there are times when a lot of the fish might get foul-hooked, so it is up to the disciplined sportsman to know when to persist and when to desist. My experience is that you are more likely to foul-hook fish than to get them fairly in the mouth, but then I know of several instances when firm hooking in the mouth has been achieved and when the fly has been taken so greedily it has almost been swallowed. Sometimes the fish will merely roll at or over your fly as if it were nothing more than a mild irritant – there is often little apparent effort to take it. At other times you may detect no response whatever and may well find that nothing is happening except that your fly occasionally scrapes the back of a fish. It is in such conditions that you need some sporting discipline, for there can be no satisfaction in taking an unfair advantage and stabbing the hook somewhere into the fish other than in its mouth. Those fish that do take properly in these conditions, however, seem to do so with a degree of aggression rarely found at any other time.

The only other Hebridean water where I have limited experience is the Blackwater River on the Garynahine Estate in Lewis. Here the river alternates between rock-girt pools and semi-stagnant lochans or lakes. Even when carrying extra water there are some parts of the river which are virtually stagnant and for all intents and purposes it should be treated as an elongated lake or loch. I was there in July

Fishing on the Blackwater river at Garynahine, Isle of Lewis, Hebrides.

1985 and was successful in catching the first salmon of the season. It fell to a size 10 Connemara Black cast upstream on my 10-foot fly rod under an overhanging bank and then slowly handlined back again. I did not see the fish take but I felt the resistance and gave a firm strike. It was a fresh-run little salmon of 4lb with the sea lice still on it.

Fish hooked in the outlet pool in an estuary seem to be little bothered by moving in and out of fresh and salt water. With the changes required in body chemistry one would assume that these fish might not cope so readily, but there is no apparent distress when making the change in either direction. Fish seem to be able to swim straight out of the salt water and into the fresh on the slightest whim. They can then stay in fresh water for several hours before being hooked and promptly charging back to the salt water again.

In many instances the presence of salmon and sea trout in the Hebridean estuaries entices predatory seals close inshore to forage amid the migrating fish for an easily acquired meal. For some strange reason, although there is supposed to be a world shortage of seals, we seem to have more in Britain than is good for our general fish resources. Indeed, the many impassioned pleas for seal conser-

vation have resulted in the reduction or abolition of the culls and a great overall increase in the number of seals to eat our fish. On several occasions I have watched seals come into the bay and spread their general alarm and mayhem among the shoals of fish. Once I was standing on the castle parapet when I saw a seal emerge with a small salmon held firmly across its jaws. A shout caused the seal to dive, letting go of the salmon as it did so. Seconds later a salmon charged into the sanctuary of the seaweed almost at my feet. The water was so clear that I was able to take several photographs and note the seal's teeth marks on the fish before it slowly moved away.

On yet another occasion my host was fishing the sea pool and he hooked a small salmon. The fish fought well in the tidal bay and was just beginning to tire under the strain of rod and line when it apparently gained a second wind and shot off towards the open sea. Slowly but relentlessly it headed for the distant headland where the Atlantic tides rolled restlessly around the swaying kelp. Here it

Note the teeth marks of a seal on this salmon which shot into the shallow water in the bay at Amhuinnsuidhe at Arthur Oglesby's feet.

appeared to pause awhile, but just at that moment the large head of a seal appeared above the water line with a salmon held firmly across its jaws. Slowly the seal submerged again and the apparently relentless draw of the salmon continued. Of course, my tale ends just as the last trace of my host's backing was about to disappear off the reel with an inevitable straightening of the hook. That seal certainly got an easy supper that evening.

LINE COLOUR

To return to the more practical aspects of catching salmon and sea trout in lochs and lakes, however, we must spend a little time on the vexed question of line colour. While I do not think it to be of paramount importance in fishing the average river or stream, on lochs and lakes, and particularly those of Ireland and the Hebrides, I am partly convinced that line colour is important. I recall one year when I arrived at Amhuinnsuidhe to find that one of the other guests had arrived without an adequate reel and line. Travelling by air and with a consequent light baggage load, I was not over-equipped with tackle, but I lent the reel and line I had intended using myself to the other guest and I made do with a rather old and tatty back-up line which had got frayed at one end. This was of light-green colour while my good-quality line was white. My first reaction was that it would all be totally unimportant but at the end of the first day I was the only member of the party to come back with a fish or two.

By the middle of the week I was becoming embarrassed by the fact that my catches were outstripping those of everyone else. Even my wife, who normally beats me salmon-wise, was way behind, and it took me until the Friday to start wondering if it had anything to do with the colour and state of my line. That day I elected to spend most of the time with my cameras, but I pleaded with my wife to take my outfit and spend the day with that. As if to confirm my suspicion, she came back with more fish to her rod than were taken by anyone else that day. The colour of the line compared favourably with normal weed and reed colouring while the frayed end caused it to sink slightly lower than would have been the case with a fully floating line.

Those who became aware of my speculations quickly tried fishing with sink-tip lines, but they did not seem to have the same effect and

produced no result worthy of close analysis. Bidding my host farewell at the end of our stay, I thought to leave the reel and line with him. I don't suppose for one minute that he has tried it since, but I don't dare ask for it back again.

FLIES

In recommending fly selections for loch and lake fishing I am well aware that many of my readers will feel that the use of the right pattern will be of paramount importance. Sadly, I doubt if it matters one jot, but there are some patterns I would put on my leader in preference to others. For most stillwater salmon I think that it is a mistake to go for flies that are too lightly dressed. The ideal seems to be a fly that is slightly bushy and dabbles tantalisingly in the wave when it is being slowly lifted for the next cast. The Goat's Toe as tied by a regular visitor to Amhuinnsuidhe – Mr Peter Cowper-Coles – is proving to be a popular pattern on this account. It has a bushy black hackle, a black peacock herl body and a red tag at the tail. Such patterns may be tied on singles, doubles or trebles and a little size 10 or 12 treble finds great favour with many regular guests. Other patterns I have tried with success in the same size include the Connemara Black, Invicta, Grouse & Claret and the Heckam Peckam, but I have no doubt that other patterns fished in the preferred manner – preferred by the fish that is – would be equally successful.

DAPPING

Dapping is a frequently used method on many stillwaters, particularly for trout on the loughs of Ireland or the sea trout of Loch Maree. It can be a way of catching plentiful sea trout, but surprisingly rarely is it a reliable method for salmon. Oh, the fish will occasionally come to it in the same manner as they do to a dropper on a wet-fly cast, but they rarely take properly. However, it is a method to which I have only given occasional trial and I am therefore not fully competent to make any profound comment. One of the vexed questions that arises on the technique of dapping is knowing the precise moment to strike. Here again we seem to have

had to endure many handed-down comments from our experts – dogmas that seem to originate in the old lore. I can promise my reader one thing, however: any attempt to feed slack line at the moment of the take will almost certainly ensure that you won't so much as feel the fish that took your fly, let alone hook it.

As a method of fishing for sea trout dapping has some mild fascination. You sit in the boat, all the time guiding your fly back onto the water surface as it blows about in the breeze. Of course, it is essential to have a good wind ripple on the water and to be using the proper dapping tackle. A long double-handed salmon fly rod will often suffice to get the necessary water command and there are now plenty of synthetic floss lines on the market which have all the qualities of the old silk ones. A very short leader will do and it may be of fairly substantial strength and thus offer more control of the fly. In most situations the fish will not see the leader anyway and will only have eyes for that great, bushy fly bobbing on the wave.

In all forms of fly fishing on stillwaters, whether for salmon or sea trout, every rise seen should be responded to by an instant strike. It might just occasionally be possible to react quicker than the fish, but you are unlikely to pull the fly away from a fish very often. Certainly, by the time you *feel* a fish it is almost impossible to pull the fly away from it. The one thing you must bear in mind, however, is that the long cast and the fast retrieve will bring more offers from sea trout while the short cast and the slow retrieve will give you a better chance with the salmon.

STOCKED STILLWATERS

When I first became keen on angling in the early 1930s it was almost impossible to go trout fishing and catch hatchery-reared fish. Most were from wild-bred stock and it was possible to go to some upland burns and becks and catch all you could carry. There were few limits in those days and angling pressure was never very high. Since the war, however, the demands on our angling resources have increased almost beyond measure and we now rely almost entirely on the produce of the hatcheries to stock our rivers and lakes. Indeed, it is now a rare event to catch a wild-bred trout and one has to journey to the more remote parts of the kingdom to find a wild brown trout. Even our hallowed salmon rivers, such as the Spey, have populations

of escapee rainbow trout from hatcheries. The day seems to be coming, therefore, when the capture of a wild-bred trout will be a thing of the past.

In recent years we have also seen the continued trend towards the artificial farming of salmon. Sea trout have yet to be exploited and developed in this manner, but it is a safe bet that by the turn of the century we shall be farming and marketing many different types of fish. By 1985 there were already at least two stillwater salmon fisheries in existence, stocked with hatchery-reared fish and in that year I came in for some mild rebuke in the correspondence columns of *Trout and Salmon* for suggesting that the future for salmon fishing, for some at least, might involve fishing in a totally artificial environment, and that it should never be allowed to happen. If these critics had been around in the 1930s, would they have reacted in the same way to predictions that by the end of the century we should all be catching hatchery-reared trout and that wild-bred fish would hardly be found except in the more remote places? Thank God in fifty years I shall be little more than rotting bones and will not have to suffer the indignity of being asked to fish in a stewpond.

The artificial salmon fishery at Lichfield. Here impeller pumps stir the water into a current.

Arthur Oglesby fishing on the Dub Pool of the Upton Bishop
salmon fishery at Ross-on-Wye.

The development of artificial salmon fisheries is a natural
consequence of increased angling activity and the necessity for
providing salmon fishing for those who cannot get away to the
classic rivers or who cannot afford the expensive rents demanded.
Throughout history every need has eventually been met by the
entrepreneur. Salmon fishing is no exception and through the
invitation of Mr Tony Chattaway, whose skill and enterprise
realised the vision, I visited the fisheries at Ross-on-Wye and
Lichfield shortly after they opened. Salmon fresh from the sea
cages were starved for a few days and then transported in tankers
from Scotland and released into the freshwater impoundments.
Great care has to be exercised in the transportation of these fish, for
they are prone to suffer descaling, which causes them to absorb
water like a leaking boat and quickly die.

After release, the fish take a little time to recover from the
trauma they have experienced and may do several things. They may,
for instance, recommence their feeding cycle and for a while be
easily caught by the anglers. Theirs has not been a natural migration
into fresh water; they have merely been transferred into fresh water

at a time when all their instincts were to feed on every morsel of food available to them in the sea cages. Had they started a natural fast and developed the urge to migrate into fresh water for spawning it might have been a different tale.

On the other hand, the release into fresh water occasionally seems to trigger off signs of the start of appetite suppression. When this happens, the capture of these fish may in many ways reflect the tactics required to entice wild salmon to the hook. It is too early for me to make pedantic statements concerning the best ways of catching hatchery-reared fish which have been released into still-waters. Obviously it is not a type of fishing which has any great appeal for me, but it is filling a long-felt need for some and I have little doubt that we shall shortly see a new and eager type of pundit who will soon be telling us all about it.

Throughout this chapter I have tried to demonstrate that in specific instances and at certain times of the year there is a great similarity in the behaviour of salmon and sea trout. Indeed, I often neither know nor care which species I have hooked until I have it firmly in play or safely on the bank. But there *are* several striking differences in behaviour, and in the next chapter I shall examine some of the specific problems associated with the capture of sea trout on rod and line.

14
Sea Trout

There was an early morning chill. The kitchen light at Cragg winked invitingly from the distant fell. I thought of hot coffee and whisky and debated whether to pack up and go home. Then, with dramatic suddenness, a heavy splash – somewhere out in the darkness to my left, up near the head of the pool. 'Splosh' would fit it better: the sound a big fish makes when it lunges on the surface before sinking back to its lie. I could guess to a foot where it had risen: by a sunken rock under some sycamore branches on the far bank. An age-old lie for a big sea trout.

Hugh Falkus, Sea Trout Fishing

It would not do to assume that because sea trout and salmon are so closely related their behavioural aspects are also very similar or that they can be treated as the same species. There *are* instances, as in loch and lake fishing, where you may with similar tactics catch salmon or sea trout and not be too aware of why you do so. I often catch sea trout while I am salmon fishing and, conversely, when I am sea-trout fishing, particularly during a late evening in June or July, I am often quite content just to hook and play salmon. During July of 1975, for instance, there was never an evening when I was not immersed in a pool on the Spey by 10.30 p.m. Every evening also, without exception, the first fish I hooked was a salmon. Oh, I caught a few sea trout later on, but I suspect that I was playing my salmon at a time when the sea trout should have been taking at their best. But there are differences both in the behaviour of the fish and in the best techniques for tackling them.

IDENTIFICATION

Many years ago when science seemed content to simplify rather than baffle, it was fashionable to classify salmon as *Salmo salar*, sea trout as *Salmo trutta* and the brown trout as *Salmo fario*. These simple classifications satisfied the angler and adequately defined three

Despite their apparent forked tails, these are Hebridean sea trout from Loch Voshimid.

distinct but closely related species. Eventually, because the sea trout is basically a brown trout turned mariner, it had to share the classification *Salmo trutta* with the brownie. The marked colour and behavioural differences we see in sea trout and brown trout are totally disregarded by the scientist.

Many anglers with limited experience find great difficulty in recognising what to them appear to be only subtle differences between salmon and sea trout. Even today it is possible to see photographs in books and articles where the fish is clearly not of the species claimed in the caption. All too frequently I see photos in coarse fishing magazines of an angler holding up a tatty-looking stale salmon, claiming that he has just caught a specimen brown trout. Such misidentification is nothing new. Indeed, there was a time when all migratory fish tended to be lumped under one heading – salmon. Even today in fishmongers' shops it is traditional to label sea trout as salmon trout. Back in the middle of the last century all migratory fish on the Yorkshire Esk were classed as one species. I am told that if you were enquiring about a specific fish or fishes you had to ask most critically whether they were salmon, sea trout, bull

Milan Halenar with his sea trout of 24lb from the river Em, Sweden.

trout or brownies.

It is when fresh-run sea trout are being compared with fresh-run salmon of similar size that most novices seem to have a problem. The first thing to note is the shape of the tail. Even when straightened the salmon's tail will still have a slight concave fork in it. The tail of a mature sea trout, on the other hand, will be fairly straight and in large fish it may even be slightly convex.

The next test is to pick the fish up by the tail with a moistened hand while the fish is still moist. It will be a safe bet that the sea trout will slip from your grasp while a salmon may be held. There are other signs – such as scale reading and the position of the eyes in relation to the maxillary – but I rely on a combination of the shape of the tail, the thickness of the wrist and the general overall appearance. Most fresh sea trout look fatter, pound for pound, than salmon. As a consequence, a sea trout usually looks a little shorter

Sea trout of nearly 3lb from the River Kent, Cumbria.

than a salmon of similar weight. Spots and marks on the flanks and gill covers also give some guidance – most sea trout have more spots beneath the lateral line than salmon.

When you have gained a lot of experience at recognition you may well wonder why you had any initial problems at all. Only occasionally am I slightly puzzled these days, and then I usually suspect some general mayhem in the hatcheries, when a hatchery operative, whether for devilment or lack of experience, occasionally interbreeds a salmon and a sea trout and produces some hybrid mule. I hope that the photographs will help you with this important identification.

HABITS

As a start, therefore, it will not do to assume that sea trout are brown trout and that the techniques for catching browns will be equally successful in catching sea trout. It may indeed be that, over the passage of time, resident brown trout in particular had good reasons (probably overpopulation combined with lack of food) for migrating downstream and feeding in the sea. It is well established

A sea trout jumps at Sleights weir on the Yorkshire Esk.

that the family *Salmo* are anadromous and quite capable of alternating between salt water and fresh as they please. Like salmon, of course, nature compels them to travel back into fresh water to spawn. If they were to shed their spawn in salt water it is possible that the specific gravity of sea water would cause the eggs to float and thus render them incapable of being fertilised.

A sea trout, therefore is a brown trout which, for reasons best known to itself, has migrated to the sea, found a vast feeding ground and has come back to the river of its birth as a fine sporting fish and a culinary delight. Thus we have a new kind of trout – a trout which shares some behavioural patterns with its close brethren salmon and brown trout, but which, through evolution, has developed into a separate race with a characteristic behaviour of its own.

Although much is now known about the life-cycle of the salmon, there are still too many assumptions where sea trout are concerned. We presume that they spawn at a similar time to both salmon and brown trout and in similar locations. Their emergence from the redd is also based on a time and temperature basis, and they go through the alevin, fry and parr stages in much the same manner as salmon. No one seems quite certain how long they are likely to

remain as parr and then change into smolts, but it is assumed that it takes about three years – an assumption which, I suspect, could be totally wrong.

On reaching the smolt stage the fish don a silvery coat, move downstream after the fashion of migrating salmon smolts and disappear, as it were, into the vast ocean. Here it seems that even less is known about sea-trout movement than about salmon. Rumour suggests that once the fish have reached the estuary they do not travel very far. Indeed, there is another type of sea trout, also known as slob or bull trout, which seem to spend most of their lives in or near the estuary and which come back into the rivers at a similar time to some late-running sea trout. The boffins tell us that these fish are merely very old sea trout which have acquired different colouring. In certain instances I think that the two are dissimilar, but those bull trout which I used to catch on the Yorkshire Esk looked just as though they had travelled no further in the sea than the seaweed beds near the estuary. They had a similar appearance to those codling which live on or near rocks close inshore and lacked the silvery beauty of a fresh-run sea trout.

Of course, the longer a sea trout stays in fresh water the more it begins to resemble a bull trout or an old brownie. Many competent anglers visiting the Spey with me in the early months of the year have frequently knocked a sea-trout kelt on the head in the almost certain belief that it was an old brownie going back a bit. But I hope that my photographs illustrate all too clearly the difference between a fresh sea trout and a recently run bull trout.

There is ample evidence that sea trout can and do make some remarkable migrations. Hugh Falkus, in his excellent book *Sea Trout Fishing,* draws our attention to an instance where a sea-trout kelt, tagged on the River Exe in Devon, was recaptured 266 days after liberation in the estuary of the River Tweed. He then goes on to express the opinion that sea-trout smolts probably do not migrate very far until they have made an early return to the river as herling or finnock, but that many older and mature sea trout probably rove more widely. This seems reasonable, although it is known that sea trout are able to make many spawning returns to the river of their birth. This behaviour is uncharacteristic of the salmon, however, which will be fortunate to survive much more than one spawning return. All in all I suspect that there is a deal of speculation involved in our assessment of the life-cycle of sea trout while at sea and that

we are not fully aware of their behaviour patterns until the fish
come back to the rivers again.

As I have noted, there is some evidence to suggest that after
migration as smolts the young sea trout spend only a short time in
the sea and then come back as herling or finnock during the autumn
of that same year. They may come in merely to keep the mature sea
trout company, as it were. There is little evidence to suggest that
they spawn on this occasion, but in such a river as the Spey they
seem quite prepared to overwinter and not move back to the sea
again until March or April of the following year. Indeed, there are
many anglers who derive great pleasure in catching herling or
finnock during the early months of the season. I am not fully
convinced that it is ethically correct to catch them at all, but they
can be great fun on an early spring day and may be quite acceptable
on the table. Although they tend to be lean from a shortage of food it
seems fairly certain that they are not kelts and this may be sufficient
justification for anglers catching and killing them.

In addition to being known as herling and finnock these same fish
have other local names. In Ireland, for instance, they are frequently
known as white or lammas trout. In Devon they answer to peal and
in Wales to sewin. The north country offers a title 'whitling' and it
is this latter name which appeared in an Act of Parliament in 1844
and was probably the most widely known name in those days. Much
information may be gleaned from *The Life of the Sea Trout* by G. H.
Nall and published by Seeley, Service & Co. in 1930 or *The Sea Trout
– A Study in Natural History* by Henry Lamond and published by
Sherrat & Hughes in 1916. I suspect, however, that a lot of the
information we have on sea trout may be erroneous. It is not a fish
with the same charisma as salmon and consequently it has not
enjoyed the same detailed research which has gone to its more blue-
blooded relation.

After the return of the finnock or whitling to the sea there is a
slight breathing space before the first of the summer runs of mature
sea trout enter our rivers. A lot depends on the river system, its
overall length and the availability and temperature of the water. On
a river like the Spey, for instance, it may be as early as April when
the first runs of sea trout make it into the river. Often by early May
you could be catching beautiful fresh-run sea trout as high upstream
as Grantown. Certainly by the end of May and into early June the
runs and sporting activity are reaching a peak. No doubt these runs

An early season sea trout is played on the Spey.

continue to be augmented throughout the summer, but the rivers then become very dependent on rainfall to top them up from time to time and, as with salmon, there is a marked deterioration in the appearance and quality of the fish the longer they stay in fresh water. By August and September the sea trout in the upper reaches above Grantown are barely worth having and would be best left unmolested to fulfil their prime task on the spawning redds.

Mature sea trout can grow to some remarkable weights. The British record, a fish of 22½ lb, was caught on the Dorset Frome in 1946, but this is not an exceptional fish for some rivers and in Sweden's River Em they catch a lot of twenty-plus pounders every year. My picture of Milan Halenar of Stockholm shows him proudly holding a specimen of 24 lb which he took from the Em in the

autumn of 1985. It is a beautifully shaped deep fish most worthy of becoming glass-cased. The average British sea trout, however, will vary markedly in size with the specific river system. In the old days, when I used to spin for sea trout on the little Yorkshire Esk, it was rare to catch a fish under 3lb. My first sea trout there weighed 5lb and there was a late run of bull trout which could go anywhere up to 15lb. Alas, I am reliably informed that such fish are no longer found in the Esk. Indeed, on a recent visit, merely to watch fish leaping over the weir at Sleights, I did not see anything of consequence except a few diminutive sea trout of little more than 1½lb.

On a river like the Spey, on the other hand, the sea trout may be said to average about 2lb. There are smaller fish just as there are a lot of larger fish, but my best Spey sea trout fell just short of 7lb and was taken in the semi-darkness of a June evening several years ago. In the Hebrides the school sea trout tend to be about 1lb while there is a sprinkling of other fish up to 5lb and the oddity almost up to double figures. On many of our other rivers where sea trout abound, such as those on the west coast of England, Scotland and Wales, it is usually late June or July before the first runs come in. Most of these runs will be induced by a good spate and the sea trout often join forces with a summer run of salmon and come in on the same tides. This is the time when many of our spate rivers give us our first chance of sport – rivers like the Cumbrian and Yorkshire Esks, Lancashire's Lune and Wales' beloved Dovey. It is frequently a short season, and hard work is called for to get the greatest benefit from nature's bounty.

During the early days of the runs into fresh water it is quite possible to catch fish on similar flies to those we might use for wet-fly trout fishing. Indeed, there have been many occasions on the river Lune when I have been there following a summer flood and have tackled up with a 10-foot trout fly rod, a no. 7 floating line and three flies on a 6lb test leader. On one memorable day I just happened to be there when a run of sea trout came in. It was an occasion when I had that great all-round sportsman, Jim Deterding, fishing with me. On one cast all three of his flies were taken by sea trout. He remembered to net the bottom fish first and was eventually successful in getting all three into the net. There was a short spell that evening when the fish went semi-berserk to get at our flies. There were no monsters, but we must each have caught a

'Is this really happening to me?' Jim Deterding playing three
sea trout on the River Lune at Newton, Lancashire.

score or more before they went quiet or, more likely, moved on
upstream.

For as long as the water holds up with a tinge of colour and for as
long as the fresh fish come in, it is possible to have superb sport in
daylight. There comes a time, however, and often very soon after a
summer flood, when the water clears and falls back to a bare trickle.
This is when the sea trout tend to be confined to the deeper pools.
They seem to love the sanctuary afforded by overhanging trees and
they then become almost uncatchable during the hours of daylight.
This is the time to alter your cycle and rhythm of life. Now the best
times to be searching for sea trout will be between the hours of dusk
and dawn. And, when the sea trout fever hits you hard, there is
nothing that will keep you in bed – not even a new wife!

As soon as the magic of the flood has passed and the river has
fallen back to summer level any temptation to seek sea trout in
daylight must be resisted. You are more likely to frighten the fish
and it may be possible to scare them so much that they will move out
of the area. Of course, in very small streams it may be that there are
few places for them to go, but they are quite capable of moving
through water barely deep enough to cover their backs and I have
watched them many times, during the late season, skittering their

way through shallow pools and on upstream. Bear in mind also that
fish seen during daylight on our larger rivers may well move with the
onset of darkness. In many instances it is a mistake to start fishing
too early – 10.30 p.m. is soon enough on most June and July nights
on the Spey and it makes sense to start with a floating line and two
flies on the leader. I tend to stick to the traditional sea-trout
patterns, such as the Invicta, March Brown, Mallard & Claret and
Blue & Silver, but I am not at all convinced that the pattern
matters one jot, particularly in the half or full darkness of a summer
night. The size might matter a lot more and there is some sense, as I
shall hope to show, in fishing deep with a sunk lure once the surface
rise has finished and the fish have gone down.

Many ideal sea-trout evenings come when a myriad of natural
insects can be seen dancing in the car headlight beams. They might
follow a shower of rain or when there is a soft, warm breeze from
the south or west so that natural flies may hatch in abundance. The
first signs of sea-trout movement may be tell-tale plops, gulps or
jumps in the air as the fish move into the glides or tails of the pools.
Providing it is sufficiently dark it may then be permissible to ease
your way into the water and start casting. Initially it will help if you
start on the rough streams and leave the glides until later. You
should use all the skills of the hunter, wade cautiously and do make
certain that you are on a piece of water which is totally familiar to
you or one which you have thoroughly reconnoitred in daylight. You
must wade with the confidence of a blind person walking around his
house. There must be no risk of stepping into an unknown deep hole
or getting caught by an overfast current and being swept downstream. Try to avoid tell-tale ripples spreading from your body as
you wade. These ripples will not matter too much later on when it is
totally dark, but they might initially induce the fish into cautious
mood and diminish your chances of a good catch.

Usually, following a recent run of fish, the sport at this time can
be little short of hectic. There will be just sufficient light to see
where your flies are alighting and to respond instantly to the fish
seen attacking them. As the night darkens you might have to rely on
the feel of the take rather than the vague sight of it. Somehow,
though, throughout the gloaming period, there is something magical
about that vicious pull at your fly, when you are suddenly attached
to an express train and your reel screams in protest. It may only be a
game little fish of two or three pounds, but it could be one of double

'The first signs of sea trout movement may be tell-tale plops,
gulps or jumps in the air as the fish move into the glides on
tails of the pools. It may then be permissible to ease your
way into the water and start casting.'

figures that will test your skill before it is brought safely to the net.

The snag with most forms of night fishing for sea trout is that
once a fish has been hooked you will usually have to wade out to the
shallows or the bank to land it. It may be difficult to see the fish in
the dark and I have known occasions when successful netting has
taken quite some time. Then there is the problem of finding your
way back into the river to the precise spot where you first hooked
your fish, in order to continue. Invariably you don't make it to the

exact spot and you may well spend some time fishing down over
water you have already covered. Alternatively, the bad light might
cause you to miss the best portion of the water and not get the bag
you might have done. Nowadays, therefore, on the specific occasions when I go sea-trout fishing at night, I have a large polythene
fertiliser bag, originally intended to hold 50 kilos or more, which I
attach to the top of my breast waders and then weigh down with a
stone in the bottom. With this I can wade down a pool, hook a fish
and play it from where I stand. I might have to play it a bit longer
than might be necessary if I were going to beach or net it; but by the
time it is played out it is but a simple matter to lead it to where I am
standing, grasp the fish behind the gills, remove the hook and
instantly drop it into my waiting sack. Then, from the precise
position where I first hooked that fish, I can continue casting in my
search for the next one. You may suggest that this is not an ethical
way of doing things and that you prefer to use traditional methods
with a net. The choice is yours!

So long as the sea trout continue to show interest in small flies
fished on the floating line, I think that this is an easier way of fishing
than by any other method. There comes a time on most sea-trout
nights, however, referred to by Hugh Falkus in sporting metaphors
as 'half-time', when the fish go off the take and apparently go down
for the night. It is at this stage of the proceedings that many anglers –
myself often included these days – having drawn the wrong
conclusion that it is all over, pack up for the night. Were you to take
time out for a quiet period of reflection, rest, or a chat with a friend
over a cosy dram of Scotch, you might well change over to the
sinking line and a large sunk lure and continue fishing through to the
dawn.

The fact that the fish have gone down does not eliminate the
chances of one of them taking a lure near the bottom. In fact some
of the largest sea trout you might encounter could come *after* the
magic period of the rise in the 'first half' and the period of 'half-
time' when sport goes dead, in what is known as the 'second half'. I
recall a pitch-black night on the Lune many years ago. I had four
nice sea trout in the bag before the fish went down and I then
tackled up with a sinking line and a large tandem lure. It was about
1 a.m. before I started fishing the same water over again and I had
not been casting for many minutes when the rod was nearly pulled
out of my hand as, with a crashing leap, a monstrous sea trout

jumped in the darkness. My leader snapped with a twang and the line catapulted back to me and festooned itself around my face. Within a split second my encounter was over, a brief brush with one of the most vigorous fish I have ever felt or heard. It would be silly to speculate about its weight or whether it might have been foul-hooked, but I should dearly love to know.

On another occasion I was fishing the Lune in the company of Hugh Falkus. We were sharing a rod and a large bottle of Scotch. At Hugh's insistence we abandoned fishing with a floating line around midnight. Then, fishing a sinking line and one of his tandem lures, we took it in turns to wade out into the shallows at the tail of a pool. For the next hour or so we each caught a sea trout at every cast. We followed the ritual of netting by toasting each fish as it came ashore. We continued to take turns to cast with the result that by about 3 a.m. we had over twenty sea trout on the bank and we were already developing slight lists alternating between port and starboard while deep wading. The irony of this particular incident came when a friend drove down to the river just before dawn to ask what we were fishing with and how we were doing. When told that we were using the sunk lure and were catching a fish at every cast, he boldly retorted that we would do much better on the floating line. For the life of me I could not understand his logic. Surely it cannot

Popular sea trout lures for use on sinking lines.

be possible to do better than catch a fish at every cast?

It is a long time now since I have spent an entire night on a sea-trout river. It is simply that the inclination to fish for twenty-four hours a day has long since gone. It is not so bad if you can adjust your lifestyle to go fishing through the night and take an adequate rest during the daytime, but to attempt to fish for salmon during the day and then attack the sea trout at night requires more stamina than I now seem to possess.

In my experience catching sea trout falls into two distinct categories. In the early days of the run and during those late evenings when they are to be seen rising boldly, they are one of the easiest fish to catch. But there comes a time when they become cautious and not only difficult to tempt to the hook but almost impossible. Even then Hugh Falkus suggests that there is not a night in the season when you might not get an offer. Moonlight is generally regarded as being bad for the fish and any drop in air temperature below that of the water is said to tend to put fish well down onto the bottom. But even then there is still a chance with the big sunk lure and it is a mistake to assume that under the cover of darkness you might not get a chance.

A disadvantage of some heavily-fished association water is that the fish tend to be over-molested. Some anglers don't mind intimidating fish with sunken lures and seem quite content to stab the hooks into any point on a fish's anatomy. Legitimate fishing of such places becomes a highly speculative operation and one that I cannot now be bothered to undertake. Far better that you seek some barely accessible place well off the beaten track and concentrate your attention there.

As if to reinforce this view I recall a gentleman who came on one of my midsummer courses on the Spey. He complained to me at breakfast one morning that he had been out the previous night searching for sea trout, but that the best pools were being ham-mered into foam by the scores of anglers who were fishing the best water. I told him to forget about those known best places for sea trout and concentrate on the small streams and stickles away from the crowds. He went out again that night and it was a joyous grin I got at breakfast time the following morning when he proudly announced that he had just caught three sea trout.

During much of my time on the Spey in June, July and August I used to adopt a routine of fishing for salmon during the morning, taking lunch at the hut and then retiring to my bed almost until

Grace Oglesby beaches a small sea trout on Pollowick, on the
Spey at Castle Grant.

dinner time, when I would casually finish my dinner, have another
brief cast for the salmon in the main pool until 10.30 p.m., and then
concentrate on the sea trout. I never did make any monumental
baskets of fish, but it was not unusual to come back to base with five
or six fish for a couple of hours' work. Only rarely did I stay out
much beyond 1.30 a.m. but there were occasions when I would take
a temporary rest about 1 a.m., have a dram in the hut, and then
continue until dawn. June nights are not over-long in Strathspey and
when I was much younger it was no great hardship to stay up until
dawn and watch the world come back to life under the eastern sky of
a new day.

In general terms the darker the night the better will be your
chances of a good basket of sea trout. But perhaps this statement
needs some qualification and the short nights of June present a
different situation from the much longer nights of August and
September. Frankly, were I to fish for sea trout in September, as I
used to do on the Yorkshire Esk many years ago, I would rarely
bother starting later than about 6.30 p.m. and would then call it a
day just as darkness was falling at about 7.30 or 8 p.m. Never once

did I persist until midnight even, and all the reports from those who tried indicated that they usually wasted their time.

It is important in night-fishing to have a good torch handy and one or two leaders already assembled with the appropriate flies tied on. I used to have at least two leaders ready and loosely draped around my hat. One would have a duo of flies for use with a floating line while the other would have a single tandem sinking lure. It is a dark night indeed when you cannot get sufficient light to see to change leaders merely by holding your line and leader up against the sky. Failing that, you should retire well away from the bank and use a torch.

It is said that shining your torch on the water is the one sin you must not commit if you hope to catch fish at night. In practical terms I don't think that it matters too much. One of the biggest sea trout I ever caught on the Lune, a fish of 6lb, was taken a few minutes after a friend had driven his car down the river bank on dipped headlights. Of course, it makes sense to lie low and use a torch only when you have to. Most certainly you do not want to be flashing it over the water like a miniature lighthouse beacon.

Casting at night poses problems for some anglers, but satisfactory night fishing will only come to those who have developed their casting so that they do it automatically. Initially it might help to make a few daylight casts over the piece of water you are going to fish at night. Get the feel of how much line you need to cover the water. Better still, tie a thread of cotton round the line at a point where the correct length to cover the water is just at your fingertips. When pulling line off the reel for casting you will quickly feel your previously assessed limit.

Just occasionally, and for no apparent reason, you might find yourself attached to what seems a very large fish. It might fight with less verve and panache than your average sea trout, but it could be a salmon that has taken your fly and will make a very welcome addition to your basket. It would not do to assume that all offers from sea trout will come with a vicious slash or pull at your fly. I have known some of my biggest sea trout to take so delicately that I might have assumed that little more than a floating leaf had merely touched the fly. All suspected offers should be treated with a firm strike. Quite often the gentle takes come from those fish which have been in the water a long time, while the slashing, vicious rises and offers come from fish which are fresh-run and in an abandoned mood to take anything that crosses their path.

Playing fish at night also poses problems of its own. You may not be able to see your line or gain even the most remote clue exactly where your fish is. I have sometimes detected my fish apparently charging hard upstream only to hear it seconds later in a crashing leap somewhere downstream of me. The fish may turn and change direction with the speed of lightning and you may never be sure what to do until it is more subdued and getting nearer the time when it might succumb to the waiting net. Hugh Falkus once hooked a sea trout of 13lb which beached itself on its very first run. The battle was over and the fish was knocked on the head in less than a minute.

Sometimes it may be a profitable exercise to apply white or luminous paint to the rim of your landing net. Even then it is not easy to see it in the pitch darkness of a moonless, cloudy night. You might think it should be possible to hand-tail a sea trout in much the same manner as I have described for salmon, but remember that the sea trout has a thicker wrist to its tail and that the tail section is liable to collapse and the fish slide out of your hand. If you must get the fish out by hand it is much simpler to wait until it is fully played out and then grasp it firmly behind the gills with forefinger and thumb. In order to do that, of course, you have to see the fish, but if all visual aids fail you and you can neither see to net it or grasp it with your hand then there is only one sensible thing left to do. Shine your torch on it so that you can see exactly what you are doing.

Most tactical considerations in fishing the fly for sea trout involve the same basic downstream-and-across tactics you would normally use for salmon. At night the sea trout usually chooses to lie in different water from that chosen by salmon, but there may a movement into shallower water by both species and it is important to know, or be told, just where the best places for sea trout are.

There is nothing worse than stumbling about in the dark wondering where to go and what to do. Ideally, you should be on or near the water long before dark and a good half-hour before you start fishing. This will enable you to watch the water carefully, and, when the fish movement starts, to take note of where the fish are. Sometimes they will decide to move and the thoughtful angler will have been at pains to reconnoitre and have some clue to where they might move if the sport in his immediate vicinity suddenly goes dead.

I recall a late evening spent in the tail of Pollowick on the Spey, a portion of that pool also known as Green Bank. In summer this pool is usually too low and too slow to bother with in daylight. Indeed,

the fish may not even be there in daylight, but will move in at the onset of dusk and darkness, cruising around in the shallows, and they can be seen foraging about chasing flies and moths. I waited until it was past 10.30 p.m. before I eased my way into the pool. A few short casts explored the water in the immediate vicinity of my wading ripples to no effect. Longer casts eventually had me covering most of the water and it was not long before I heard a splash and my rod hammered into a tight bow. The reel sang and there were more jumps before I got the fish under control and brought it over the rim of my waiting net. This fish was quickly followed by numbers two, three and four, but thereafter, and well before what I considered would be half-time, the water went dead and I could not catch another thing.

Moving back upstream, I decided to have another cast or two in the main stream of Pollowick. I had not been fishing very long before the rod arched over again and I was into number five. Another two came to the bank before I called a halt and I could only conclude that the fish that had been in Green Bank when I started my operations had moved into the stream of Pollowick – although there are endless other possible explanations.

Many of the really good sea-trout places on the Spey are also good salmon taking places during daytime. In fact, there are many evenings when I go fishing for sea trout neither knowing nor caring what I may catch. The tail of Dunbar Pool on the No. 3 Castle Grant water is a known good lie at any time when May is out. It is also a super place for sea trout. Much the same applies to a pool known as Slopeaka on the No. 1 Castle Grant beat: a superb pool for salmon throughout most of the season, but also a wonderful place for sea trout just on dusk.

As the river gets low, one of the main attractions of any pool or piece of water is the shelter it affords the fish under the long hours of daylight and the possibility of a hot sun. Sea trout, and most fish species for that matter, love to be under the shelter of overhanging trees. In such locations, provided there is a bit of streamy water, they may occasionally be caught in daytime on a low water. Take care only to fish in the very broken runs at the neck or tail of a pool and do remember that the same tactics regarding effective water command will apply as much with sea trout as they do with salmon. It usually helps to throw a long line and to wade cautiously.

Although some sea-trout anglers are quite content to use the

Grace Oglesby plays a leaping sea trout on Loch Ulladale,
Harris, Hebrides.

same double-handed rod as they would use for salmon fishing, I
much prefer to fish with a 10-foot or a 10½-foot single-handed rod
in carbon fibre. It has been my good fortune to test several
prototype rods for both sea trout and salmon and I see little need for
the rather cumbersome and stiff-actioned built-cane rods which
used to be so popular when I first started fishing for sea trout.
Except for boat fishing, where the longer rod has an advantage in
tripping the flies over the wave, I see little reason for going any
longer than 10 feet.

In all types of fly fishing for sea trout it pays not to be too
regimented on the choice of fly pattern and size. Many of the flies
now used with great success on our reservoirs for trout will often
catch sea trout. I am thinking specifically of those lure-type flies
such as the Muddler Minnow and the Baby Doll. Although I have not
tried a Dognobbler I would not mind betting that at times it
would take sea trout almost as well as any other lure. The tandem

lure as devised by Hugh Falkus, however, is a good, reliable pattern. It may be tied in a tandem arrangement of single sneck-bend hooks or you may, sometimes with greater effect, tie in a treble hook at the tail in lieu of a single. Don't be afraid to make your lures big. Sometimes the very big lure offers just the right formula or image for a big sea trout.

The best of the sea-trout season is all too short. Usually you will be able to confine your useful fishing to the months of June, July and August. Indeed, it may still be possible to catch some fish in September and October, but most are getting past their best and are not worth eating anyway. It may have been permissible to fully exploit the resource a few years ago when nature, in her great bounty, seemed able to cope with the heavy predations of mankind. But there is now too much indiscriminate fishing and because the sea trout lacks the charisma of a salmon it lacks the attention it deserves from those involved in conservation. There is also a tendency merely to hope that the Almighty will continue to provide without any other assistance.

15

Fly Fishing through the Season

The Ancients wrote of the three ages of Man: I propose to write of the three ages of the fisherman. When he wants to catch all the fish he can. When he strives to catch the largest fish. When he studies to catch the most difficult fish he can find, requiring the greatest skill and most refined tackle, caring more for the sport than the fish.
Edward R. Hewitt, A Trout and Salmon Fisherman for
Seventy-Five Years

THE EARLY SEASON

Let me start by taking you up to the banks of the River Tweed in time for the opening day there on 1 February. Let me assume that you have access to a beat in the vicinity of Kelso; that the water is a few feet above normal, but running clear; that there is an icy chill in the air and that the water and air temperatures are similar at around 35° or 40°; that you know or can see that the river has a good stock of spring fish; and that, initially, you are going to fish from a boat.

For the first two weeks of the season on Tweed you will be bound by a fly-only rule so there will be no temptation to consider other methods and little difficulty in deciding to put up your 15-foot carbon fly rod, a no. 11 sinking shooting-head line and a stout leader of about twenty-five pounds test. You will possibly choose a rather garish-looking tube fly of between two and a half and three inches and, since he will know the strength of the current and the depth of the pools better than you, you may seek your boatman's advice on the weight of this fly and whether it should be mounted on a light, polythene tube or a heavy brass tube. He will then move you out in

Breaking ice on the Wintercast Pool of the Tweed, where
fly-only rules apply for the first two weeks of the season.

the boat and when you are positioned on the edge of the current he
will suggest that you start casting.

Initially it will help to make a few short casts out towards the
opposite bank, pulling a yard or two of line and backing off the reel
at every cast until your boatman suggests that you have sufficient
line out. Always remember, however, that the longer cast will
enable your fly to get further down in the water and that holding up
the rod point in the expectant erection position, immediately
following your cast, will keep more line off the water, as it starts its
swing, and thus lets the fly sink further down anyway. Don't be in
too much of a hurry to strip the backing in for the next cast. Let the
fly dangle for a second or two behind the boat and then only casually
pull in the first two or three loops of backing. There may be many
instances during the cold weather of early spring and late autumn
when fish will slowly follow the fly and only take it as it is being
withdrawn back upstream. Sometimes, but more particularly in the
autumn, I have had my fly snatched when I have been handlining the
backing in at full speed.

All the time you are fishing try to take careful note of how much

your boatman moves the boat between each cast. Most times, when you come to the best taking places, he will let your fly cover the area more thoroughly. In any event maintain your same rhythm and style and don't forget about the slight pause before you start the retrieve for the next cast.

By 11 a.m. you are getting down to the middle of the pool on which you started, the current is easing a little, and you sense that your fly may be going down a little too deep. Frankly, this won't matter so long as you are not actually scraping the bottom too frequently, but if this does occur then it will be better if you change your fly for one of the same length and colouring as your original choice but tied on a lighter tube.

At the very next cast you feel an exciting tug on the line and a fish is on. It pulls and thrashes on the surface and eventually starts to come towards you with, perhaps, a little greater ease than you might have thought normal. Although quite bright-looking, the fish looks a little lean and your boatman offers the early remark, 'It might be a kelt.' The fish is duly netted and a close look inside the gills reveals that they are covered in maggots. Some of the fins are ragged and

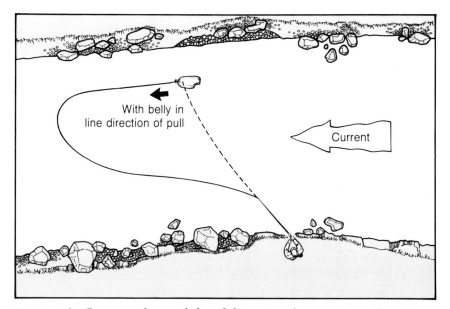

Fig 31   If a fly snags when sunk line fishing, its release may be effected by merely paying off line so that the current forms a downstream belly. A subsequent strike will frequently release the fly from its snag.

torn and the vent is distended. You do not need to be very clever to deduce that it is a kelt and you promptly remove the hooks and put it back.

Bear in mind that not all kelts will be quite so easy to identify. Some may fight with a deal of stamina and may look a lot more handsome than stale fish which, although they have not spawned, have been in the river a long time. Take care also to check whether any fish you catch is a baggot or what Tweed fishermen call a kipper. These are respectively unspawned or partially unspawned female and male fish and used to be encountered fairly frequently several years ago when I fished the Tweed in February.

While most baggots are quickly identified by the fact that they begin to extrude eggs fairly quickly when handled, there will be times when they carry sea lice and when the eggs may not be shed until after you have knocked the fish on the head. Kippers (unspawned male fish) are more easily identified and usually have a partial hook or kype uncommon in fresh-run springers. They may also show slight discoloration and some may only be partially spawned and still seeking another mate to complete final and total orgasm. Remember that both are classed as unclean fish and it is unlawful to kill them.

With the kelt safely returned it is not long before you feel another slow draw at the fly. The line just stops rather solidly and you may wonder, as I frequently do when I hook a salmon on the sunk line, whether it is a fish or whether I have merely snagged on the bottom. But you then feel that electric movement as the fish backs away. It may be that there is little initial activity and your boatman will have ample time to row slowly for the shore. In these early months, and particularly on the Tweed, he will know that it is not likely to be a very big fish and that the chances of it taking you a long way from where you hooked it will be slight. Nonetheless, he will maintain the boat just out from the bank until he is convinced that you are in full control. Only then will he row for the shore, tether the boat to the bank and stand by with his waiting net.

At this stage many anglers feel some compulsion to get out of the boat and onto the bank so that they can move up and down the river in order to follow the fish as it moves. Frankly, you will not impress your boatman if you do this. The experienced angler will sit tight and continue to play the fish from the boat. In a dire emergency, when the fish makes a long run, it will be a simple matter for the

boatman to get back in and move you to a new position. Far better, therefore, that you remain seated and continue to play your fish from where you are. There is nothing more likely to frustrate a boatman than to have you on the bank running back and forth as the fish moves while he dashes hither and thither trying to net it for you.

Eventually, as your fish begins to tire, it will thrash on the surface in the vicinity of the boat. Don't be in too much of a hurry at this stage and do make sure that your reel can always run free should the fish make a sudden lunge for deeper water.

In a very short while now your fish begins to tire and to flounder onto its side. It is while it does this that you should suddenly take command and lead it like an unwilling dog over the rim of the waiting net. Your boatman will do the rest and he will raise the net the instant you lead the fish, head first if you can, over the net. Hey presto! You have a handsome springer of 8lb to start your season.

After lunch your boatman decides to rope you down a pool which is a little more shallow. There is a nice edge to the current where running fish might choose to lie temporarily. He suggests that you put up an intermediate weight sinking line, but with the same fly you had on when you caught your fish, which will enable your fly to move over the shallower water without getting hung up.

If, as your week progresses, the river drops fractionally, this will be a pool where you might profitably wade. Throughout your week note how the river rises with melting snow or rain or falls after overnight frosts, and how the changing water height affects the tactics advised by your boatman. You should take special note of the places where you actually hook fish, the time of day and the height of the water. This knowledge, stored in a recess of the mind, will eventually make you almost totally independent of your boatman in deciding tactics for any given day. By that time you may even be able to suggest a specific course of action to suit yourself or the prevailing conditions, but it will not be knowledge which is easily won.

During this time you may expect the weather to do all of the most diabolical things it is possible to endure. For instance, the river could be in roaring flood and not worth a cast. Alternatively, it might even be frozen over or so covered in a form of slushy ice, known as *grue*, as to be virtually impossible to fish. Sometimes it is just feasible to make the odd cast in heavy grue, but it may prove difficult to get the line to sink and not continually get fouled up on

the moving ice floes. Putting the rod point under the water immediately after the cast sometimes gets your fly clear of the grue and into a position where it might attract a taking fish.

In flood conditions, of course, your fishing activity will tend to be confined to that portion of the river immediately under your own bank. Here again it may be thought that a short cast will suffice, but do always bear in mind that the longer cast will get your fly down further in the water and in times of flood you will want your fly down anyway, despite the fact that the fish you hope to catch may be only a few feet out from the bank. Effective water command is one thing, but at times of very cold and high water you also have to think in that third dimension – the depth of the water.

SPRING

On your return from the Tweed with a nice catch of fish for your deep freeze, you begin to get excited about the real spring – when you hear the dawn chorus of birdsong and when daffodils spread their colours into the warming winds. You have planned a visit to the Spey in late April or early May. It is on a good beat downstream of Grantown and your gillie advises you, from long experience of his piece of water, to bring a 15-foot double-handed fly rod with both floating and sinking lines, and a wide variety of fly patterns and sizes, as well as a 10-foot trout fly rod with appropriate line, leaders and flies.

Unless the river is running big from melting snow, which it could well be at this time of the year, you will be fishing in breast waders and you might also need a wide variety of clothing to cover rapidly changing weather conditions. In the April of 1984, for instance, there were several days when Strathspey, with a shade temperature running into the seventies, was the hottest place in Europe. During late April 1985, on the other hand, we still had to suffer some bitter north-east winds with heavy snow showers.

You must also be aware of the wide range of water temperatures at this time of year – as much as ten degrees in a week. One day it could be down to 42°F and seven or eight days later it could be up to 52°. By the same perverse law, as devised by Mr Sod or Mr Murphy, it might equally have moved from 52° back to 42° a week later. This means that you should be constantly ready to change tactics as the

Idyllic spring fishing conditions perhaps, though it must be remembered that water levels and temperatures do change rapidly at this time of year. The angler must be prepared to alter his tactics accordingly.

conditions dictate. Most times you may prefer to start with your 15-foot carbon-fibre fly rod and a no. 11 floating line. This will certainly simplify your Spey casting and enable you to cover all the likely water without too much effort. You might have to share the services of your gillie with four or five other rods on the beat, but he will allocate a section of the river to you and then show you the best taking lies. At lunch time you will change places with another rod and fish his piece of water in the afternoon. These changes will continue all week so that you get an opportunity of fishing all the water available on the beat at least once during your week.

Having been prepared for a wide range of water and air temperatures, you must also expect the river to rise or fall as a consequence of the effect of temperature or rain on the deep snow-ridden corries of the Cairngorm mountains. A warm wind or rain can materially affect the amount of water released into the river, as can nothing more than a strong south-westerly wind putting a wave on Loch Insh and forcing the water into the river. All these factors may cause

water temperature and height to fluctuate quite markedly. You may find that you are fishing quite comfortably with your floating line one day and then, the day after, you are fishing in exactly the same style as you did on the Tweed in February. Unless there is a gauge on the river, it might not be too easy to take a mental note of the rapidly changing conditions. The fish too will tend to be very unsettled by any change in temperature and water flow and it will be the angler who is prepared to fish hard in the most appropriate manner who will do better than the casual fisherman who likes to potter.

Having been allocated a pool for the morning you should be at pains to study exactly where you are to wade. Ask the gillie or a person with wide experience of the water to give you any hints on exact lies for a particular height of water. Make sure that you know the best wading and entry and exit positions and don't take any chances. I have yet to lose one of my spring guests on the Spey, but it is an ever-present threat to the unwary.

Whenever the water gets exceptionally cold or higher than average, consider trying the sunk line. Don't be too worried about neglecting the traditional small fly of the spring. Unless the weather is very warm and the river very low, even when fishing with a floating line it is a mistake to fish with flies that are too small. Show the fish something that is readily seen. Most of them will be fairly fresh-run and the ability (or the sheer luck) to cross a resting fish will be much more important than your choice of fly. Stick with size 4s or 6s on the floating line and with little less than 2-inch tubes on the sinking line.

Your day-to-day tactics for fishing at this time of the year may only be governed by your experience or the advice of the gillie. Most Spey gillies prefer the floating line to the sinker and they despise anyone who wants to spin. It brings to mind that lovely quotation from the Good Book which urges us to 'Consider the lilies of the field, they toil not neither do they spin.' My corruption of this delightful verse might read: 'Consider the gillies of the Spey, they toil not neither do they spin.'

It took me many years to come to terms with the fact that the Spey is essentially a fly water and that over a season the floating line will do better than the sinker – but there have been notable exceptions. I dare not predict from one day to another, let alone over a week or a season, just how the spring will be in Strathspey. I am there every year from mid-April to the end of May and I cannot

recall any two years when the climate has followed the same routine. But it is a time when you might serve a useful apprenticeship to salmon fly fishing on the Spey – providing you take the several years I have stipulated to do it.

Meanwhile, let me run through the form on a hypothetical late April day on, say, the Polchraine Pool of the Spey on the No. 2 Castle Grant beat. Let me assume that there is a light breeze from the south-west, the sky is partially obscured, and the daffodils are just about into full bloom. A cock chaffinch chants cheekily from a nearby branch, wheeling plovers, oystercatchers and curlews add their chorus to the spring symphony and up the strath you notice a solitary osprey hovering high over the river near Cromdale bridge. The river gushes round the central arch at Cromdale and the gauge registers one foot ten inches.

Consulting your gillie, you ask from which bank at Polchraine you might have the better chance. Traditionally, as the river bends slightly to the right, you may think that the right bank and the inside bend will offer the best chances. Indeed, there is some superb water in both the neck and the tail at this side, but there is a lot of slack water in the middle which may be best fished from the left bank and it will be difficult to decide for the best. You must also consider the direction of the wind and the light, should the cloud clear and the sun emerge. Usually you will try to avoid fishing with the light at your back. In this position it will surely be shining into the eyes of the fish you hope to tempt.

With water height as described, I would not mind too much from which side of Polchraine I fished. The right bank offers slightly better casting positions and helpful prevailing breezes, while the left bank demands Spey casting with limited wading. There is little doubt, however, that the right bank offers easier fishing for the novice and you quickly opt for that.

It is 10 a.m. before you are fully clad in breast waders and ready with your tackle. The water is at 48°F while the air has already made it to 52°F. You have chosen a no. 11 double-taper floating line and the same 15-foot carbon-fibre fly rod you used earlier in the season. A 12-foot length of level 14 lb test monofilament serves as your leader and you soon select a size 6 double- or treble-hooked Munro Killer as being the fly most popular at this time of the year. You wade out slowly into the neck of the pool and make a few short casts. Slowly you lengthen these until you are covering a nice

Polchraine, River Spey, looking downstream from the high
bank. Note how the bulk of the current goes down the left
bank. Indeed, it does fish well from this side on a normal
height, but there are also many times when it fishes superbly
from the right bank – providing that you wade deep.

section or arc of the water at your side of the river. As soon as
effective water command has been attained (about twenty-five to
thirty yards) you maintain that casting distance and merely take a
pace or two downstream between each cast.

As you move out of the fast current, where your chances of a fish
might be better in a lower water with a higher temperature, you
note that your fly is now swinging round very nicely into a portion of
deeper water as it comes almost onto the dangle from where you
stand. You cover this area most carefully and are excited to see a
quiet head-and-tail rise just a few yards downstream of where your
fly is moving. Two casts later, when your fly is in the vicinity of

where you saw the fish, you momentarily feel something check your fly as it swings round to the dangle.

More than likely the fish you saw was the one which made a pass at your fly. Without serious thought or consideration you make the same cast again, hoping for a firm take. Most times, following such action, nothing happens and you just move on downstream, cursing your luck but hoping for another fish which will take more boldly. Sometimes I adopt this procedure myself, but there are times when I am in an inquisitive mood and then I rest the fish which apparently pulled my fly. I strip in the line without altering the amount held on the reel, which – provided that I don't move my feet in the meantime – will enable me to instantly place the fly exactly where it was before. More often than not I will do little more than rest that fish for five minutes and then try again with the same fly. Occasionally I might change the fly for one a size bigger and then make it move a little faster over the lie of the fish by handlining or with a downstream mend. The fish has already demonstrated that it has all the hallmarks of a taker and you should not give in too easily and presume that it will be uncatchable.

After several changes of fly and odd periods of waiting you eventually conclude that the fish is no longer interested. You continue on down the pool and you are just coming to that portion where the water goes fairly slack on the right bank, and you are perhaps wading more deeply than you enjoy, when the line tightens and your rod arches over into a tight bow – a springer is on! Initially the fish does little more than let you feel its weight. It backs away in the current while you quietly maintain the bend in the rod and ease yourself out towards the bank. Far better that you make the bank as soon as you can. This way you will be able to move with more haste should the fish run your line down to the backing.

Once on the bank you should not give ground downstream unless forced to do so. Maintain a steady strain on the fish and only let it take line when you feel that the tackle is being strained to near limits. At all times seek to be winning back line from the fish and never let it rest or lean on your tackle, so to speak. Constant pressure and harrying will tire it all the more quickly, but be ever ready to yield line when you have the fish coming in fairly close to you. Many a fish gains its freedom in the final stages of play when the angler is overconfident that all is nearly finished.

Slowly the fish begins to tire and it starts to wallow on or near the

surface. This may be the time to wade back into the water and stir up some of the mud or gravel with your feet to reduce visibility in the water. You must now maintain a constant pressure to pull it into the area of turbid water. Eventually the fish lies on its side more frequently and it is during one of these moments that you ease it into the edge and then, when it is lying quietly on its side, lift it up by the tail and heave it onto the bank. Your first fish of the season on the floating line, a lovely thirteen-pounder, has become a reality.

If at any time in the spring you get tired of salmon fishing, it will make an interesting diversion to try for the resident brown trout. This is not the place for detailed and rapturous praise of the Spey brown trout, but there may be many late April and May days when, around noon, there is a prolific hatch of large spring olive duns that will bring the trout and the remaining stock of finnock into prize-fighter trim. Hatches around lunch time will initiate a great response from the fish and I can recall many a blank day salmon-wise which has been transformed into one of memorable sport by a diversion with the trout. Invariably my first sea trout of a season is taken when I have been having the odd lunch time cast for a brownie and when – bang! – a fish has taken my fly and the line is down to the backing before you can say 'sea trout'! Caught in late April or May, when they are fresh-run in from the sea, they are about the most sporting fish you can encounter. They might only represent the initial vanguard of the main late-spring run, but every one caught at this time has to be a bonus.

Two 2¾lb brown trout taken by Arthur Oglesby in one morning from the Spey at Castle Grant. Both had been feeding on salmon parr.

LATE SPRING

If you find that mid-spring fishing is too unpredictable it may pay to delay your visit to the Spey until late May or June. Most certainly the pools will now be full of resident spring salmon and there will be a sufficient head of sea trout to make fishing for both species well worth while. Most of the snow on the Cairngorms will also have melted and the river will be beginning to settle down to normal summer level. In most situations you can now put your sinking lines to one side and concentrate entirely on the floating line. Initially it might make sense to continue with your double-handed rod, but you should be ever watchful for the water to drop away, when, with deep wading, the single-handed rod with a lighter line and smaller fly could be more effective.

Often on the Spey the river begins to fall away by mid-May and air and water temperatures start to move into those levels more associated with summer. I am thinking of times when the water temperature gets into the low fifties and air temperatures stay in the mid-sixties for a long portion of the day. Now most of the salmon that were running a month ago will have settled into the main holding pools and catching them begins to sort the men from the boys. The best of the fishing may now be restricted to the periods between dawn and lunch time, and again, a more interesting spell, between dinner time and the onset of full darkness. Even then it is important not to conclude that afternoon fishing is always a waste of time; I have already related how one May afternoon got me four fish when all my guests had gone back to the hotel for an afternoon siesta. There was a similar afternoon on the left bank of Polchraine when I hooked and landed all four fish which came to my fly, but that was during the bonanza year of 1978 – a time, perhaps, when it did not matter too much what we did.

SUMMER

After your spring visit to the Spey you are faced with several summertime possibilities. In most situations June will bring a start to the dog days of fishing, but it will offer superb opportunities for sea trout at dusk and on through the short hours of darkness. Many of the salmon will be getting slightly past their best and it may need

rain to lift the river out of the metaphorical doldrums and back into life. You may alternate with double- and single-handed rods as the conditions dictate and there may be times, following a summer flood, when it will pay dividends to resort to the sinking line and fly used back in February.

But June is a lovely time to be on such a river as the Spey and there were many years when I literally had to tear myself away in order to swan off to Norway for my annual pilgrimage to its famous Vosso river. By the time we get into July we really are into the dog days of British fishing. Good alternatives are still to be found in Norway, Iceland and Canada and if you can get access to some of their good rivers you will be there at the best time of the year.

However, July does offer good opportunities in the smaller spate streams of the west coast and the Hebrides. I have already recounted some of the fun we have at Amhuinnsuidhe Castle during early July and the way the sport may vary with salmon and sea trout and from year to year. It is a fascinating time of the year to be in such a paradise – although one may never dare predict the ferocity of the winds or the horrendous level of the rainfall. Perhaps we should invent a special inclemency scale for Hebridean weather, with zero representing a zephyr-like calm under cloudless skies and semi-tropical temperatures, and 100 representing twenty-four hours of continuous rainfall with storm-force winds and freezing temperatures.

AUGUST

There are many years when I follow my Hebridean visit with an August return to the Spey, but this can be a very dour time for fish and when we confine most of our efforts to the early mornings or late evenings. Invariably I fish with a floating line on a single-handed rod but there are times, as the river rises after rain, when the sport goes flat. While a slight rise of water in midsummer, particularly after a fairly long spell without rain, might bring some fish, it is quite likely to bring down some peat water from the hills which will increase the acid level of the water and make the fish a bit reluctant to take. When foam on the water suggests excessive acidity, you may on occasion revert to the sinking line with advantage. I have already related how one July afternoon produced five fish for me

A sea trout coming to the net on Loch Voshimid.

when the rest of our party, myself included, had drawn blank for the previous three days.

In August few rivers in Britain offer regular sport. Oh, there will still be good opportunities in the Hebrides and on some of the west- and north-coast lochs of Scotland, but almost everywhere else will be dependent on new rain to lift the rivers and give them a veritable shot in the arm.

Depending entirely on rainfall, many of the smaller rivers should now be getting their main runs of summer salmon, grilse and sea trout. In those halcyon days when I had regular access to the Lune and the Yorkshire Esk it was great fun to have the boot of the car loaded with tackle and to be hanging on the end of the phone waiting for the word that all was right. Many a time I have been hightailing it over the Whitby moors or the Pennines just on dawn so as to be well in time for what a keeper or a friend had predicted as

being the magic moment. Usually it was important to down tools at the precise moment as instructed, for the river could be back down to summer level again in a matter of hours rather than days. Usually I made arrangements to stay near the river for as long as it held up and the good conditions lasted. There is little doubt that the ability to do this gives you a head start over those who have to adhere to the disciplines of an appointments book or routine business.

There was one memorable occasion when I went to the Lune just as quickly as I could. It was at a perfect height and I quickly caught three fish weighing 18, 9 and 8 lb. I stayed over that evening in the local pub to await guests joining me on the following morning. Sad to relate, they missed the magic moment and fished all that day for not so much as a pull.

AUTUMN

While all salmon and sea-trout fishing is a bit of a lottery, it is never more so than in summertime, when we rely on flash floods to bring some of our rivers into trim. September is a more predictable month – the dog days are virtually over – but on the classic rivers it often means catching stale fish that have been in the river for some months. On a little river like the Yorkshire Esk, however, which frequently does not get its first fish of the season until July or August, September might well provide an opportunity of intercepting a run of fresh fish. Sadly, most of my Esk fish were caught on baits and spinners. It was never a good fly river following a flood.

Many of the old school of salmon fishermen feel that all angling for migratory fish should cease at the end of August. They reckon that the spring- and summer-run fish are now past their best and that, despite the apparent freshness of an autumn-run fish, both males and females are likely to be full of near-ripe eggs or milt. This is often a valid point, but in so many situations a lot of us now have to rely on the autumn run to get any fish at all. There is also little doubt that on a river like the Tweed we are likely to get not only some very handsome fish in the autumn, but also some of the biggest fish we will encounter in the season.

October is a great month to be on one of the lower beats of the

Tweed. Once again, a fly-only rule applies. Because of the residual heat left from the sun's prolonged spell in the northern hemisphere, daytime temperatures may be higher than in the spring, while the hours of darkness and daylight resemble those of late February or March. This suggests that, while you may still fish with the floating line, you might not be so concerned with very small flies as you were in July, August and part of September. Indeed, if there is good October rainfall and a few overnight frosts, you might well resort to the sinking shooting head and the same large tube flies you used in February and March. Always bear in mind that water temperatures must be related to air temperatures. In no circumstances do I like a day when the water is warmer than the air, but even then there may be a chance of fish if you resort to the sinking line and the large fly.

In late October and early November I journey north for my annual visit to the Upper Floors beat of the Tweed just upstream of Kelso. This water is regarded by many as the finest beat on the whole river but, as with any other piece of salmon water, it is possible to spend a week there and catch nothing. We need the river to be at the right height and to know that there has been a run of fish. In 1980, the first year I had access to this lovely water, I fished hard all week for nothing. My wife managed one fish, but the river was at flood level over most of the week and fishing was almost a complete waste of time. The following year we did slightly better, but it was not until 1982 that I hit a mild bonanza.

I had taken the TV camera crew up for the shooting of a sequence for the Benson & Hedges series. They were booked in for just two days and I have already recorded how I caught a fish or two for them. But it was on the evening that they departed that I guessed that, with any luck at all, I should have a very good catch on the following day. On that Wednesday morning even Bob Paterson, my boatman for the day, asked me just how many fish I would like. By lunch time I had five on the bank and he suggested that I should get another five that afternoon. My last fish of the day took my fly in the failing light and at 22 lb it was my biggest fish of the day. It brought my total to ten fish weighing an average of 14½ lb.

Although I once caught more salmon in a day on a spinner, that was my best day on the fly and the greatest weight of fish I have ever taken in a day. All were caught on my 15-foot 'Walker' with a sinking no. 11 shooting head and one of the large tube flies so popular on the Tweed in early spring and late autumn. The river fell

a little more during the rest of the week and I caught quite a lot more fish. But that day produced the most magic moments and, following the rise of water we had endured three days before, it was almost predictable.

Three Lune fish: 18lb, 8lb and 9lb.

16
Great Moments
with Great Fish

I do not really understand the compulsions of salmon fishing, but I am well aware that I am gripped by them. Looking forward to a good day's salmon fishing can still keep me awake the night before, turning over the possibilities in my head and wondering whether my hooks are sharp enough.

William B. Currie, Days and Nights of Game Fishing

Although much of my earlier life as a fish-hungry angler was spent pursuing salmon and sea trout with all manner of lures and baits, there are few occasions nowadays, if any, when I want to fish for salmon and sea trout in any other style than with the fly. It is not that I have developed any superior attitudes to those anglers who are prepared to catch fish on baits, it is just that methods other than the fly now have no appeal for me. I suppose that in many ways all my wildest salmon-fishing dreams have been totally fulfilled. I have been fortunate to fish in some of the most exclusive waters in the world and my largest salmon came out at fractionally under 50lb. All this means that I am now well past the stage when any fish caught is a noteworthy event.

Much of my enjoyment now comes from helping others. My life seems to hinge around those weeks when I run my fishing courses at Grantown-on-Spey and I get just as much satisfaction from taking photographs or movie film of fishing sequences as I do from catching fish. It all adds up to a great longing just to be beside a salmon or sea-trout river, feel its pulse and tempo, as it were, and sometimes just sit and wonder at it all. There is another sense in which I occasionally feel slightly guilty about killing fish, for I do think that mankind has abused this wonderful resource almost to a point of total irresponsibility. That aside, there have been moments of great excitement when I have hooked a salmon or a big sea trout – although it is not necessarily the biggest fish that provide the greatest thrills.

While I cannot condone the deliberate foul-hooking of fish, there is no doubt that one so hooked will often take off like an express train and provide some sensational excitement. In fact, one of the surest indications that a fish is foul-hooked is its initial behaviour immediately you feel that it is on. If at that instant it leaps or goes cavorting off on a long, screaming run, you will often not be mistaken if you conclude that your fish might be hooked somewhere other than in the mouth. Most times I can tell instantly if I have foul-hooked a fish and I can usually inform others with less experience, if and when I see their fish in play, whether it is foul-hooked. I am sure that many of the legendary tales of epic battles with monsters have involved foul-hooked fish. Without firm and specialised treatment in play such fish could remain hooked for hours and not give in.

The instant you realise that you have foul-hooked a fish it pays to be tough on it. Many fish so hooked get off at some stage during the play and it is much better to let them get off as soon as possible so as not to prolong the agony. Playing a fish to the limits of your tackle strength will give it every chance to get off as soon as possible and it will also give you a better chance of getting it ashore in reasonable time if it is to be one of those fish which cannot shake the hook.

One of the most memorable fish I foul-hooked on a fly was during the spring of 1978 when we had a wonderful run of fish into the Spey. I was casting with a single-handed rod and a light sinking shooting-head with a single-hook size 4 Munroe Killer. Wading deep in the Manse Pool at Castle Grant, I felt my fly touch something as I was handlining it back for my next cast. Instantly I guessed that I had snagged a fish and shouted over my shoulder to a friend that I expected a veritable firework display at any second. Slowly I wound the hand-held shooting line back onto the reel and then, as I applied tension with the rod point, the fish set off on a screaming run downstream. My friend swears that he saw smoke erupting from my reel as the fish tore off, but whether he did or not there was an abrupt stoppage of the line as my reel seized up. By this time the fish had reached a quiet backwater on the opposite side of the river and it seemed content to lie there for a short rest. Meanwhile no amount of persuasion would get my reel to function in either direction and there was nothing left to do but put the rod down on the grass and play the fish by hand.

The battle continued for many anxious minutes while I felt some conviction that it would not be long before the fish got free anyway.

Eventually, I walked off into the field adjoining the river and slowly cajoled the fish back towards my own bank. It was a bit like handling a tug-of-war rope, but slowly the fish wallowed back to my side and it was then but a simple matter for my companion to pick it up by the tail and get it ashore. It was a fresh-run fish of 14lb with the sea lice still on it.

Most instances of foul-hooking occur when the fish are taking badly or at a time when the pools are well stocked with fish. Sadly, the deliberate foul-hooking of fish is a practice all too frequently indulged in by some so-called anglers and must not be condoned. Just occasionally it happens that the best-intentioned sportsman hooks one thus and you should learn to read the signs and the display of a foul-hooked fish which, with experience, are easily recognised.

The largest fish I ever caught on a fly, the one of 31lb from the Vosso in Norway, did not give a memorable battle, but I was extremely lucky ever to get it into the gillie's net. By the time we got the fish ashore the fly was held by a mere thread of flesh – a few more seconds of prolonged play and it would have regained its freedom. The next largest fish I caught on a fly, the 29-pounder also from the Vosso, was taken on a large tube fly and a lead-cored sinking line at a time when my host had been pleading with me to put my fly rod to one side and concentrate on the spinner. He himself had spent an entire morning on the Upper Bolstad Pool with his prawns and spinners, and I had gone down just before lunch in order to watch him and see what he had done. He urged me to have a cast myself while he looked on and I was standing beside the river in my light shoes when down from the depth of the pool there came a heavy pull at my fly and a salmon was on. As is normal on many Norwegian rivers when you hook a fish while fishing from the bank or wading, I instantly got into the waiting boat with my gillie. This is a sensible precaution in case the fish takes off downstream in one long, unstoppable rush.

Initially, the fish gave a strong fight in the heavy current at the head of the stream. I kept my rod well bent – although several minutes elapsed without it having any apparent effect. Only slowly did the fish drift into the heavier part of the current and it was then not long before it started swimming downstream at an ever-increasing pace. I was unable to stop it and we had no other choice but to follow. It was a bit like having a stubborn dog on a lead except, in this instance, the fish seemed to be the master and I felt

Arthur Oglesby with his largest ever salmon on a fly: a fish of 31lb from the Vosso at Bolstadoyri in August 1967.

Odd Haraldsen playing a salmon on the Sandia beat of the
Alta, July 1985.

like the dog. Relentlessly it headed down for the rapids and the exit
into the fjord. Suddenly we were in the maelstrom, fish and boat
nearly together now, bobbing about like a cork in a storm. Quite
quickly, however, we smoothed out onto the placid waters of the
fjord and I was then able to get onto terms with my fish, terms
which would quickly move into my favour. Then, thirty-five
minutes after hooking, I had a beautiful cock fish of 29lb on the
bank.

Perhaps the Alta in the north of Norway is the true Mecca of
salmon fly fishermen. It has been the chosen destination for salmon
anglers since the mid-1800s. Successive generations of the Dukes of
Roxburghe and Westminster rented the entire river during July and
made some of the most memorable catches of large salmon ever
recorded. Charles Ritz, in his book *A Fly Fisher's Life*, records that
the biggest catch of fish from the Alta to one rod was 44 salmon
averaging 23lb taken in one day. It must be remembered that a
fishing day in Alta may run to twenty-four hours for in July there is
perpetual daylight. Another noteworthy catch in 1860 was 39 fish in
a day to the Duke of Roxburghe, while in 1926 the Duke of

Antti Parkkinen with a salmon of 56lb taken from the Alta
river in July, 1985.

Westminster caught 33 salmon in a day weighing 792lb.
    While, as on many salmon rivers elsewhere, such catches have
not been forthcoming from the Alta in recent years, it is still visited
by the present Dukes of Roxburghe and Westminster every summer. In 1979, the Duke of Roxburghe caught a lovely fish of 51lb on
the fly and as recently as 1985 a Finn, Mr Antti Parkkinen, caught a
superb fish of 56lb on a fly. Both of these fish were taken in July,
when most of the big fish are taken and when a fly-only rule applies.
    There is some special magic about the tranquility of a June or July
evening on the Alta under the lowering midnight sun. By 11.30 on
the night of 30 June/1 July 1985, the air had gone calm and a cuckoo

hooted mockingly at us from a distant hillside. During the day the temperature had made it to the low seventies, but I did not forget that I was several hundred miles north of the Arctic circle and I quickly added another sweater and a light showerproof coat against the chills of midnight before I started casting with the same fly tackle I would use on the Tweed in February or November.

My gillies rowed me carefully over one of the best lies on the Sandia beat and it was then that it happened. The rod was nearly pulled out of my hand. No time to worry or wonder about the pundits' theories on feeding slack line at this moment! The fish was hooked and it set off on a very determined run across and downstream.

Perhaps it is strange that all my experience of big Norwegian fish, particularly those that are absolutely fresh-run, is that whenever they run they usually do so in a downstream direction. Is it that their recent memory of the sea triggers off the feeling that it offers them a

The Duke of Roxburghe, looking suitably pleased with this 51lb salmon taken from the Sandia beat of the Norwegian Alta river, July, 1979.

degree of security they do not initially feel in the river, and that instinctively they make back in that direction the instant danger threatens?

With a lot of experience in playing big Norwegian salmon, and because I was already safely in a boat and thus easily able to follow the fish, it did not take much more than fifteen minutes to have it ready for the tailer. Even then we had moved downstream from the point where it was hooked by some 100 or 150 yards and it was just a few minutes short of midnight when the gillie heaved my 24-pounder into the boat. Not a noteworthy fish for the Alta or for Norway, but another nice milestone for me!

I continued fishing until 6.30 a.m. but that was to be the only offer I got that night. Upstream, on the Sautso beat, Lee and Joan Wulff were just finishing an enjoyable week in which Lee, by remarkably bad luck, had nothing to show for his efforts at all. Joan, on the other hand, had taken several fish on her 9-foot trout fly rod, with the best pulling the scale down to 38lb. But it was a memorable visit for us all and I came home wondering if I should ever be permitted to visit my Mecca again.

Although I have caught several hundred fish in Britain, up to and including three fish of 23lb on the Lune and the Tweed, my fish of 27½lb is still my biggest British fish. In the good old days of the early sixties, and prior to the disease, the Lune could always be relied on to give me the odd 20-plus-pounder, but I never seemed to be able to get one on the Spey. Over many years it was an event to get a Spey fish running into double figures. Usually I had to be satisfied with handsome little fish of between six and ten pounds. Just occasionally one or two in the double-figure bracket would go into the diary, but I fished the Spey for nearly twenty-five years before I caught a 20-pounder.

This barrier was broken on a late April day in 1980 when I had gone down to the beat to see how my guests were coping. I had not intended to go fishing, but my gillie, Eric Robb, told me that a pool known as the No. 1 Burn was unoccupied and that I ought to give it a quick cast before lunch. The day was still a bit cold so I put on a bigger fly than I had been using earlier that week, a size 2 Oglebug of my own tying. Normally, with Spey casting, this pool can be easily fished from the bank. For some perverse reason, however, I put on my breast waders. It might have been because there was a hint of rain or that I did not want to get my shoes dirty, but whatever the

reason I was soon glad that I had put them on.

Casting from the bank was easy and I had not been fishing for more than five minutes when there was a heavy pull on the line and a fish was on. I immediately sensed that it was larger than average, but its initial runs took it upstream and for several minutes I was able to maintain side strain without moving. Then the fish quite suddenly got tired of this and took off on a screaming downstream run. I had little option but to follow and, since I had to ford a small stream to keep up with it, I was indeed thankful that I had put on the waders.

Over the next few minutes that fish led me quite a dance. I really had far too many clothes on to be at all athletic and as I stumbled, lurched and tottered over the rocks and stones I began to wonder if I would ever get it ashore. It was still wallowing around in the heavy current while I was floundering about in the shallow water trying my best to get near it. It seemed very reluctant to come anywhere near the shallow water and at every attempt it would gain a few more yards in its quest to go downstream. I was nearly into the neck of the next pool before I was able to coerce it into shallow water and virtually collapse over it and drag it ashore. It weighed 22½ lb and it is still the largest Spey salmon I have ever caught.

Although the next was not a big fish – in fact I have forgotten its weight – one of my more memorable Spey fish was notable only in the way I came to catch it. I had gone down to the beat to see how my guests were coping and was driving along the riverside when I saw a fish do a head-and-tail rise in some fairly dead water at the foot of a steep bank. It was a stretch of the river where we do not normally fish but, as always, I had a rod set up ready on the roof-rack of my car and it took me only a few moments to scramble down the bank in my shoes and make a short Spey cast to cover it. I had barely worked out a modest length of line when I detected a fin protruding from the water immediately behind where I knew my fly to be. Shark-like, the fin moved in close formation with the fly, but when the fly eventually came to the dangle in a quiet backwater the fin slowly disappeared from view. That fish had at least followed my fly, but I reckoned that it would be highly unlikely to do so again.

I waited a few moments and made another Spey cast to the same spot. Seconds later the fish's fin appeared and again followed the fly round to the dangle. I decided to handline my fly quickly back to give it more movement and the fin then moved more quickly towards it. In the tense moments that followed I did not know what

to do. The fly was rapidly coming to my feet, but that shark-like fin still followed menacingly and to my great surprise and relief, just as I was about to lift the fly out of the water, the fish closed its mouth round it and was on. The subsequent fight and my antics in extracting the fish while still in my shoes were trivial compared with the excitement of the take. It was indeed a very unlucky fish!

I once caught a 13lb sea trout on a Mepps spinner, but I have not caught any very large sea trout on the fly. The biggest one I did hook cannot be claimed as my biggest for the very simple reason that I did not play and land it myself. It happened like this.

One June evening I had gone down to fish the No. 1 beat at Castle Grant as a guest of Lady Pauline Ogilvie-Grant, in the company of another of her guests, a young gentleman from New Zealand. He only had thigh waders while I put on my breast waders so that I could better cover more water in a favourite pool known as Slopeaka. My companion for the evening took Congash Burn, the pool above. By midnight I had five nice sea trout in the bag and I sauntered upstream to see how my friend was coping. Sad to relate, he had not taken a fish so I urged him to come down to Slopeaka and have a try there. Watching him wading and casting I quickly realised that he was not achieving effective water command. It seemed to make sense for me to fish it down again, so I promptly waded in behind him and started fishing.

Presently a heavy draw at my fly indicated that I had hooked yet another sea trout. Shouting to my companion to wind his line in, I quickly handed him my rod so that he could at least feel the mettle of a Spey sea trout and have one to take back to the lodge with him. The fish fought well in the eerie twilight and I began to think that my companion was being far too easy with it in not getting it played out more quickly. Anyway, to cut the story short, when he was eventually able to lead the fish over the rim of the net I discovered that I had netted a lovely sea trout of 7½lb for him.

It is always a bit of a puzzle to know just how tenacious in play any specific fish is going to be. I have had fish that have gone beserk, while others have come in like an old boot. I am sure that fish are a bit like other animals – and even humans – in that some are exceptionally fit and athletic while others are overweight, docile, very tired or out of condition. Of course, there are few specimen hunters in salmon and sea-trout fishing in the sense that there are in some spheres of coarse fishing. Normally the angler is content just

to hook a fish and concern himself with its weight only when it is safely on the bank. Rarely is it possible to fish for a specific fish you can see, and even size is much harder to detect than, say, with brown or rainbow trout seen rising regularly to passing insects.

MINOR TACTICS

If the size of the fish and their condition are largely controlled by the river location and the time of the year, other subtle factors, which I shall call *minor tactics*, can get you a fish when other anglers fail to catch them. A very dear friend of mine, a very talented angler, once fished down a pool on the Tweed one early February morning and came back to the hut for a mid-morning dram with the comment, 'They are just not taking today.' Of course I knew what he meant, but I could not resist making the response, 'In that case let us set about making them take.'

You may think that this sounds arrogant, and had I said it to anyone other than a very old friend it might well have been regarded as such. What I really wanted to demonstrate was that, while the fish might well have 'not been taking' in the normal course of events, such an assumption was not the right attitude to adopt if any fish were to be caught.

What followed gave me an early insight into the value of effective water command. My friend was a superb distance caster and after he had covered a pool it could be safely concluded that every fish in the vicinity had at least seen his fly. By their constant leaps we knew that there were plenty of fish in the beat and I quickly tackled up with a large tube fly and waded into the head of the pool at the top of our beat. I sensed that it would be one of those times when the fish would need to be intimidated into taking the fly, and that deep wading was needed to make the fly move as slowly as possible and dangle deeply and tantalisingly over the lies. By lunch time I came back to the hut with two fish, but I will concede that a multitude of other factors might have given me two fish while my friend remained fishless until the afternoon.

When you frighten a feeding trout, particularly one that is born and reared in the wild, it usually scurries off in alarm. When you disturb a salmon or sea trout, particularly in low water, it often has no other place to go than the area of water in which it is residing and

to which it seems temporarily confined. Resident trout in a stream have their own territories and bolt-holes. Migratory fish, on the other hand, are only temporary residents and have little time to get to know a pool with the same degree of intimacy as its full-time denizens, particularly during their early days in the river when they might not be in one pool for very long. Most migratory fish also have less to fear from the shadow of man anyway, and their reaction to being alarmed or alerted is not always the same as that displayed by full-time residents.

Certainly, all fish are fearful of unfamiliar shadows and vibrations but they seem not over-bothered by those to which they have become accustomed. Bridges are favourite stopping-places for migratory fish and they usually seem totally unconcerned at the shadow of the bridge or the vibrations of passing traffic. A low-flying jet, on the other hand, often causes instant panic among the fish, but it seems also to wake them into a state of full alertness, and if you rest the water for ten minutes and then fish it down you might just catch one.

The passage of canoes or other traffic on the river often produces a similar response and when canoeing takes place on the high water of spring I do not think it matters much. The snag is that many irresponsible canoeists use parts of the river as practice and marshalling areas, and I suspect that the continued disturbance this causes makes fish vacate the immediate area and swim on elsewhere – upstream or down. In a low water, on the other hand, I have watched fish move off the lie the instant the shadow of the first canoe came over them. In one instance, when I was acting as an official observer for some fishery proprietors on the Spey who were contesting the rights of canoeists to navigation on the river, we erected a deer stalker's high seat in the river and took it in turns to watch the behaviour of the fish beneath us. The canoeists, a party of schoolboys from Gordonstoun, were all there to give kindly co-operation. In all instances of canoe movement the resident shoal of fish absconded downstream into a deep dub where they jumped restlessly for about twenty minutes. Occasionally it was nearly an hour before some of the fish were back in their original lies. Whether they would take an angler's lure or fly any better after this disturbance is not known, but it does not alter the fact that while the occasional movement of canoes may be easily tolerated their constant passage throughout a day could render many pieces of

water offering hitherto good taking lies, virtually useless for sport.

We have all heard of instances when some angler, keen perhaps to prove a point on this score, has ordered his dog to swim across the river to create a disturbance and has then rested the river briefly before fishing it down and catching a fish. In the days when my labrador was an agile pup he was more at home in the water than he was on dry land. He would frequently go out swimming with me while I waded down a pool, but I was particularly keen that he did not venture into the area of water where I knew the main fish lies to be.

The acquisition of what I call *water sense* might take some little time. It is an instinct akin to that of the hunter, but it involves little more than a bountiful supply of pure common sense. Nothing in nature moves quickly and thus betrays its presence unless it is alarmed. Watch a cat stalking a mouse or a bird; or a pike lurking in a weedbed waiting for its prey to inadvertently swim within close attacking range. Of course there are instances when a quick burst of speed will clinch the contest, as with an osprey catching a trout for lunch or a falcon stooping onto a fast-moving rabbit, but in these cases too the predator is at pains to conceal his intention until the very last moment. If we wish to become successful predators, we must learn to move and think in the same fashion.

It helps if you become a keen observer not only of what the fish are doing but also of the behaviour of other animals. For many years I gave close observation to goldfish feeding in a bowl. Naturally there were factors that made any comparison with wild fish hardly worth noting. The goldfish were fed regularly and were kept in a constant environment of water temperature and light. Even so, it was interesting that at some times the fish seemed hyperactive while at others they seemed to be slightly switched off. Wild birds coming to a feeding table outside my study window have patterns and times of high activity and others when they ignore the food completely. Even cattle in a field spend some periods of the day up and about and chomping on the grass and others just lying down and chewing their cud. Experience on the Lune, where we had a field full of cattle adjacent to the river, seemed to indicate that more fish were caught when the cattle were active than when they were lying down.

Probably nothing has a greater influence on the catching of migratory fish than subtle and often minute changes in the height of the water. Often it is not easy to tell if a river is rising or falling, but

there is one sure way and it was a method I used to good effect many years ago on the Lune. This is a river which is highly influenced by small changes in the height of the water, but a slight rise can usually be detected by studying the meniscus formed where the the water's edge meets stones and pebbles.

In normal conditions, when the river is falling slowly this meniscus is concave, and the stones themselves are slightly damp above the water line. It is a sign, unless the river is exceptionally low, that fishing may be good. A convex meniscus, on the other hand, with the water bulging against the dry stones and with no signs of damp above the water line, indicates that the river is on the rise.

Of course such indicators are useless if it is actually raining, but then the careful placing of a stick, away from places where the water may be lapping up or down from wind and current, will soon indicate what is happening. The first flush of a rise may also produce a fish or two, but thereafter it is possible to fish for a long time without an offer until the river starts to turn and drop. Even then the speed at which the river drops also influences the chances of making a good catch.

In some instances, a river which drops quickly, soon confines the fresh-run fish in the main lies, and there may be a brief period of hectic sport until the river settles. A river which drops only slowly, on the other hand, may cause the fish to stay on the move for a longer period and only give you the chance of the odd, resting fish. A lot depends on the river, the geography of the specific pools on that river, the time of the year and various other considerations. Most certainly it brings me back to that ten-year apprenticeship on one piece of water which I constantly commend to you. Such experience will not be easily won.

But fishing is meant to be fun, and maybe you will be content never to become much more than an average angler. In the good times you may well catch as many fish as your fellow anglers; but in those more testing moments, when the fish are not in suicidal mood, perhaps your bag is lighter than those of anglers more closely attuned to the water and the elements. Much depends on what you want from your fishing. It may be that, like me, you will find that there is much more to the challenge of fishing than mere numbers of fish caught.

Epilogue

The average angler cannot hope to increase his opportunity to take more salmon. His increase in pleasure must come from enjoying each salmon he catches more or by having each salmon spread the pleasure it can give to more than one angler.

Lee Wulff, in a plea for catch-and-release, The Atlantic Salmon

In a recent television documentary on the decline of the salmon it was suggested that the value of each rod-caught fish to the tourist economy could be as high as £2,000, as against a commercial food value of, say, £20. If this is true, and it may well be, a good case could be made for saying that the wild salmon is too valuable a resource to be exploited by commercial netting at all. But it is not yet expedient for any political party to attack the present status quo. The fact that more jobs will be put in jeopardy by the loss of the salmon resource to the sportsman than to the commercial fisherman is not taken into account. The issue tends to be emotionally divided on the simple assumption that a cessation of commercial fishing would merely rob the poor of a job and provide more sport for the rich.

If overfishing represents the greatest threat to the future of the sport, there are other threats which must receive attention if the resource is to be properly managed. High on the list of hazards today is the phenomenon known as acid rain. This is the result of sulphur dioxide fumes, released in the combustion of fossil fuels, uniting with water to form a dilute solution of sulphuric acid. Acidity is measured in pH, or parts Hydrogen. The scale runs from 0 to 14 and the figure of 7 represents a neutral solution. Below this level the solution is said to be acid while any figure above is alkaline. Salmonid life is said to perish at pH levels below 4·5, but there have been many instances when the pH of rainfall in parts of Cumbria and south-west Scotland has measured as low as 2·6. Little wonder that there have been instances of entire runs of salmon and sea trout coming in on summer spates and perishing within hours rather than days.

In other instances a slightly less disastrous pH has enabled the mature fish to survive but has inflicted great mortality on hatching ova and young alevins. This latter type of mortality may be less easy to monitor than the demise of mature fish. It represents yet another threat to the future well-being of the species.

If there need to be drastic changes in order to achieve the successful management of the migratory fish resources there will also be inevitable changes in the type of tackle used for salmon and sea trout fishing. Doubtless the trend to the use of ultra-short rods has been halted, but I suspect that the growing army of stillwater fishermen will be reluctant to buy specific tackle for occasional salmon fishing when much of their reservoir gear will prove equally effective. Carbon fibre or graphite has undoubtedly provided the possibility of having rods giving exceptional water command, and I cannot see a time when I shall want anything more than a 15 foot rod for the spring and autumn fly fishing and a good quality 10 or 11 foot rod for the late spring and summer salmon and sea-trout fishing. The recent 'Hexagraph' construction of carbon-fibre rods manufactured on the tried and tested principles of split-bamboo cane will always be slightly more expensive than rods of tubular construction, but the more discerning anglers will seek them even if the market for tubular rods continues for many years. However, we cannot expect too much in the way of development in other items of tackle. Leaders will continue to be made of man-made fibres such as nylon and we may expect diameters to decrease while test strengths increase slightly. Fly patterns will undergo slow if meaningless change and we may see some development in floating and sinking lines to reduce the drag effect while casting, yet giving better floating or sinking qualities as desired. The ultimate, of course, would be for the line and leader to be tapered down to the required point size and strength and manufactured as an integral unit with not a single knot (except obviously at the fly) to weaken the line and leader.

In speculating on the future, therefore, I suspect that the one vital factor which may emerge on salmon fishing is that rents for the best fishing will tend to go through the proverbial roof. Any commodity in short supply tends to quickly find a high price level, and so long as we have more people seeking more leisure it will be a safe bet that costs to fish will be calculated on a cost per fish basis. But factors

such as the quality of the location, the time of year, the style of fishing and the quality and quantity of the fish to be caught will all add to or subtract from the basic price structure.

In closing, my one plea is that you learn and adopt all the better sporting ethics of fishing for migratory fish and that you do not become just another cowboy. There are far too many of these still pursuing all the fish they can catch by whatever means. The wild resource will not stand this type of exploitation for much longer and only more responsible attitudes and greater self-discipline on the part of sporting anglers will reverse the current trend.

Sadly, our stillwater fisheries seem to have bred a type of angler who thinks only in terms of catching his limit at every outing. This 'catch your limit' philosophy must be foreign to the nature of future salmon and sea-trout anglers if the resource is to survive at all. Far better to promote the slogan 'limit your catch', for we must think of fish as a bonus and be ever mindful of the motto of the Fly Fishers' Club, *Piscator non solum piscatur* – 'There's much more to fishing than catching fish.'

Useful Information

My own videos are:

Fly Casting & Game Fishing, two films on one videotape, marketed by Harvey Scruton Ltd, 4 Barker Lane, York Y01 1JR, at £19.95 inc. p & p.

The Benson & Hedges video is:

Fly Fishing, parts 1 and 2, available from Prospectus Ltd, 32 Woodstock Road, London W4, at £17.95 each.

My spring fishing courses are held at the Seafield Lodge Hotel, Grantown-on-Spey, Moray, Scotland.

The Association of Professional Game Angling Instructors can be contacted c/o Jack Martin JP, 26 Linghill, Newby, Scarborough, North Yorkshire.

Bibliography

BALFOUR-KINNEAR, G.P.R., *Catching Salmon and Sea Trout* (Thomas Nelson & Sons Ltd, 1958).

CROSSLEY, ANTHONY, *The Floating Line for Salmon and Sea Trout* (Methuen, 1944).

CURRIE, W. B., *Days and Nights of Game Fishing* (Allen & Unwin, 1984).

EDWARDS, T. L., and HORSFALL-TURNER, ERIC, *The Angler's Cast* (Herbert Jenkins, 1960).

FALKUS, HUGH, *Sea Trout Fishing* (Witherby, 1975).

FALKUS, HUGH, *Salmon Fishing* (Witherby, 1984).

GRAESSER, NEIL, *Fly Fishing for Salmon* (The Boydell Press, 1982).

GREEN, PHILIP, *New Angles on Salmon Fishing* (Allen & Unwin, 1984).

KELSON, GEORGE M., *The Salmon Fly* (Wyman & Sons Ltd, 1895).

LAMOND, HENRY, *The Sea Trout – A Study in Natural History* (Sherrat & Hughes, 1916).

MACLAREN, CHARLES, *Fishing for Salmon* (John Donald, 1977).

NALL, G.H., *The Life of the Sea Trout* (Seeley, Service, 1930).

PARRY, J. HUGHES, *Fishing Fantasy* (Eyre & Spottiswoode, 1949).

RITZ, CHARLES, *A Fly Fisher's Life* (Max Reinhardt, 1959).

Scotland for Fishing (Scottish Tourist Board).

SCROPE, WILLIAM, *Days and Nights of Salmon Fishing in the Tweed,* 1921 edn, ed. H. T. Sheringham (Herbert Jenkins 1921).

WADDINGTON, RICHARD, *Salmon Fishing: A New Philosophy* (Faber & Faber, 1959).

Where to Fish (Harmsworth Press).

WRIGHT, LEONARD M., *Fly Fishing Heresies* (Winchester Press, 1975).

WULFF LEE, *The Atlantic Salmon* (Winchester Press, 1983).

Index

Other fishing books published by The Crowood Press

Travels with a Two Piece   *John Bailey*
A collection of writing inspired by the author's journeys along the rivers of England with an ancient two piece fly fishing rod.

River Fishing   *Len Head*
How to read waters and set about catching the major coarse fishing species.

Boat Fishing   *Mike Millman, Richard Stapley and John Holden*
A concise but detailed guide to modern boat fishing.

Stillwater Coarse Fishing   *Melvyn Russ*
A guide to the maze of tackle, baits, tactics and techniques that surround the cream of coarse fishing in Britain.

Beach Fishing   *John Holden*
A comprehensive insight into the fish, their habitat, long distance casting, tackle, bait and tactics.

My Way with Trout   *Arthur Cove*
Outlines the techniques and tactics employed by the master of nymph fishing on stillwaters.

In Visible Waters   *John Bailey*
John Bailey reveals the deep insight that he has gained over nearly thirty years closely observing the lives of the coarse fishing species.

Imitations of the Trout's World   *Bob Church and Peter Gathercole*
Describes advanced fly tying techniques and explores the link between the natural and the artificial.

Tench   *Len Head*
Natural history, physiology, distribution, tackle tactics and techniques are discussed in this most comprehensive study of the species.

Pike – The Predator becomes the Prey   *John Bailey and Martyn Page*
Twenty top pike anglers experience of all types of waters.

Carp – The Quest for the Queen *John Bailey and Martyn Page*
Combined specialist knowledge from twenty-six big fish men.

Long Distance Casting *John Holden*
A guide to tackle and techniques of long-range casting in saltwater.

The Beach Fisherman's Tackle Guide *John Holden*
Covers rods, reels, accessories, rigs and maintenance.

An Introduction to Reservoir Trout Fishing *Alan Pearson*
Covers tackle, casting, flies, bank and boat fishing, and location.

Rods and Rod Building *Len Head*
A manual of rod building, giving guidance on design and the selction of rods.

Further information from **The Crowood Press (0672) 20320**